Shakespeare's ❧ COMMON PRAYERS

Morning prayer.

A generall Confession to be said of the whole Congregation
after the Minister, all kneeling.

 Lmighty and most mercifull Father, we haue erred and strayed from thy wayes like lost sheepe, we haue followed too much the deuices and desires of our owne hearts, we haue offended against thy holy Lawes, we haue left vndone those things which wee ought to haue done, and we haue done those things which wee ought not to haue done, and there is no health in vs: but thou, O Lord, haue mercy vpon vs miserable offenders, spare thou them, O God, which confesse their faults, restore thou them that be penitent, according to thy promises declared vnto mankinde, in Christ Iesu our Lord, and graunt, O most mercifull Father, for his sake, that we may hereafter liue a godly, righteous, and sober life, to the glory of thy holy Name. Amen.

The absolution or remission of sinnes to be pronounced by the Priest Minister alone, standing: the People still kneeling.

Lmighty God the Father of our Lord Iesus Christ, which desireth not the death of a sinner, but rather that hee may turne from his wickednesse and liue, and hath giuen power and commandement to his Ministers, to declare and pronounce to his people being penitent, the absolution and remission of their sinnes: hee pardoneth and and absolueth all them which truely repent and vnfainedly beleeue his holy Gospel. Wherefore wee beseech him to grant vs true repentance and his holy Spirit, that those things may please him which we doe at this present, and that the rest of our life hereafter may be pure and holy, so that at the last wee come to his eternall ioy, through Iesus Christ our Lord.

The people shall answere, here & at the end of all other prayers Amen.

A 2   Then

Shakespeare's

 ## COMMON PRAYERS

The Book of Common Prayer
and the Elizabethan Age

DANIEL SWIFT

OXFORD
UNIVERSITY PRESS

OXFORD

UNIVERSITY PRESS

Oxford University Press is a department of the University of Oxford.
It furthers the University's objective of excellence in research,
scholarship, and education by publishing worldwide.

Oxford   New York

Auckland   Cape Town   Dar es Salaam   Hong Kong   Karachi
Kuala Lumpur   Madrid   Melbourne   Mexico City   Nairobi
New Delhi   Shanghai   Taipei   Toronto

With offices in

Argentina   Austria   Brazil   Chile   Czech Republic   France   Greece
Guatemala   Hungary   Italy   Japan   Poland   Portugal   Singapore
South Korea   Switzerland   Thailand   Turkey   Ukraine   Vietnam

Oxford is a registered trademark of Oxford University Press
in the UK and certain other countries.

Published in the United States of America by Oxford University Press
198 Madison Avenue, New York, NY 10016

Library of Congress Cataloging-in-Publication Data
Swift, Daniel, 1977–
Shakespeare's common prayers : the Book of common prayer
and the Elizabethan age / Daniel Swift.
p. cm.
Includes bibliographical references.
ISBN 978-0-19-983856-1
1. Shakespeare, William, 1564–1616—Religion.
2. Shakespeare, William, 1564–1616—Sources.
3. Religion and literature—England—History—16th century.
4. Religion and literature—England—History—17th century.
5. Prayer in literature. 6. Religion in literature. I. Title.
II. Title: Book of common prayer and the Elizabethan age.
PR3011.S95 2012   822.3′3—dc23   2012005616

For Leo ❧ *Grapple them to thy soul with hoops of steel.*

Contents

*Learning cannot be too common, and the commoner the
better. Why but who is not jealous, his mistress should be
so prostitute? Yea but this Mistress is like air, fire, water,
the more breathed the clearer; the more extended the
warmer; the more drawn the sweeter.*

◆

JOHN FLORIO,
"To the courteous Reader,"
The Essays of Michael de Montaigne
(London, 1603)

A Note on Texts

For most of Shakespeare's lifetime, the 1559 version of the Book of Common Prayer was the official prayer book of the Church of England. In what follows, I quote from this version unless otherwise noted. Brian Cummings's edition of the Book of Common Prayer (Oxford: Oxford University Press, 2011) collects the 1549, 1559, and 1662 texts, and this is the most convenient modern edition.

Shakespeare's plays are quoted from the *Norton Shakespeare*, edited by Stephen Greenblatt (New York: W. W. Norton, 1997), unless—particularly in the case of *Hamlet*—otherwise noted. References to Shakespeare's plays are by act, scene, and line. The translation of the Bible that Shakespeare read and most frequently alludes to is the Geneva version. This will also therefore be my default version although the Book of Common Prayer was a vital and too-long unacknowledged place where Shakespeare, like all his contemporaries, encountered scripture.

I have lightly modernized the spelling of sixteenth- and seventeenth-century texts throughout: so that, for example, "publique" appears as "public."

Shakespeare's ❧ COMMON PRAYERS

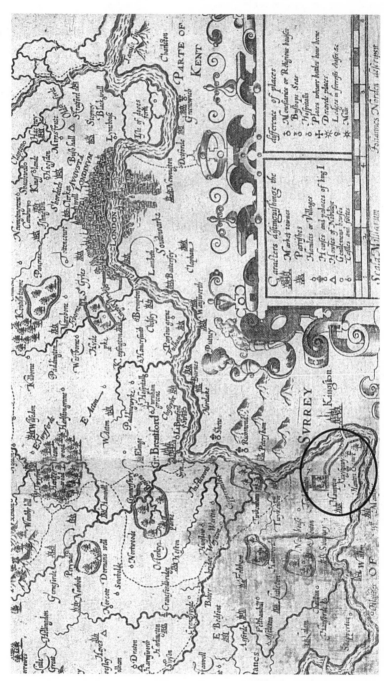

Hampton Court Palace, from William Camden, *Britain: A Chorographical Description* (1610).

PROLOGUE ❧ *A Revel with the Puritans*

I n 1603, Elizabeth I died and King James of Scotland became the king of England. It was a season of change, of the old order passing. John Stow, updating his great chronicle of England, noted the spread of plague "in divers parts of this realm, notably the City of London," and estimated that thirty thousand had died in this most recent outbreak. "God make us penitent," he wrote, "for he is merciful."[1] At the end of the year there were unusually thick mists. That winter at Hampton Court Palace, twenty miles upriver from London, the new king summoned representatives from two different worlds. He called to a conference religious men, bishops, and preachers, the orthodox and the radical, and he called men of the theater, players and playwrights alike.

The Hampton Court Conference may now seem a minor episode in the great sweep of British history, and is perhaps most famous as the occasion at which the new King James Version of the Bible was commissioned. This was completed in 1611, now a little more than four hundred years ago. But the conference was a great affair, much-discussed, much-anticipated, and its consequences ran wide. It had been called in response to a Puritan petition for further reformation of the English Church, and in particular the revision of the Book of Common Prayer, which set out the official rites and forms of public devotion. This was the central religious text of this powerfully religious age, and at his palace by the river the king, his bishops, and the

Puritans came together to resolve the issue of what to revise. These were not the only visitors. As was customary, the holiday season in the royal household was marked by revels and performances of plays, staged by theatrical companies brought up from London. One name stands out today: William Shakespeare was at Hampton Court Palace at Christmas 1603.

The clash of these different worlds was not lost upon the king. Reflecting upon his first winter in England, James wrote to the Earl of Nottingham: "We have kept such a revel with the Puritans here this two days, as was never heard the like."[2] The joke suggests the mismatch between revels and Puritans, and perhaps reveals also his pleasure in this unusual meeting.

If you had been at Hampton Court in the winter of 1603 and were asked what would echo down the centuries as the remarkable event of the season, you would not say the performances by Shakespeare. You would say the Hampton Court Conference; that this may sound odd today is only a sign of our distance from the world in which Shakespeare moved and wrote, and which first looked upon his plays. If you wish to understand Shakespeare, then Hampton Court Palace in the winter of 1603 is a good place to start: at the meeting of the great playwright and the revision of the most contested literary work of the age, the Book of Common Prayer.

THE KING'S MEN were the first to arrive. The company, with Shakespeare as part owner and resident playwright, had during Elizabeth's reign performed under the patronage of the Lord Chamberlain; but Elizabeth died in March 1603 and on 17 May the Privy Council relicensed the company as the King's Men. Two days later, their home theater the Globe was closed due to an outbreak of the plague, and by the first week of September three thousand people were dying each week in the capital. The new king was forced to delay his formal entry into London until the spring of the following year, and like the king his players stayed away. In August they were in Oxford, and in September and October in Coventry, Bridgnorth, and Bath. On 2 December they played at Wilton for the king and went on to spend Christmas at Mortlake, near Richmond, where one of the company had a house. Now the court traveled on and the weather turned. As the courtier and diplomat Dudley Carleton wrote on 22 December, upon arrival at Hampton Court they "there were welcomed with fogs and mists, which make us march blindfold." There was excitement too, for the Christmas revels were coming. On 18 December, Lady Arbella Stuart wrote to the Earl of Shrewsbury: "It is said there shall be 30 Plays." Playing was forbidden on Christmas Day, so early on the morning of 26 December—St. Stephen's Day—Shakespeare and his company reassembled to travel to Hampton Court. On the walls of the Great Hall were tapestries of the biblical story of Abraham, and a lattice of fresh branches was suspended from the roof beams. All was lit by candles, and that night Shakespeare played before the king.[3]

Other theater companies were at court that Christmas. The Lord Admiral's Men and Worcester's Men, soon to become the Prince's Men and Queen Anne's Men, played for the royal family. But the King's Men played first and most frequently, and their new patron and their schedule indicate that they were the principals. They played on 26 December and again the following day; they played on Innocents' Night, 28 December, and on 30 December before Prince Henry. They played twice on New Year's Day and were gone by Twelfth Night. On 18 January the records note their payment: for "six interludes or plays before the kings majesty and the prince" the sum of eighty pounds. This is only proper, but something more than this suggests that the players found royal favor: a fortnight later, another payment to the King's Men. "His Company being prohibited to present any plays publicly in or near London by reason of great peril that might grow through the extraordinary concourse and assembly of people to a new increase of the plague," the accounts explain and note a payment of thirty pounds, "by way of his majesties free gift."[4] These revels were a success.

This is as far as the records go for this Christmas season; there is much we do not know. Despite diligent detective work by literary historians, we do not know for sure which plays were here, but a cautious consensus has emerged. It seems likely that *A Midsummer Night's Dream*, Jonson's *Sejanus His Fall*, and the anonymous *Fair Maid of Bristow* were played for the king, and possible that the King's Men also performed *Twelfth Night*, *Troilus and Cressida*, the two *Henry IV* plays, or *Henry V*. In his study of Shakespeare at court, Alvin Kernan claims that *A Midsummer Night's Dream* was played at a matinee on New Year's Day for the nine-year-old Prince Henry and that *Hamlet* was performed on 26 December, as it "would have been the likely choice to open the season on the night after Christmas."[5] These are possible candidates, although unproven.

The archives are thin, and this is as far as we can know; but there is much we can reconstruct. We have put Shakespeare in a time, but he was also in a place. If we do not know which plays were performed, we do know the context in which they were performed. If we do not know what Shakespeare saw or thought about at Hampton Court in late December and early January, we do know what struck his contemporaries, for the palace was exceptionally well documented. This is a different style of recovery, speculation but built upon a simple physical law. What you see is a function of where you stand. At this moment, we know where Shakespeare stood, so we may trace much of what he saw and heard.

The palace was spectacular. Philip Julius, Duke of Stettin-Pomerania—a Baltic state on the border between Germany and Poland—visited in 1602. In his diary he noted the paintings, furniture, and particularly the tapestries—"exquisitely wrought in good gold-thread and best silk, that not easily will be found anywhere in such quantities as in this palace"—and concluded that this was "the principal royal residence in all England." He was mistaken. Elizabeth had not been in residence at Hampton Court since the summer of 1599, three years earlier, but his assumption testifies to the grandeur of the place. All were struck. Paul Hentzner, touring England in 1598, was awed by the tapestries—"in short all the walls of the palace shine with gold and silver"—and a small bejeweled antechamber, "the cabinet called Paradise" where "every thing glitters so with silver, gold and jewels, as to dazzle one's eyes." Hampton Court was designed to impress. "A royal palace of the Kings, a work in truth of admirable magnificence," as the geographer William Camden described it, noting that it had been "built out of the ground by *Thomas Wolsey* Cardinal, in ostentation of his riches." Such rivalry did not please Henry VIII. In the euphemistic account by John Stow of the events of the year 1526, "At this time the Said Cardinal gave to the King the lease of the Manor of Hampton Court," and Wolsey was charged with treason and died soon after.[6]

Henry continued to expand Hampton Court, adding the Great Hall—in its windows stained glass, which portrayed the Tudor family tree—and an astronomical clock, which to this day tells the hour, the phase of the moon, and the time of high water at London Bridge. Most of all he added art. Henry bought eight enormous tapestries narrating the history of Abraham by the famous Brussels weaver Wilhelm Pannemaker; he filled the royal apartments and the Privy Chamber with biblical allegories by Hans Holbein and his contemporaries. Each subsequent Tudor monarch added to the collection. Mary, who spent little time here, left a small portrait of her husband, Philip of Spain. Elizabeth added a dour series of portraits of her councilors—Walsingham, Leicester, Sir Nicholas Bacon—and an enormous canvas depicting the calling of St. Matthew, looted by the Earl of Essex at the siege of Cadiz. On 28 December 1603—while Shakespeare was at Hampton Court—James sat for a portrait by Nicholas Hilliard, which he gave as a gift to the Danish ambassador.[7]

All was deliberate, poised. When in 1611 John Speed came to describe Hampton Court in his *Theatre of the Empire of Great Britain*, he called it "a City rather in show then the Palace of a Prince," for these halls and walkways work most powerfully not as housing but as vision. Here, the Tudor dynasty defined itself in the eyes of the world, and insisted upon the elaborate, expensive dream of kingship.

This is not self-indulgence. It is politics. In listing the "curiosities" of the Great Hall, Hentzner specifically mentions "a portrait of Edward VI," and as he continued his tour he recalled "two chambers, called the presence, or chamber of audience, which shone with tapestry of gold and silver and silk of different colours; under the canopy of state are embroidered in pearl, *Vivat Henricus Octavus*." Four years later the Duke of Stettin-Pomerania emphasized one painting from the collection. He describes "the likenesses of the three prince-electors, offering Henrico Octavo the empire," which is one of a series of four huge canvasses commissioned by Henry; the others show Henry at the Field of the Cloth of Gold, Henry meeting the Emperor Maximilian, and a group scene of the royal family. Elizabeth added four portraits of herself to the palace collection.[8] When you walk these halls you walk beneath royalty.

By 1603 Shakespeare had completed his cycle of English histories. He had spent much of the last decade thinking about the mutually constitutive relation between monarchy and display expressed upon the walls of the palace; he had long considered royal style and its ends. "What have kings that privates have not too, / Save ceremony, save general ceremony?" King Henry asks himself one night, among his troops, on campaign in France. The worry of kings is a strain that runs thick through that cycle, a fear of the hollow within all their great display, and it surfaces here in *Henry V* (1599) as a sudden fear, almost vertigo. He pleads:

> O ceremony, show me but thy worth.
> What is thy soul of adoration?
> Art thou ought else but place, degree, and form,
> Creating awe and fear in other men? (4.1.220–21, 226–29)

Hampton Court was such a show, a gesture of place, degree, and form, tuned to inspire awe and fear in other men, and it was, as Henry sees, all surface, a sheen of dazzle and gold.

The play asks the question of the palace and the palace answers. For each rich scene there is one austere image. In the Great Hall,

Hentzner noted a portrait of Henry, and "under it was placed the Bible curiously written upon parchment," and he is here describing a small painting of 1535 by Joos van Cleve, in which Henry holds a scroll inscribed with a quotation from the Gospel of Mark: "Go ye into the world, and preach the gospel from every creature," it commands, and this portrait celebrates Henry's endorsement of a new translation of the Bible. In the last decade of his life, Henry commissioned Girolamo da Treviso the younger to paint a more inflammatory scene. The image, *The Destruction of Popery by the Evangelists,* depicts an aged pope lying on the ground while being stoned by Matthew, Mark, Luke, and John. It is a violent painting. The four have hard, workmanlike faces, and as a whole the picture is so leached of color as to be almost black and white. Coming to this painting, after the rich shine of Holbein, is still a shock. It hung here throughout Elizabeth's reign. These are severe, Protestant images, and they promise that these kings are holy too. After all that gold thread and best silk this is not so much a contradiction as a balance. Hampton Court Palace is how kings of England showed what they believed kings to be.

Hampton Court was famous too for another kind of spectacle, for the Great Hall had been the scene of Elizabeth's extravagant Christmas revels. There are records of payments to playing companies at Christmas in 1572, 1573, 1574, 1579, 1580, 1582, 1592, and 1593; the 1576 revels were particularly grand, when six different plays by three different companies were presented to the queen. That year the records show fourteen separate transports up and down the river between 26 December and 8 January, for while the players boarded at Kingston during the season, there was constant traffic between London and the court as props and costumes went back and forth by carriage or by boat. The dry lists still convey how splendid this must have been. There are accounts for "Buttons of green silk and gold," and "lace of the same employed by John Arnolde upon a scarf for one of the gentlewomen masquers." There were blue and green tinsel, feathers and flowers, sixty bushels of

honeysuckle, and calls for "more Roses." How splendid, and how
fun: in 1573, a payment to "Roger Tyndall for Lending his Armor
and for his servant attendants to arm & unarm the children in the
play of Q[ueen] Fabius."[9]

This is the tradition that James resurrected over his first winter as
king of England. As Dudley Carleton wrote on 15 January 1604: "The
first holy-days we had every night a public play in the great hall, at
which the K[ing] was present, and liked or disliked as he saw cause,"
and went on to note that "he takes no extraordinary pleasure in this.
The Q[ueen] and Prince are more the players friends." The Venetian
ambassador Nicolo Molin agreed that the season was customary
rather than innovative. "All these last days have been devoted to
fetes, banquets, jousts, as is usual in England from St. Stephen's to
Twelfth Night," he wrote on 28 January, and perhaps these observers
felt the weariness among the splendor. This year the Christmas
revels had purpose: they were designed to show continuity between
the new Stuart court and Elizabethan custom, and one night the
revelers came close to reanimating the dead queen. As Arbella Stuart
wrote on 18 December, "The Queen intendeth to make a Mask this
Christmas, to which end my Lady of Suffolk and my Lady Walsingham hath warrants to take of the late Queen's best apparel out of the
Tower at their discretion."[10] The courtiers took clothes from the dead
queen's wardrobe, and they danced.

This is a startling image, and it flirts with the radical suggestion
that a monarch's clothes are only clothes, borrowed from one, worn
by another. In a tender, sad scene in the second part of *Henry IV*
(1598), Prince Hal comes to his sleeping father and by the bed he
sees the royal crown. "O majesty," he addresses it:

> When thou dost pinch thy bearer, thou dost sit
> Like a rich armour worn in heat of day,
> That scald'st with safety. (4.3.158–61)

He is considering what it is to bear the crown—its weight, its
pinch—and he cannot resist; he reaches out and wears it for a

second, although his father is not yet dead, and so before he is the king he playacts as one. Kings may be undone by what they put on. "Why do you dress me / In borrowed robes?" demands Macbeth when he is named Thane of Cawdor, and kingship fits him equally badly. It fits him, that is, like a costume on an actor, not as that which is true to him. As the play proceeds, his discomfort grows.

> Now does he feel his title
> Hang loose about him, like a giant's robe
> Upon a dwarfish thief

observes Angus, close to the end (1.3.106–7; 5.2.20–22). No writer in literary history has written with keener acuity about the costumes of kingship than Shakespeare. He did not borrow the image from Arbella Stuart, nor did he craft it wholly new. Now the revels read the plays and the plays read them back.

We have the certainty of archives and the speculation of criticism, and when we travel from one to the other we move between classes of evidence. A court letter does not tell the same story as a self-conscious literary work, and nor does it even tell the same style of story. But we must, too, be wary of any simple hierarchy of records. Like all literary historians of this period, I have relied heavily upon the account books of the Elizabethan and Jacobean royal revels, edited by Peter Cunningham: they are a wonderful, rich archive and the sole source for much of what we know about Shakespeare's life at court. As Shakespeare's biographer Katherine Duncan-Jones coyly notes, "the 1604–5 Revels Accounts seem almost too good to be true," and the problem is that perhaps they are.[11] The Shakespeare Society published Cunningham's *Extracts from the Accounts of the Revels at Court in the Reigns of Queen Elizabeth and King James I* in 1842, and by the late 1860s many suggested they were suspicious: particularly two lists of plays, including those by "Shaxberd," performed in 1605–6 and 1611–12. They were too clean, too convenient, too perfectly that which one might wish for. James Halliwell-Phillipps argued they were fake in his *Outlines of the Life of Shakespeare* (1881), and John Murray's *English Dramatic Companies 1558–1642* (1910) reprints the records while in a footnote describing them as "forged." By the early 1920s, however, they were widely considered to be real. E. K. Chambers argues for "the genuineness of the 1604–5 list" in his canonical *Elizabethan Stage* (1923), and the following year W. J. Lawrence defended them at length in the *Modern Language Review*.[12]

The most recent consensus is that the records are authentic. There is, however, another lesson here, about the proximity of fantasy in all archival work, and the peril of drawing too perfect a line between the imagined and the historical. Shakespeare was at Hampton Court and he played before the king; and stories, plays, and works of art may tell us history, too.

THE ONE EXTANT theatrical work that we know was played before James at Hampton Court is Samuel Daniel's *Masque of the Twelve Goddesses*, which was performed by eleven ladies-in-waiting and the queen herself in the Great Hall on the evening of Sunday, 8 January. Some artworks of this age look still alive today. The school of Holbein portraits on the walls of the palace have lost none of their polished depth. They are dazzling still but the tapestries that hang next to them now seem only decorous. The court masque as a form is closer to a tapestry than a portrait. They are panoplies of frozen gesture, awkward with symbols, and this masque is a conventional phantasmagoria of allegorical figures and classical goddesses, descending, singing, and processing. It reads as the excuse for a dozen courtly ladies to dress up. And yet one phrase, spoken near the beginning, bears an unexpected echo. The character of Night— "appareled in a black vesture set with Stars coming from below"— wakes her son Sleep and pointing to the audience instructs him "make their slumber to beget strange sights." She goes on to elaborate what the waking-dreaming audience here may see:

Strange visions and un-usual properties,
Un-seen of latter ages, ancient rites;
Of gifts divine, wrapped up in Mysteries,
Make this to seem a Temple in their sight:
Whose main support, holy religion, frame,
And wisdom, courage, Temperance and right:
Make seem the pillars that sustain the same,
Shadow some *Sibyl* to attend the rites.[13]

They are to imagine a temple here, a church and its priest. The reveling went on past midnight. A little more than three days later, early on the morning of Thursday, 12 January, James opened a conference to discuss precisely those issues that the masquing Night had promised: ancient rites and their expression of the divine; the properties of sacraments or, in Greek, "mysteries"; the framing relation between religion and the Temple of the state; and the role the imagination must play at the finish of all acts of worship. The Hampton Court Conference had been planned for three months, but the masque was written specifically for this occasion. Perhaps James, known both for his sense of humor and his love of theological debate, greeted these lines with a laugh.

The immediate confluence of revels and conference was a coincidence. The conference had been planned for 1 November, but 1603 saw outbreaks of plague across the country, so it was postponed. It was prompted by two linked concerns. First, all were curious about the new king and particularly the shape of his belief. James's treatise on kingship, *Basilikon Doron*, had been published, with fortuitous timing, within days of Elizabeth's death. The Venetian ambassador, Giovanni Carlo Scaramelli, reported on 20 April 1603 that "There are hopes that the King may become Catholic," but then in a letter four days later conceded that such hopes were unfounded. "His Majesty's religion," he wrote, "is not, as was said, Calvinist, but Protestant, as may be gathered from a book published by his Majesty in the English tongue, and sent to press here within an hour of the Queen's death."[14] Scaramelli was not the only one to read *Basilikon Doron* for traces of the new king's faith, nor was his conclusion universal. On 24 May 1603 the Jesuit exile Robert Parsons wrote that he had just finished reading *Basilikon Doron* and "it exceedingly comforted me . . . with great contentment of all sorts of men, upon hope that our new king will in time prefer to be rightly informed in religion."[15]

Second, the arrival of a new monarch was taken, by people across England, as a season of renegotiation of the country's laws. The new king was petitioned to reform or reissue the monopolies on saltpeter, gunpowder, and many other goods; one plea, presented to James immediately upon his coronation, listed twenty-seven "things grievous and offensive to the Common Wealth which may be reformed by your Highness," including the sale of offices and the tax rate.[16] Most of all his petitioners sought reformation of the state religion. James was petitioned, both on his entrance into the kingdom and at his coronation, by a group who signed themselves simply "the Catholics of England": they defended the traditional faith as "conformable to natural form and Reason . . . agreeable to the sacred text of word and gospel" in contrast to the "discontented minds innumerable" of reforming theologians and worshippers.[17]

The most influential petition presented to James, and the one that provided the immediate prompt for the Hampton Court Conference, was the Millenary Petition. It claimed to be from a thousand disenchanted Church of England ministers, although no signatures were attached, and it sets out the conventional Puritan critique of the late sixteenth-century English Church. Puritanism was not a perfectly distinct movement, but historians routinely describe Puritans as those who followed "a form of heightened Protestantism" and were disappointed by the remnants of traditional Catholic practice within the Elizabethan church.[18] Describing themselves as "all groaning under a common burden of human rites and ceremonies," these ministers sought the further reformation of the English Church and specified four areas of particular urgency. First, the Book of Common Prayer required revision and clarification; second, "That none hereafter be admitted to the ministry but able and sufficient men"; third, that bishops no longer be permitted to collect revenues from multiple church properties, known as "benefices"; and fourth, that the structures of ecclesiastical discipline be reorganized. The Millenary Petition ends with a challenge. "These, with such other abuses yet remaining, and practiced in the Church of England," it claims, "we are able to show not to be agreeable to the scriptures, if it shall please your Highness further to hear us, or more at large by writing to be informed, or by conference among the learned to be resolved." It circulated widely and many manuscript copies survive.[19]

Shakespeare had long been aware of the troubling politics of common prayer: of how the expression of piety might mask abuse and of the taut relation between state power and worship. In *Richard III* (1592), Buckingham stage-manages the rise of the villainous Richard to the throne by placing in his hand a prayer book. "See, a book of prayer in his hand," he tells the assembled aldermen and citizens: "True ornaments to know a holy man" (3.7.88–89). The invocation of liturgy works as a powerful political gesture precisely as it invokes a communal piety, but communities are formed by their exclusions as well as their inclusions, and in one of the cruelest scenes in *The Merchant of Venice* (1596) Portia punishes Shylock by forcing him to convert to Christianity. "That same prayer doth teach us all to render / The deeds of mercy" she tells him, but of course her prayer is not the same as his (4.1.196–97). Common prayer is, as the Millenary Petition insisted, never as common as it appears.

The conference began like a Shakespeare play, in confusion and rumor. At nine o'clock on the morning of Thursday, 12 January, a swarm of bishops, "summoned by letters," gathered at Hampton Court. "The night before, they heard a rumor that it was deferred," notes William Barlow, the Dean of Chester, in his official account of the conference, and yet they came nonetheless as they "thought it their duty to offer themselves to the King's presence." Here were Archbishop Whitgift, and bishops Bancroft of London and Bilson of Winchester, the official respondents; the bishops of Durham, Worcester, Chichester,

Exeter, Carlisle, and Peterborough, and seven cathedral deans, and yet once all had presented themselves to the king they were told to leave "and return on Saturday next following."[20]

The bishops return on the morning of the 14th, and when they arrive at the presence chamber, "there were found sitting upon a form, D. *Reynolds*, D. *Sparkes*, M. *Knewstubs*, and M. *Chaderton*, Agents for the Mileine Plaintiffs." John Reynolds was president of Corpus Christi College, Oxford, and dean of Lincoln; Thomas Sparke was a former archdeacon, Lawrence Chaderton the Master of Emmanuel College, Cambridge, and John Knewstub a popular Suffolk minister. Each was known to be sympathetic to the Puritan cause for further reform, and they had been invited by the king; here began a curious dance of inclusion and exclusion, of conservation and innovation. For now the king, hearing that all were assembled, issued the command "that none of any sort should be present, but only the Lords of the Privy Council, and the Bishops with five Deans." The bishops were called to the king in a privy chamber and the petitioners left outside. Having excluded the Puritans—who represented one rationale for the conference—the king addressed the remaining clergymen. His intention was, he declared, "like a good Physician, to examine & try the complaints, and fully to remove the occasions thereof, if they prove scandalous, or to cure them, if they were dangerous," but lest this make him sound too radical, the king assured all present "that he called not this assembly for any Innovation." Now, sworn both to cure and to change nothing, they pass copies of the prayer book back and forth. They discuss, and then lightly edit, the general absolution, and go on to debate at length whether women or laypersons may perform baptism. Concluding that they may not, they alter the baptismal rubric to reflect their decision.

On the second day of the conference—Monday, 16 January—the four Puritans arrive between eleven and twelve, and today, there is an additional figure in the room: the young prince Henry, who sits on a stool and watches. Now Reynolds expresses his hope that "the Book of Common Prayer, might be fitted to more increase of piety," and asks for particular moments of clarification. He is interrupted by the bishop of London, who demands that the Puritans again be banned but is overruled by James. Again the dance, of heeding and ignoring; having overruled the bishop of London James trades condescending jokes with the others—"*A Puritan is a Protestant frayed out of his wits*"—and today, following Reynold's objections to mistranslations in the Bible, James agrees upon the need for a new English version. This was to be published in 1611 as the King James Version. The third day—Wednesday 18 January—passes much like those previous. The Puritans are kept away for the morning, and the bishops and king return to the baptism rite; the Puritans are called in, later in the day, to finish discussion of one line in the marriage rite—the presence of the word "worship"—and James concludes with a speech. "His Majesties gracious conclusion was so piercing, as that it fetched tears, from some, on both sides" is William Barlow's unlikely summation.

The description so far comes all from Barlow's report, which is necessarily a partial source: James's biographer Alan Stewart describes it as "a cloyingly Anglican vision of the Hampton Court Conference."[21] It preserves an air of free-floating contention common to all accounts. The Puritans listed abuses, which were answered or mocked by the bishops and then in turn upheld or overruled by James. This structure was irregular. It was closer in form to an academic disputation than an ecclesiastical council, and perhaps to call it a conference overstates its dignity for it sounded at times more like a bad-tempered squabble. On the second day, having heard the Puritan objections, James declared: "I shall make them conform themselves, or I will harry them out of the land, or else do worse." What Barlow underplays is how heated this became. According to the Venetian ambassador Molin, "the debate has been acrimonious," and Sir John Harington in a private letter agreed. "The spirit was rather foulmouthed," he noted.[22] Included as an appendix to Barlow's report is an anonymous letter, which records the king as declaring "he had as lief an Ape, as a woman should baptize his child."

On the first day James spoke first, and the accounts of precisely what he said—as with all elements of the conference—vary. Barlow does not record the phrase, but according to an anonymous manuscript account "A Brief relation of ye conference 1603 held at Hampton Court" and now in the British Library, James then declared: "religion was ye soul of a kingdom, and unity ye life of Religion." This is a bland enough sentiment and a conciliatory pose, and in a letter written a week after the Conference the bishop of Durham Tobie Matthew described the moment to Thomas Hutton, the archbishop of York. In Matthew's version, however, one word is different: there James declares "that Religion was the soul of a Kingdome, and *amity* the life of Religion."[23] This may seem slight, this shift from "amity" to "unity," but the tension between the two is the tension of the conference. All men may act the same and follow one liturgy, but this does not necessarily say that all like it. Here is the struggle: between preferring and obeying, and between power and faith.

THERE IS A scene beloved of all biographers of Shakespeare: when he came to the court for great royal revels and there perhaps saw the monarch. But the meeting his biographers always describe was not at Hampton Court and nor was the monarch James. In the summer of 1575, Queen Elizabeth visited Warwickshire on a royal progress, and she spent nineteen days at Kenilworth Castle with the Earl of Leicester. There were fireworks for the queen and elaborate entertainments, speeches by mythical and classical figures, acrobatics, and bearbaiting. The castle is twelve miles to the northeast of Stratford, and Shakespeare was then eleven years old. Samuel Schoenbaum notes that it is "not implausible" that Shakespeare's father took him to see the festivities. Katherine Duncan-Jones notes that even if they stayed in Stratford, "The whole Shakespeare family, among many others, could gaze with wonder towards the brightly lit castle from a nearby viewpoint." Peter Ackroyd allows that this coincidence of future playwright and royal entertainment is "at least suggestive. And a pretty story does no harm." Park Honan, who is possibly Shakespeare's dourest biographer, pours cold water. "There is no evidence," he insists, that Shakespeare's father "took William or Gilbert to the royal entertainments at Kenilworth in 1575." Having said this, however, he goes on to observe that all in Stratford would have "heard of the Queen's arrival with her courtiers, ban-dogs [large guard dogs, often mastiffs], and bears," and adds as proof an echo in one of the plays. On 18 July, there was a pageant of the Lady of the Lake, with a mermaid and a mechanical dolphin, and in *A Midsummer Night's Dream* Oberon reminds Puck: "Once I sat upon a promontory / And heard a mermaid on a dolphin's back."

The purplest version of this meeting is told by Stephen Greenblatt in *Will in the World*. The queen's progress, he argues, "seems to have strongly marked his vision of the theater," and like Park Honan he quotes the lines from *A Midsummer Night's Dream*. But he goes one step further than this. He places Shakespeare not only at Kenilworth but in sight of the queen, and the sight he glimpses—"arrayed in one of her famously elaborate dresses, carried in a litter on the shoulders of guards specially picked for their good looks"—bred a fascination that lasted Shakespeare's career, with "the intoxicating pleasure and excitement that royalty aroused."[24] Such proximity is irresistible.

Each of these biographical fantasies begins with the fiction of some kind of meeting, and yet the far-better-documented coincidence between monarch and playwright at Hampton Court during the Christmas season of 1603–4 has been ignored. It appears in biographies as one upon an itinerary of palaces played, as if the King's Men really wished that they were at the Globe, and if the conference is mentioned at all, it is soon dismissed. For Alvin Kernan, in a study of Shakespeare at court, "Much of the conference was taken up with the kind of trivial legalities that intrigued the donnish king."[25] This is the echo of a larger pattern of overlooking. Modern historians tend to understand the Hampton Court Conference as a non-event; they narrate what ended here and emphasize what did not happen. "With good reason," writes Nicholas Tyacke, "the events surrounding the famous Hampton Court Conference in January 1604 have been described as the 'end of a movement.' The movement in question, of course, is the concerted Elizabethan attempt to remodel the English Church along more Protestant lines."[26]

The Hampton Court Conference in this telling is the evening of the English Reformation, the fading of the old Puritan dream of further purification of the church, and historians of the period emphasize how deliberate this was. As Kenneth Fincham and Peter Lake have argued, "the Hampton Court Conference was primarily a premeditated attempt to settle the issue of Puritanism once and for all by driving a wedge between the moderate and radical wings of Puritan opinion." Those moderates were integrated into the church, and the extremists expelled; following the conference, ninety beneficed clergy were deprived of their livings. As strategy this depends upon the illusion of accommodation. The conference implied the possibility of further reform while simultaneously ending it, and all historians seem to agree that here a kind of trick was played upon the Puritans. They never were going to achieve the reforms they sought. Frederick Shriver describes the air of "rehearsed drama" of the conference, "which makes one suspect that it was a kind of enacted proclamation." Patrick Collinson concludes, in the seminal article on the conference: "the Jacobean religious settlement [was] little more than an endorsement of the Elizabethan *status quo*."[27]

Describing what happened at Hampton Court as irrelevant was always a polemical construction. On 5 March—six weeks after the conference—a royal proclamation was issued, which gave James's opinion of the proceedings. "We cannot conceal, that the success of that conference was such as happeneth to many other things, which moving great opinion before they be entered into, in the issue produce small effects," it begins and continues in a voice heavy with royal pomp:

For we found mighty and vehement Informations supported with so weak and slender proofs, as it appeared unto us and our Council, that there was no cause why any Change should have been at all in that which was most impugned, the Book of Common Prayer, conferring the form of the public service of God here established.[28]

The conference was unnecessary, the proclamation insists; the Puritan objections were heard and judged irrelevant, and the Book of Common Prayer would not be changed.

Anti-Puritan mockery found full expression in the official account of the conference. Barlow's *The Summe and Substance of the conference* was commissioned by Bancroft and appeared in August 1604, and it rehearses the tone of lazy scorn that would soon become historiographical orthodoxy. "Our men stumble and strain at these petty quillets, thereby to disturb and disgrace the whole Church," comments Barlow, and his version was reflected in another contemporary account, which simply concludes, "Dr Reynolds and his brethren are utterly condemned for silly men."[29] The first historian to mention the Hampton Court Conference was John Stow, whose great historical survey the *Annals of England* was published the following year. He glosses over the conference in three short paragraphs, giving only date and participants, while on the next page he devotes twice as many lines to a staged fight between a mastiff and a lion that took place in London on 13 March 1604.[30]

The trouble with this anti-Puritan narrative is not simply its disregard for a faithful reporting of events. It comes at a greater historiographical cost for it hides from us some of the cares of this distant world. The conference, as the literary historian Jesse Lander has observed, "aroused such intense and sustained interest" that Barlow's *Summe and Substance* was reprinted twice in 1604 and again in 1605, 1612, 1625, and 1638.[31] People were curious about what had transpired, and for good reason. The same proclamation, quoted earlier, which declares that the conference was unnecessary because the prayer book did not require revision, was printed a second time in 1604 as a preface to the new edition of the Book of Common Prayer, which in fact revised certain key phrases to which the petitioners had objected. James, that is, had listened to the Puritans.

There exists also an account that lays out a version of events dramatically different to the received orthodoxy. The anonymous "Declaration of the conference had before the kings most excellent Majesty and divers of his most honorable privy counsel" survives in a single manuscript in the British Library, and it tells a story of ecclesiastical faction and vindicated complaint. In it, the summoned bishops are opposed to James. "The BBs [Bishops] of Canterbury, London, and Winchester fell down upon their knees," it recounts, "and humbly beseeched his Majesty that there might not be any alteration of any thing before prescribed." James's reply is blunt and reworks the familiar physician metaphor. "It was no reason that because a man had been sick of the pox 40 years, therefore he should not be cured at length," James replies, and goes on to hear out the listed "corruptions in the Communion book."[32]

This is the hidden history of the Book of Common Prayer: a history of passionately contested revision and of manic sensitivity to a verb or a turn of phrase. As the church historian and Anglican priest Judith Maltby has written, "there was probably no other single aspect of the Reformation in England which touched more directly and fundamentally the religious consciousness, or lack of it, of ordinary clergy and laity, than did the reform of rituals and liturgy."[33] The architecture of the Book of Common Prayer was imprecisely finished, and its enormous political and cultural importance in early modern England was a function precisely of its malleability and the endless possibility that it could be rewritten. In the spring of 1604, following the Hampton Court Conference and the reissue of the prayer book, with correspondent injunction that all ministers of the Church of England must subscribe to the liturgical form, two groups of English priests again petitioned the king with objections. In a letter appended to a petition addressed "To the right Reverend fathers in God the Lord Bishops of the Church of England," the nonconforming minister John Burges pleaded to James: "Give me leave once to swear to your Majesty by ye god of gods, that never anything in my memory has more grieved the subjects, then the present course against ye ministers."[34]

Less than a year later, in early 1605, a group of London ministers published their *Survey of the Booke of Common Prayer, By way of 197 Quares grounded upon 58 places*. In opening their list of liturgical criticisms, the petitioning priests dare to instruct the king. "Vouchsafe to examine the book of Common Prayer," they plead, "which is, as it were, the Helena of Greece, and cause of all these controversies."[35] Shakespeare's contemporaries likened the prayer book to Helen of Troy—the most beautiful woman in the world, the face that launched a thousand ships, and the cause of great wars—and claimed that its revision caused them griefs "greater than anything in my memory." The Book of Common Prayer was the devotional centerpiece of an age that was passionately religious, and its fluidity is the sign of its cultural centrality. You do not have to care about early modern England, its literature and history, or its structures of belief. But if you do choose to attend to it, then you must begin by tracing what mattered, not by holding onto what appears relevant now.

Magna Carta, the United States Constitution, the Communist Manifesto: these are literary works which imagine and upon which are built models of society. Human history is illegible without reference to certain founding documents, and this is the status of the Book of Common Prayer. It mattered more deeply than any other written text of its age precisely because it was where and how the age defined itself. And something more than this: the prayer book is not only a political document for its claims are not only of this world. Rather, this is a work that traffics in the salvation of the soul, and so each fine revision is not stylistic nicety. For the population of Elizabethan and Jacobean England, every edit and change of phrase looked toward eternity.

This is the first lesson of the Hampton Court Conference: about the depth of care that once inhered in the precisions of liturgical revision. The second lesson suggests the extent to which liturgical controversy was a literary pursuit. At the beginning of the conference, James demanded clarification on certain points, and among them listed the issue of private baptism: Did they "intend a permission, and suffering of women, and private persons to baptize?" A reply was offered by the bishop of Worcester and left uncontradicted by any of the other bishops present. As Barlow recounts, "Here the Bishop of *Worcester* said, that, indeed, the words were doubtful, and might be pressed to that meaning, but yet it seemed by the contrary practice of our Church, (censuring women in this case) that the compilers of the Book, did not so intend them, and yet propounded them ambiguously, because otherwise, perhaps, the Book would not have then passed in the Parliament" (14–15).

Thomas Cranmer, as archbishop of Canterbury under Henry VIII and Edward VI, was the chief architect of the first version of the prayer book, issued in 1549, and from the start he intended it to be "an ambiguous book"; subsequent editions compounded rather than clarified its original ambiguity.[36] The Elizabethan prayer book was ratified by the 1563 Convocation, which established the ecclesiology of the Elizabethan church. Convocation discussed and decided against clarifying the prayer book, precisely because a strategically vague theology allowed a wider range of confessional factions to worship together.[37] This policy of theological ambiguity intensified as the Reformation continued.

The Hampton Court Conference reveals that a full account of the religion of this period requires a reader attentive to literary nuance because liturgical texts are literary works. One Puritan petition presented to James attacks the prayer book on the grounds not of what it says but what it might imply. "To our best understanding it seemest to contain in it some untruths," it declares, and goes on to give the example that the prayer book "alloweth baptism in a house merely private and seems thereby to nourish superstitious opinion."[38]

Or in the words of another roughly contemporary pamphlet: "the reader may . . . be occasioned by this rubric to think that there be more sacraments than Baptism and the Lords Supper."[39] In each case, the admonitioners' concerns lie less with the words themselves than with how they may be read: that which "seems," that which "the reader may be occasioned to think." In reply to pamphlets such as these, Thomas Hutton—a Cornish priest and well-known defender of the Anglican orthodoxy—insisted that critics of the prayer book were overreading. "How exact and strict some are in their verdict," he wrote: "they pass against what they imagine, not what they can prove blame-worthy."[40] This exchange concerns the degree of license allowed the individual in reading religious works, and while the extent of imaginative freedom permitted to the reader is disputed, both the contesting Puritans and the orthodox Hutton concur that the act of reading is personal, not universal and transparent. These men were scrutinizing the prayer book with closer attention and concern for ambiguity than any literary critic would dedicate to the plays of Shakespeare today. Liturgical controversy in this period is a style of literary criticism. Perhaps revels and Puritans were not so distinct as they may seem.

The geographical and temporal coincidence of royal revels and liturgical debate at Hampton Court in the winter of 1603–4 is a bountiful symbol, but it is also, in the end, a coincidence. Shakespeare at Hampton Court is the same person as Shakespeare in London or at the Globe: immersed in and constantly receptive to the currents of contemporary debate, both limited and freed by the intellectual assumptions of his culture, and the perfect product of his time. But he is also, by virtue of his immediate context, cast in a specific light, which reveals an unexpected set of contours to the plays and their formation. If we are to recover Shakespeare's plays— and part of the burden of literary criticism is the recovery of that which is apparently lost—we may begin with the book in which his contemporaries found an index of the controversies and knowledge of his time: the Book of Common Prayer. For there, in its ambiguities and its fierce contestations, Shakespeare in turn found the ready elements of drama: dispute over words and their practical conse- quences, hope for sanctification tempered by fear of simple mean- inglessness, and the demand for improvised performance as a desperate compensation for the failure of language to do quite what it may appear to promise.

Perhaps the deepest fantasy of literary scholarship is to catch Shakespeare at the moment of invention. What follows will sketch out a sequence of collisions between the playwright and the prayer book in order to portray the writer at work. I trace his use of one set of materials in one strand of his career and in doing so argue that the Book of Common Prayer is his great forgotten source. All the chronol- ogies of the plays are uncertain, but here is a general trend: from his tentative use of liturgy in early comedies to the great engagements of his mid-career, that extraordinary period of creativity of 1599–1603. At first, in *The Two Gentlemen of Verona* (before 1591?) and *The Taming of the Shrew* (1593), he explores the relation between marriage and dramatic plot, and in *Romeo and Juliet* (1595) and then more intensely in *As You Like It* (1599) finds dramatic tension and structure in the resolution of the two. The marriage rite resurfaces in a cluster of "problem plays" written at the start of the seventeenth century, but at this time his interest too turns toward the church ceremonies for the departed, as set out in the connected rites of Communion and burial. In *Hamlet* (1600) and again in *Macbeth* (1605?) he brings back the dead. *Macbeth* is the play most marked by liturgy, and here the rite for baptism provides a powerful symbolic vocabulary of politics and guilt. There he apparently exhausts the dramatic depths of the prayer book, or perhaps he has by this time learned all that he can, and just as he adopted and worked through each of these rites in turn only to drop them, so does he after *Macbeth* put aside the Book of Common Prayer. The plays move on from the particular engagement with lit- urgy that defines this sequence. He does not return again to these explorations, and so the story I am telling here does not give total coverage of his career. It is instead an account of one rich period, in the tired last years of Elizabeth's reign and the first years of the new king, James. Because it is a story of recurrent interest, of repetition transformed in the imagination, we might also in the end consider it a story of obsession.

This book follows Shakespeare's arc of study. He builds in careful sequence. His order is not the same as that of the Book of Common Prayer. There, the rites are arranged to follow the shape of a human life, marriage following baptism and being in turn followed by death. Nor does Shakespeare consider all the prayer book equally; he focuses upon and returns frequently to particular moments while ignoring others. Here, two chapters consider the marriage rite, which was the first he explored; these are followed by two chapters about the rites of Communion and the burial of the dead, to end in two chapters on Shakespeare's exploitation of the contradictions and ambiguity inside the rite for baptism. My story culminates in *Macbeth*, but first, in the following chapter, I survey the larger culture of the prayer book and its role in Shakespeare's world to suggest why this influence might have been forgotten for so long. Although Shakespeare stands apart, we can know him only in his meetings. Although the plays appear to be miracles, they are the product of human work and of human time.

CHAPTER 1 ❧ *The Only Book of the World*

"Do not for ever with thy vailed lids / Seek for thy noble father in the dust," Gertrude counsels her son: "Thou know'st 'tis common—all that lives must die, / Passing through nature to eternity." Hamlet's father is dead, and the prince trapped now in what looks like an excess of mourning; his mother's gesture toward shared experience—all men lose a father—is meant as consolation. For Hamlet, however, this suffering is precisely what sets him apart. In the following lines, he will point to the particulars of his grief. "'Tis not alone my inky cloak," he notes, for he is wearing black, and "I have that within which passeth show." But his immediate response, in the moment of exchange, is a formal repetition. "Ay, madam, it is common," he answers (1.2.7–74, 77, 85).

Where Gertrude is comforting, Hamlet is mocking. He is quoting her, speaking in quotation marks, so where they are joined by the phrase they are divided in its usage. But this is not quite all, for both in turn are borrowing from a single source. "We therefore commit his body to the ground, earth to earth, dust to dust, ashes to ashes," declares the priest in the rite for the burial of the dead set out in the Book of Common Prayer, but the body will not remain there long. Quoting the book of Job, the burial rite instructs "that I shall rise out of the earth on the last day"; in advising her son not to seek his father in the dust, Gertrude is simply following the liturgical commonplace that he will not there be found (Cummings, 171–72). Her shared language informs her instruction: all men share one general fate, and the grounds for grief are too the grounds for joy.

For Hamlet too, an older script stands behind his expression. According to the sixth chapter of Ecclesiastes in the King James Version, "There is an evil which I have seen under the Sun, and it is common among men." Hamlet only moments before has punned that he is "too much i' th' sun"—and here again, another echo, for Claudius has claimed him as "Hamlet, and my son"—so his responses toy with scriptural phrases, of commonness and sons. Folded inside the individual gesture is a tangle of old speech, as if the sensation of uniqueness may be voiced only in quotation.

The word is tense with its own contradiction. Later in the play, and faced with another son mourning his father, Claudius will offer, "Laertes, I must common with your grief," and here he takes the word as a verb, the activity of sharing equally.[1] That which is common is joint or standard; it is usual, ordinary. "I am more than common tall," claims Rosalind in *As You Like It*, and in *Measure for Measure* the Provost says, "Here in our prison is a common executioner." But this sense may shade into its opposite and where before it indicated inclusion, here it can also work as a marker, a barrier between groups. In numbering French prisoners taken after Agincourt in *Henry V*, Exeter counts "lords and barons, knights and squires, / Full fifteen hundred, besides common men," and those common men are excluded from the reckoning. It may suggest a hierarchy or its opposite; it may be praise or blame. When the rebel Jack Cade in *Henry VI* promises "All the realm shall be in common," this is an ideal; when Bertram in *All's Well That Ends Well* dismisses Diana as "a common gamester to the camp," this is an insult.[2] This struggle between meanings begins with the etymology of the word. The Oxford English Dictionary notes that "common" may arise from "*com*—together + *unus*, in early L[atin] *oinos*, one," and so here it means company; or it may derive from "*com*—together + *munis*," and this second term arises from "bound, under obligation," the opposite of "immune." The word may mean a neutral state or the particular consequences arising from that state. In sharing it considers the conditions that divide.

IN ENGLAND FOR almost one hundred years between the issue of its first edition on 7 March 1549 and the government decree of 4 January 1645 that made its use illegal, the most influential literary work was the Book of Common Prayer. These dates are a neatly bracketed but wide-open window, and they include the whole reign of Elizabeth I and of James I; the lifetime of Shakespeare, John Donne, Ben Jonson, Philip Sidney, and Christopher Marlowe, and the composers William Byrd and Thomas Morley. This is perhaps the most famous and certainly the most sentimentalized sweep of English history, and it was also an age deeply marked by the religious struggles of the Reformation. The Book of Common Prayer was its definitive devotional text. It established the correct form of church services, the sacraments of baptism and Communion, and the rites of marriage, burial, churching, and confirmation; it set the cycles of morning and evening prayer, and the schedule of scriptural readings, each proper to their day. Daily prayer orders the day and the year, but the rites measure a life, from the baptism of a newborn child to the burial of the dead. The prayer book gives an architecture to human time.

The Book of Common Prayer was cheaper and more widespread than the Bible. It is impossible to gauge the modern equivalence of historical prices, but we may estimate the prayer book's cost by contemporary comparisons. In 1549, a royal proclamation set its cost at 2 shillings and 2 pence with no binding, 3 shillings and 3 pence bound in sheepskin, and 4 shillings in calves' leather. By the end of the sixteenth century, due to the mass diffusion of copies, its price sank to about 10d, and it continued to fall. In 1623, the first Folio of Shakespeare's plays cost £1, making it approximately twenty-five times as expensive as a prayer book; a Quarto of a Shakespeare play cost 6d, and a penny bought you a standing-room ticket to the public theater. The prayer book was more expensive than a chicken and less than a pound of sugar. It was just less than a day's wages for an actor.

The three most frequently reprinted books of Shakespeare's age were a version of the psalms by Thomas Sternhold and John Hopkins, first published in 1562; a catechism called *The ABC*; and the Book of Common Prayer, and these last two are really one, for *The ABC* is heavily based upon the prayer book. The Book of Common Prayer went through approximately 525 editions between 1549 and 1729 in English alone, and it was published also in French, Latin, and Welsh. Perhaps a million copies were printed in this period, and the population of England in 1600 was roughly 4 million. This book was everywhere and in so many forms. It was revised and reissued in 1552, 1559, and 1604, in folio, quarto, octavo, and even smaller versions; in black print and Roman type, with one column or two. Its liturgy and devotions were reprinted in special forms of prayer and thanksgiving: in 1572, following the St. Bartholomew Day Massacre in Paris, during which thousands of French Huguenots were killed; in 1599, marking the departure of troops to Ireland; and in 1604, commemorating the entry of James into England to assume the throne. New versions appeared in times of plague, drought, and the threat of Spanish invasion. In 1605, for example, a special edition was issued to give thanks for the deliverance of the king from the Gunpowder plotters. At forty-six pages, this quarto version incorporates into the standard order lengthy new prayers written specifically for the occasion: these are conventional effusions of piety and joy.[3]

Even outside its printed versions, the language of the Book of Common Prayer flowed through the great flood of devotional works that dominated early modern publishing. As the print historian Ian Green notes, "No other vision of prayer came near to having the same degree of penetration in the country at large, and among Protestants of all levels."[4] Its cadences echo through the popular devotions and supplementary prayers issued by the church; the prayer book's particular balance of exposition, confession, and petition came to structure a whole generation of devotion. Indeed, in the eyes of some, the

English were focused upon the prayer book to an unhealthily exclusive degree. The English Puritan recusant Henry Barrow, writing from exile in the Netherlands in 1590, found in it a synecdoche for all that was wrong with the Elizabethan church. As he mocked:

> By this Book are the Priests to administer their sacraments, by this Book to church their women, by this Book to bury the dead, by this Book to keep their *Rogation*, to say certain Psalms and prayers over the earth and grass, certain gospels at crossways &c. This Book is good at all affairs; it is the only Book of the world.

Thinly veiled under Barrow's withering emphasis is the charge of idolatry, but his hottest contempt is reserved not for the feebleness of English worshippers but for the object of their worship. The Book of Common Prayer is, he insists, his syntax tripping over his disgust, "a stinking patcherie devised apocrypha *Liturgy*."

Barrow's charges tug in two different directions, and their tension is the tension within the Book of Common Prayer. He objects first to its pretense to being a compendium of all English church worship: its claim to be common. "By this Book," he repeats, and "By this Book," mocking the idea that one book could do all. Yet at the same time he presents it as insufficiently particular, for it is not wholly its own work. He calls it a "patcherie," a jumble of pieces, and goes on to describe its most damning quality. "For the thing it self," he insists, "it is evident to be abstracted out of the Popes blasphemous MASS-BOOK."[5]

Barrow is correct. The main author of the first prayer book was Thomas Cranmer, and he drew upon a range of sources. The 1549 Book of Common Prayer was partly based upon Cranmer's 1538 Latin breviary, which prescribed the daily round of prayer and readings from the Bible. This 1538 breviary in turn took as a major source a 1535 breviary written by the Spanish cardinal Francisco de Quinones, which had been commissioned by Pope Paul III, a bitter enemy of Henry VIII, so this great document of Protestant English emancipation from traditional European Catholicism was built upon a text designed precisely to bolster the European Catholic church.[6] Inside this apparently simple work lies a tangle of competing intentions.

The Book of Common Prayer was marked by mobility. Its fluid state, potentially revisable, was the result of its rough genealogy. The word "liturgy" derives from two Greek words: "leitos," meaning "public," and "ergon," meaning "work." Liturgy is by definition public: not the work of a single author but created in committee and informed by a long history of shared devotional practice. Its family tree resembles a forest running wild. There had been religious service books as long as there had been Christianity in Britain. The faith was first spread by Roman missionaries, who used a service book called the "Sacramentarium" or "Liber Sacramentorum," which contained the Rite of the Mass and the sacraments, and which is mentioned in the works of Tertullian, writing in about 208. By the early sixteenth century the English church endorsed many variations upon the Roman rite. These uses—that of Salisbury, for example, or of Hereford—commemorated local saints and days. But in 1534 the Act of Supremacy placed the church under the direct jurisdiction of Henry VIII, and this new centralized institution required a standard liturgical form.

The direct genealogy of the Book of Common Prayer lies in the new service books and liturgies prepared for Henry VIII during the Reformation: a thicket of texts, overlapping and often contradictory, at times doctrinally at odds but all concerned with the invention of a national English Church. In 1539 the bishop of Rochester, John Hilsey, prepared a *Manual of Prayers*, which included polemical attacks upon traditional Roman worship, and in 1541 the printer Edward Whitchurch in London issued the two-volume *Portiforium, Secundum usum Sarum noviter impressus*. This Latin breviary followed traditional language and form, but it excluded the pope from all prayer and was, according to the liturgical historian and typographer Stanley Morison, "the original liturgical book of the English Rite."[7] In 1542 Cranmer began to reform service books through Convocation, and in 1544 he issued a liturgy in English, followed by a volume of *Devout Prayers and Collects* in 1547. On 28 January 1547

Edward VI succeeded to the throne and, on 11 April, Compline—the prayers that end the day—was sung in English for the first time in the Chapel Royal. By November, English was being introduced into the Mass. This year, Cranmer wrote the first volume of homilies— set prayers and devotions for the English Church—and the following year issued his English *Catechism*. In March 1548, Richard Grafton published "The order of Communion," a quarto text of Communion in English. In January 1549 the Act of Uniformity established the Book of Common Prayer as the country's only legal form of worship. "All and singular ministers in any cathedral or parish or other place within this realm," the act declares:

> shall, from and after the feast of Pentecost next coming, be bound to say and use the Matins, Evensong, celebration of the Lord's Supper, commonly called the Mass, and administration of each of the sacraments, and all their common and open prayer, in such order and form as is mentioned in the said book, and none other or otherwise.

On 7 March Whitchurch published the first official edition.[8]

The 1549 Book of Common Prayer is the first version, but it grows from a great many immediate predecessors. It is a document of compromise, with many fathers and origins. Reformation in England was never a single process. As late as 1560, the English Church printed a Latin version of the prayer book called *Liber Precum Publicarum*. The 1549 book was a careful blend of the novel and the traditional, of Catholic language and Protestant theology, of new meaning and old structure. The form was conventional. This prayer book follows the traditional division of Breviary (for Morning and Evening Prayer), Missal (for the Collects, Epistles, Gospels, and Communion), Processional (for the Litany), and Manual (for the other rites). "It preserved the basic pattern of parochial worship, matins, Mass, and evensong" notes Eamon Duffy, the influential ecclesiastical historian who has done most to uncover the popular experience of sixteenth-century English worship, but he goes on to stress the new prayer book's radical doctrinal agenda. At the Mass, for example, the new liturgy abandoned all that had previously defined popular Eucharistic piety—the parish procession, the elevation at the consecration of the Host, the peace, and the sharing of holy bread—meaning that the experience itself was transformed in both content and meaning.[9] In fury at this innovation, people rioted across England. Rebels besieged Exeter, and in East Anglia rioters demanded the restoration of traditional service. Four thousand people were killed in the southwest as government troops put down the rebellion.

Revision began immediately. The first prayer book of March 1549 was followed by a new pontifical—the form for consecrating archbishops and bishops, which the English church had adapted from Rome—later in the same month, and in 1550 *The booke of Common praier noted*, which set the liturgy to music by John Merbecke. On 1 November 1552 a second prayer book became the official text. This version presented a liturgy more clearly marked by the Protestant tendencies of the Edwardian church, with less ceremony or suggestion of holy transformation. To preempt resistance it was accompanied by a second Act of Uniformity, which warned that "a great number of people in divers parts of this realm [were] following their own sensuality," and enforced use of this book on pain of imprisonment: six months for the first offense, a year for the second, and for the third the rest of your life in jail.[10] The 1552 prayer book remained in use until the death of Edward on 6 July 1553, at the age of fifteen. In the autumn, his successor and half-sister, Queen Mary, repealed all liturgies uses, and at the start of the new year an injunction returned divine service to Latin.

The history of the prayer book is a history of struggles: between rival forms and uses, between languages and revisions, between the accessions and theological tastes of monarchs. Publication ceased during the reign of Mary, who remained a Catholic and wished to restore the English Church to Rome, but following her death and the accession of Elizabeth to the throne in November 1558, the prayer book returned to the English Church. In 1559 her version was issued; it lightly diluted the more extreme Protestant elements of the 1552 edition, presenting instead a liturgical compromise, and was made standard by a new Act of Uniformity. When James acceded to the English throne in 1603 he too sought to mark the prayer book and after the Hampton Court Conference issued a new version in January 1604. The changes were minor; this edition largely followed its predecessor. The 1604 prayer book remained in use in the English church during the reign of James's son Charles. Following the out-break of civil war in August 1642 the king's army carried copies of the Soldiers Prayer Book, a manual of prayers based on the Book of Common Prayer. In 1644 the Westminster Assembly authorized the use of an alternate form, the *Directory of Public Worship of God*, and public use of the Book of Common Prayer was made illegal on 4 January 1645. The prayer book was by now a compromised docu-ment, filled with traditional devotional forms; it was associated, too, with the royal church and for both of these reasons proved abhorrent to the republican army.

What this narrative of dates and editions reveals is that the Book of Common Prayer was from its beginning a book in dramatic flux. More than this: these are not successive revisions, or improvements; rather, they are rivals. It exists in order to instruct a set of practices, which take place outside itself. Its chief concern and its central ratio-nale therefore were and are the ways that others will use it, so the prayer book cautiously presents itself to all worshippers. The 1549 version ended with a brief self-justificatory essay called "Of Ceremonies, why some be abolished and some retained," but following popular resistance the essay was moved to the front, a commanding position it retains in all successive versions into the twentieth century. It is a subtle and carefully crafted piece of writing, aimed simultaneously at those who object to the prayer book's retention of traditional ele-ments and those who dislike its novelty:

> whereas in this our time the minds of men are so diverse that
> some think it a great matter of conscience to depart from a piece

of the least of their ceremonies, they be so addicted to their old customs; and again on the other side, some be so newfangled that they would innovate all thing, and so do despise the old, that nothing can like them but that is new; it was thought expedient not so much to have respect how to please and satisfy either of these parties, as how to please God, and profit them both. (Cummings, 215)

While ostensibly presenting liturgical controversy as a minor quibble to be risen above, the preface responds to both charges. Against those who find the prayer book traditional are balanced those who find it too novel; and to each the prayer book offers salvation. The Book of Common Prayer is designed to contain the various minds of its worshippers in corporate forms of devotion. It is a work, therefore, premised upon agreement, but one aware of the presence of disagreement. Accommodation is deep in its DNA, runs through its design.

The book, like the day, begins with Morning Prayer. In 1549 this is called "Matins," and opens simply with the priest saying the Lord's Prayer, but the 1552 edition changed the name to Morning Prayer and expanded the service. The priest "with a loud voice" reads at the opening a quotation from scripture upon the theme of contrition: "I do know mine own wickedness," from the Psalms, and "Correct us, O Lord," from Jeremiah, among others. "Dearly beloved brethren, the Scripture moveth us in sundry places, to acknowledge and confess our manifold sins and wickedness," the priest explains, and asks the congregation "to accompany me with a pure heart and humble voice" in saying the General Confession.

Each movement of the service builds upon the one previous. The opening emphasis upon the priest's voice in turn informs his instruction to the congregation that their voices should be "humble," and where one voice has been speaking on behalf of the group, now all those present follow him in saying aloud and together:

Almighty and most merciful Father, we have erred and strayed from thy ways, like lost sheep. We have followed too much the devices and desires of our own hearts. (Cummings, 103)

This moment establishes many of the rhetorical habits of the prayer book. The General Confession, which was added by Cranmer to the 1552 version, opens with two pairs of hendiadys, which is itself a figure of speech involving two elements. "Almighty and most merciful," it begins, and "erred and strayed from thy ways," with its internal rhyme, and from this doubling foundation builds to a simple simile: "like lost sheep." The passage is dense with allusion to Scripture. It is not quoting, yet is meant to sound like it might be, as the prayer book appropriates biblical commonplaces. "Strayed from thy ways" recalls the biblical command to "walk in the ways," a phrase scattered through the Bible, most frequently in the Psalms. It echoes through the prayer book, from the opening of Morning Prayer—"we might walk in thy laws" (Cummings, 49)—to surface again in both the Communion rite and the Catechism at confirmation. The trail of echoes continues. In the Bishop's Bible (1568), Psalm 23 begins, "God is my shepherd, therefore I can lack nothing," and here is one original for the "lost sheep"; "The clear sight of the eye, is better than that the soul should walk after desires of the lust" advises Ecclesiastes 6:8 in the same translation, and we are not far from "devices and desires." For each new image, an older pattern; in every phrase, an allusion.

The echoes build into a structure of recollection, where words and images gain rhetorical force through repetition. All is familiar, for all is familial, and the relation between the prayer book and Bible is genetic, an issue of genealogy. These are not simple quotations. The General Confession is neither new nor old. It is instead a tight palimpsest of phrases, remembered and reworked. This liturgy performs its ideal of commonness even on the level of style.

The prayer book's curious mix of echo and originality, of convention and invention, is entirely purposive. "A ritual which has never been performed before may seem to those present not so much a ritual as a charade," notes the sociologist Roy Rappaport, and concludes that as a consequence, in order to gain popular acceptance, "'New' rituals are likely to be largely composed of elements taken from older rituals."[11] The prayer book was human work and never perfect or fixed. Even those who praised it during its first century began with this concession. Preaching in early February 1588, Richard Bancroft—then a canon of Westminster, later archbishop of Canterbury—defended the church hierarchy against recent attacks. "As touching the Communion book, you know what quarrels are picked against it," he began, and went on, "although for mine own opinion there is not the like this day extant in Christendom." There is a curious defensiveness here, caution in the ideology. In 1594 the anti-Catholic polemicist Andrew Willett defended the prayer book precisely for its contradictions. "Be it acknowledged, for this time, that the Book of Common Prayer hath some defects and imperfections," he began, but goes on to demand, "what humane work is absolute?"[12] Early defenders did not overlook its flaws. Rather, they celebrated it as the best among alternatives; they praised it by acknowledging the strains and traces of its composition.

Not all great art pretends to be perfect or original. "'Tis common," says Gertrude, and Hamlet agrees, with a whispered shift of emphasis, "Ay, madam, it is common."

SHAKESPEARE'S ENGLAND WAS a culture bound by ritual. In the opening scene of *Titus Andronicus*, the captured queen of the Goths Tamora pleads with the Roman general Titus to spare her sons, whom he has captured in the wars. His reply is oddly gentle. "Patient yourself, madam, and pardon me," he begins: "These are their brethren whom your Goths beheld / Alive and dead, and for their brethren slain / Religiously they ask a sacrifice." Those who would find brutality in Titus's response should look first to his apology, and then to his choice of the word "religiously": this is formality, not barbarity, although this makes it no less stark. As Friar Laurence plots with Juliet how they may stage her funeral, he pauses to remind her that they will do it properly "as the manner of our country is / In thy best robes, uncovered on the bier / Thou shalt be borne to that same ancient vault."

In *Much Ado About Nothing*, Friar Francis instructs Leonato that in burying his daughter Hero, he must "do all rites / That appertain unto a burial." Claudio, who does not know that Hero lives, is struck by the funeral monument and vows that he will continue to mourn. "Yearly will I do this rite," he declares. Laertes's howl over the grave of Ophelia, whom he considers improperly buried—"What ceremony else?"—is the voice of a society that found solace in decorum and which held as sacred the correct performance of church rites.[13]

These might be the traces of an orthodox age, one playing by the rules. Set ritual appears by its nature to serve the conservative ideology of a restrictive state or institution: it demands order, repetition at the cost of individual expression. Yet it is precisely in requiring the involvement of the worshipper that the prayer book diffuses its single authority. In each of the lines quoted earlier, a character vows to follow the set text of prayer, but in each the impetus to ritual is driven solely by that character's desires and schemes. The prayer book is where the wildness of individual will encounters regular form, where personal need meets proper expression, and both are altered by it. In a seminal essay Lisa Jardine and Anthony Grafton define early modern reading as "transactional." It involves, they argue, "the conjunction of reading practice and application to specified goals."[14] Readers are not locked inside that which they read. Rather, they are freed by it, endowed with a vocabulary and a set of meanings, each twisted to new purpose.

What scholarly work that has been done on reading in the Elizabethan Age has tended to consider only the educated gentry, those who possessed large libraries and who were therefore less constrained in their choices. It has left out common readers.[15] Yet hundreds of sixteenth- and seventeenth-century prayer books are now preserved in archives in England and America, and many contain emendations, notes, lists, handwriting exercises, and love letters. Reading, like all social practices, is a habit trapped in time, and the marginal annotations of long-dead readers are some of the few traces left to us of the ways in which Shakespeare's contemporaries read.

The literary historian William Sherman estimates that one in five surviving books published between 1475 and 1640 is marked in some way, and notes that these marked books are less likely to have survived because they are more vulnerable to decay.[16] I have consulted prayer books in libraries and archives in England and America, and Sherman's statistic is perhaps too low, at least for the Book of Common Prayer: of the twenty-two copies in the Cambridge University Library published between 1549 and 1616, nine include substantial annotation. Prayer book annotation was a common enough activity to be the punchline of a joke in Philip Sidney's *Arcadia* (1590), in which the foolish Mopsa writes a poem about Cupid in her prayer book and is mocked for her sentimentality.[17]

Annotations fall loosely into three groups.[18] The largest consists of worshippers who inscribed their prayer books and psalters with simple, repetitive handwriting exercises, dates, and notes. Robert Bird of Corfe Castle in Dorset wrote his name and initials repeatedly into his 1597 folio prayer book; the annotations are dated 1611 and also include the alphabet and single letters scattered at random through the pages.[19] In 1631, someone began a love letter to Elizabeth Lettisham on the frontispiece of her prayer book. "Sweet hart and better come read me this letter," it begins. The remaining lines have been crossed out. On the next page, Timothy Levett added a math lesson. "In the bible are 1100 60 14 chapters," he wrote, and scratched small crosses next to each book counted.[20] In 1728 and 1729, William Smallman wrote his name—"William Smallman His Book"—repeatedly across the pages of his 1552 folio prayer book; Mary Lane wrote her name and a list of ingredients—"an Ounce of conserve of Roses / an Ounce of Conser of Slipp / an Ounce of Syrup"—inside the front cover of her 1604 prayer book.[21]

These annotations are possessive, marking each copy as the property of an individual. Such rough jottings suggest that people approached their prayer books with familiar ease, though other notes suggest a more practical use. Many are inscribed with genealogies, such as the folio 1549 Book of Common Prayer, now in the Bodleian, that includes the births, deaths, and marriages in the family of William and Anne Preist of Cambridge between 1591 and 1654, and the 1571 Psalter, now in the British Library, whose front and back covers tally deaths and marriages in the Knollys and Saunders families between 1617 and 1659.[22] The descendants of Ranulph Crew of London listed family births, marriages, and deaths between 1559 and 1664 in their 1559 folio prayer book.[23] The gestures of this first group are particular, sentimental, and local. They incorporate into the prayer book the detail of a life.

Second, the liturgy was emended to reflect contemporary events. The royal collect that dates from the 1552 prayer book asks, "That it may please thee to keep Edward the sixth, thy servant, our King and governor."[24] In subsequent editions, the name and gender of the monarch is altered, but this means that the litany may fall out of date. A Bodleian copy of the 1552 prayer book was therefore corrected to include the name of Elizabeth, "our queen," in the litany; in a 1596 folio prayer book now in the British Library, "O Lord save the Queen" is carefully changed to "King" after the accession of James I.[25] Other volumes are updated according to a more enthusiastic monarchism. The 1604 prayer book asks, "That it may please thee to bless and preserve our gracious Queen Anne, prince Henry and the rest of the kings and queens royal issue." Manuscript additions to a 1599 prayer book in the British Library insert this prayer into the Elizabethan litany; in a 1606 quarto prayer book in the Bodleian, Henry's name is crossed out and replaced with "Charles," indicating that it was written sometime between the death of Henry (son of James I) in 1612 and the death of Anne (wife of James I) in 1618.[26] These emendations suggest a general sense that prayer books must be contemporary. The Book of Common Prayer was not, in its material form, held sacred; rather, it required attention when it faltered or fell into anachronism.

Occasionally, prayer books were revised according to the theological specifics of the day. In an octavo 1604 prayer book now in the Bodleian—the third edition printed after the Hampton Court

Conference—annotations mark where changes have been made to the text of the new edition, highlighted by marginal notes reading "Conf. H.C."[27] Sometime after 1662, Martha Cary carefully altered her 1615 folio prayer book to incorporate all changes made to the Restoration version. Though the changes between the two editions were theologically negligible, this would have been an enormous work. On every page, with careful hand and two different colors of ink, she has recorded even apparently irrelevant changes to titles, to the instructions to the priest, to the title page.[28] Although it may now appear paradoxical, this second category of prayer book additions gestures toward the enormously high cultural value placed upon the precise phrasing of the liturgy and simultaneously the popular understanding that this cultural value was a product of the malleability, not stasis, of the liturgical text.

The third type of manuscript annotations personalizes the prayer book's devotional structures. Robert Bird drew simple devotional lessons from his reading of liturgy. Under the reading for Good Friday in his 1597 prayer book, he noted, "The days and hours pass away so doth the life of man." This simple Christian lesson is not a conventional exegesis of the reading for the day, which is the description of the final meeting between Pontius Pilate and Christ from the Gospel of John; rather, it is Bird's personal moral drawn from his reading of the liturgical text. Later, under the reading for the nineteenth Sunday after Trinity, he summarizes, "Learning without profit": the warning against sterile knowledge is a fair gloss on Ephesians 4:17, which is the set text for the day. This particular moral clearly had resonance for Bird. He later begins, but does not complete, the phrase.[29] A 1586 Book of Common Prayer now in the Huntington Library in California is heavily annotated with broad devotional lessons such as, "The Whole Life of a Christian is nothing else but a Continual trial of his constancy in his Continual warfare" and, "It is faith which must make us Cheerful in Afflictions / It is faith which must make us patient in Trials"; in the left margin is a list of extraliturgical scriptural references to what were for this worshipper key texts.[30] A 1600 octavo prayer book now in the New York Public Library was bound with seventy extra blank pages, which are covered with meditations, copies of the psalms, and scriptural quotations. The manuscript additions here outweigh the set liturgy, which was taken as an inspiration for flights of personal devotion rather than the formal limit of worship.[31]

Other readers more explicitly rewrote the prayer book's teachings according to individual devotional taste. During Elizabeth's reign, an anonymous worshipper annotated his Book of Common Prayer along lines that suggest a tentatively traditional faith. In this 1552 folio, manuscript marginalia translates a small number of the English verses back into Latin. The Holy Ghost, excluded from the reformed Collect, is here reinserted in the margin while a short prayer is added to the instruction for the administration of Communion. The new prayer, which hopes that "The body of our Lord / The blood of our Lord . . . brings my body and soul into everlasting life," returns a traditional theology of real presence to the reformed version of the Mass.[32] In a 1599 folio edition, a set of annotations added between 1612 and 1618 revise the scriptural translations to apply them directly to the individual reader. The plea in Morning Prayer—"Turn thy face away from our sins, O Lord"—is rephrased in a marginal note: "Hide thy face from my sins." By rewriting the prayer, this worshipper addresses God directly; by replacing the prayer book's communal "our sin" with "my sins," he individualizes it. Later, the prayer follows Jeremiah in the plea: "Correct us, O Lord, and yet in thy judgment, not in thy fury, lest we should be consumed and brought to nothing," and here again the passage is underlined. In the margin, in pale handwriting, the plea now runs: "Correct me, but with judgment; not in thine anger lest thou bring me to nothing."[33] For this early Stuart believer, the prayer book was a rough guideline to private devotion rather than a set of communal instructions. The set liturgy—quoting the Bible—provides a direction and a vocabulary; the individual worshipper in turn quotes and adapts these.

In her 1661 edition, Mary Littleton wrote in the margin, "My god my god why hast thou forsaking me."[34] The phrase is scriptural but not liturgical; for Littleton, this line must have carried some now-unknown personal relevance that drove her to include it. During the reign of Queen Mary, Francis Muscott attempted to update his Edwardian prayer book. This is a fairly eccentric project. The 1552 prayer book that he held in his hands was specifically premised upon an anti-Catholic sacramental theology, and Mary herself banned it as soon as she acceded to the throne. Muscott nonetheless added marginalia to the Communion service—"By Body and Blood unto everlasting life"—which introduced a Marian sacramentalism to the reformed rite, and in the litany he altered Edward's name to Mary's.[35] For Muscott, as for all of these Elizabethan and Jacobean worshippers, there was no simple doctrinal binary between Catholic and Protestant prayer. The annotations and marginalia in these prayer books—some touching, some eccentric, some almost blasphemous—reveal two dimensions of early modern faith. Devotion, which is the daily practice of faith, was for all of these worshippers an active process. It was also articulated through the creative manipulation, not the mechanical repetition, of set verbal forms.

Here is a vibrant history of use and adaptation, and it has only partly been told. At the start of the section on liturgies in Pollard and Redgrave's *Short Title Catalogue*—the standard listing of English printed books from 1475 to 1640—a brief note explains:

> Most bibliographers are hesitant to deal with liturgies from the period before, during and after the Reformation. For the Latin-Rite liturgies the variety of texts is the main source of confusion; for Anglican liturgies it is primarily the multiplicity of editions. For both the problem is compounded by the sad state of the majority of copies, some surviving only as fragments rescued from bindings and others having undergone contemporary, near-contemporary, or modern mutilation and/or sophistication: "made-up" copies in every possible sense.[36]

These worn-out books graphically suggest a kind of active, busy reading. Tugged and handled, bound and rebound, carried through daily lives: these were not tucked into the hush of a library, secluded up on a dry shelf. Liturgy travels in a wild richness of forms. "In medieval England," Bruce Holsinger has noted in a recent and powerfully persuasive essay, "liturgy formed a boundless provocation to and repository of literary production and invention," and he traces the tropes and vocabulary of liturgy as they appear through a range of derivative works. For example, John Skelton's "Philip Sparrow,"—likely published in 1509—opens with "a familiar incipit from the funeral liturgy put in antiphonal dialogue with a series of vernacular interrogatives and responses." Liturgy, Holsinger concludes, "more often functions as provocation to new cultural production than a conservative hindrance to aesthetic and stylistic creativity."

This story of richness as told by Holsinger comes to a sudden stop with what he calls the "uniformity and finality" of the Book of Common Prayer.[37] He is perhaps too hasty in his sense of an ending. The readers I have surveyed above are surely the signs of an ongoing and playful cultural appreciation of liturgy. In presenting the prayer book as a "monolith," Holsinger assumes its fixity: that it froze all innovation and achieved its own perfection. Here he may be in part influenced by the ways scholars divide historical periods. Holsinger's field is medieval liturgy, and the prayer book is a product of the subsequent early modern period. One of the conventional dividing markers between these two time frames is the invention of print, which is conventionally described as an agent of standardization and fixity: a fifteenth-century technological innovation that in turn created a sixteenth-century intellectual revolution, as it permitted Protestant ideas to disseminate, in identical format, across Europe. This argument was most forcibly advanced by Elizabeth Eisenstein in her influential and controversial book *The Printing Press as an Agent of Change*, but it has been recently and equally forcibly questioned by Adrian Johns.[38] Textual corruption is not only endemic to all sixteenth- and seventeenth-century printing, and therefore also to the prayer book;

it is also precisely compensated for by Elizabethan and Jacobean techniques of devotional reading.

Johns's *The Nature of the Book* refutes Eisenstein's hypothesis on two separate counts. Fixity—the notion that print reproduced identical copies without variation—was not, he argues, one of the qualities of print until at least the late eighteenth century. He reports the claim that the first book to be printed without errors was not until 1760; while necessarily unsubstantiated, this testifies to the chaotic state of early modern printing.[39] In 1614 Robert Parker printed a quarto prayer book and psalter with continuous pagination, suggesting that the two separate volumes were intended to be bound together. This edition contains at least two textual errors. The twenty-ninth verse of Psalm 37 is printed here as "The *righteous* shalbe punished: as for the seed of the ungodly, it shalbe rooted out" while the first line of Psalm 60 runs "O God, thou hast cast us *not*."

The same edition remained in print until at least 1632, when a version with the same errors was reprinted; but in a copy of the 1614 edition, they have been emended in an anonymous hand. In the corrected version, Psalm 37 declares that "the *unrighteous* shalbe punished" while Psalm 60 pleads "O God, thou hast cast us *out*."[40] Were fixity to have been a requirement of printed books, this edition would have been discarded. The individual who emended this version clearly did not assume so, and his simple corrections suggest that printed forms of liturgy allowed—even demanded—the active participation of the reader. For Eisenstein, typographical fixity was a prerequisite of the advancement of learning precisely because the reader is not an active participant: "the thoughts of readers are guided by the ways the contents of books are arranged and presented." This mechanistic narrative, in which words on pages guide readers to think in set ways, does not acknowledge the work of readers in completing books. As Johns has it, in Eisenstein's version "printing itself stands outside history," meaning that "readers consequently suffer the fate of obliteration: their intelligence and skill is reattributed to the printed page."[41] Unreliable texts require vigilant readers, while errors on the printed page—anyone with even a basic grasp of Christian theology would see immediately that the psalms do not suggest that the righteous should be punished—in turn license worshippers in their own personal practice: that is, to manipulate and rework the words they find on the page, according to their own common sense and devotional preferences. For Robert Bird, Mary Littleton, Francis Muscott, and the anonymous readers whose annotations I have quoted, the prayer book was an invitation to begin conversation.

THE PRAYER BOOK hopes for commonness but founds this dream upon exclusion. In later chapters I refer to the particulars of resistance to the liturgy—the theological scandals that animated the revisions of the book, the keywords that were hated and fought—but here I sketch its grandest separation. The prayer book struggled, throughout this period, with its twin and rival, the commercial theater. Plays were the other great common work of the age, both written collaboratively and performed before crowds. It was against the theater that the Book of Common Prayer sought to define itself.

The first prayer book of 1549 was accompanied by an Act for the Uniformity of Service and Administration of the Sacraments, which made it a criminal offense to "in any interludes, plays, songs, rhymes, or by other open words, declare or speak anything in the derogation, depraving, or despising of the same book or anything therein contained or any part thereof." In April 1559 the Elizabethan church issued a third edition, and the text of this act was now included as a preface at the start of the volume. For the first offense, the fine was one hundred marks; for the second, four hundred; and for the third, he who has violated this stricture shall "forfeit to our sovereign lady the Queen all his goods and chattels and shall suffer imprisonment during his life." One hundred marks is a significant sum. In *The Comedy of Errors*, the apparently wealthy merchant Egeon is fined "a thousand marks," which he does not have; the worth of all the goods he is traveling with, notes the Duke of Ephesus, "Cannot amount unto a hundred marks" (1.1.21, 24). Yet this was apparently insufficient discouragement, and throughout the first year of Elizabeth's reign new rulings sought to separate liturgical rites from dramatic entertainments. Following a proclamation "By the Queen" of 16 May 1559 the crown will now "permit none to be played wherein either matters of religion or of the governance of the estate of the Common weal shall be handled or treated." Plays must avoid religious topics. The royal Injunctions of 15 June 1559 set out the Articles of Enquiry for diocesan visitations, and those conducting inspections of local devotional practices were empowered to investigate "whether any minstrels or other persons do use to sing or say any songs or ditties that be vile or unclean, and especially in derision of any godly order now set forth and established." Plays may not mock the liturgy. During the 1570s, a series of statutes issued by the Diocesan Court of High Commission in the North forbade that "the administration of the sacraments of Baptism or of the Lord's Supper be counterfeited or represented," and when in 1604 the new Jacobean church reauthorized the prayer book, it again included the preface which specifically banned the dramatic parody or interpretation of church rites.[42]

As John Donne wrote in 1608, "No law is so primary and simple, but it foreimagines a reason upon which it was founded," and each recurring insistence upon this apparently simple ruling—that church rites may not be played upon the stage—implies its undoing.[43] We only need a law against that which is at least potentially common practice, and in attempting to isolate the theater from liturgy the laws betray the deep complicity between these two forms. They share a genealogy: the origins of Elizabethan commercial theater lie within the liturgy of the late medieval church. One of the first known liturgical dramas was the *Quem queritis*, recorded by the bishop of Winchester in 965 in the *Concordia Regularis*. Liturgical drama spread through Spain in the early twelfth century, prompted by Holy Week rites, which center upon the adoration of the Host; in thirteenth- and fourteenth-century England, the Corpus Christi cycles placed the sacraments on stage. "To play the whole story," writes V. A. Kolve in his study *The Play Called Corpus Christi*, "is in the deepest sense to *celebrate* the Corpus Christi sacrament, to explain its necessity and power." The East Anglian Croxton *Play of the Sacrament*, in which the transformation of the Mass is enacted on stage, is the most famous English example of this mode of drama. There is no necessary contradiction between devotion and playgoing.[44]

Studies of the Elizabethan stage, however, tend to assume that the collaboration of drama and liturgy ended with the Reformation. As the influential literary historian David Bevington has written, "the popular theatre of Elizabeth's early reign demonstrated its vitality and potential for growth by adapting itself to the trend of the times towards secularism," as if faith and plays were antagonistic. The literary scholar who has most influentially discussed the relation between late medieval liturgical drama and Elizabethan commercial theater is Louis Montrose. In his study *The Purpose of Playing* he sets out a powerfully seductive narrative, which incorporates elements of both continuity and change. "By 1580, the Corpus Christi play was no longer a vital cultural practice in Elizabethan England," he declares, and goes on to argue that the Elizabethan state appropriated the vibrant energies of traditional sacramental drama into its specifically Protestant and monarchic royal pageants, progresses, and Accession Day festivals. Alongside these state rituals, and working in concert, the commercial theater occupied the medieval church's role as a space where the trials of daily existence could be addressed. One form replaced another. As Montrose explains, "the secure establishment and royal licensing of a fully professional, secular, and commercial theatre in later Elizabethan London was contemporaneous with the effective suppression of the religious drama."[45]

A repeated law is an inefficient law, and the frequent rulings quoted earlier suggest a limit to Montrose's enthusiasm; perhaps religious drama was not so effectively quashed. The turbulence of early modern liturgical controversy is animated by the proximity of plays and devotion. According to the great stage historian E. K. Chambers: "During the earlier part of Elizabeth's reign, Sunday was the usual day for plays. The trumpets blew for the performances just as the bells were tolling for afternoon prayer; and writer after writer bears testimony to the fact that too often the yards and galleries were filled with an appreciative crowd, while the preacher's sermon was unfrequented."[46] Here is a provocative competition, and polemicists could not keep church and theater apart. Both those who praised common prayer, and those who swore down upon it great condemnation, acknowledge the neighborliness of these two cultural forms.

When English Protestant reformers came to describe traditional Catholic worship, they turned to a theatrical vocabulary. As Calvin declared in a digression during his exegesis of Job: "We have none of all the fine masquing knacks that are in the papacy," and reformers warmed to the theme.[47] "Many times the thing that the priest saith in Latin is so fond of itself, that it is more like a play than a godly prayer" declared Thomas Cranmer in 1549; for Thomas Becon, one of Cranmer's chaplains, the traditional Mass is "a scenical and stage-like Supper"; for Andrew Willett, the rite is "but a kind of juggling trick" as "they do make nothing else but a Pageant-play of the Sacrament."[48] The analogy became a cliché of Protestant polemic but not exclusively so. In the controversy between the Anglican apologist John Jewel and the traditional theologian Thomas Harding during the 1550s, Harding compares Jewel to a playwright—"Sophocles was a poet, that is to say, a feigner and deviser of things that be not true, but fabulous: ye also are feigners and devisers of novelties, and followers of new devices, that be false. Sophocles was a tragical poet: ye are tragical divines"—and Jewel replied in kind. "O M. Harding, Sophocles himself, if he were alive, were not able with all his eloquence to express the tragical dealings of your company," he declared. "Your whole life and religion is nothing else but a tragedy."[49] The theater, as the most public mode of literary creativity, provided a neat analogue for the falsities of a rival theology, so both Catholics and Protestants used it to damn the other.

The Reformation unmoored a previously stable relation between liturgy and drama, but this is not to say that all relation disappeared. When in 1633 the Puritan lawyer and pamphleteer William Prynne surveyed the history of the popular stage, he found many things to dislike, but what irked him most were those plays "whose stile, whose subject matter is ordinarily satyricall and invective, being fraught with bitter scoffs or jests against Religion, Virtue, and Religious Christians." Prynne insists upon what the repeated statutes assume: that the plays staged in early modern London were not only inflected with religious controversies and vocabularies but were also stylistically and thematically specific in their appropriation. Prynne gives only one example of the "bitter scoffs or jests against Religion," and it is a liturgical parody. As he recounts:

> It is recorded that one Porphyry a Pagan stage-player, that he grew to such an height of impiety, as he adventured to baptize himselfe in jest upon the stage, of purpose to make the people laugh at Christian baptism, and so to bring both it and Christianity into contempt: and for this purpose he plunged himself into a vessell of water which he had placed on the stage, calling aloud upon the Trinity: at which the Spectators fell into a great laughter.[50]

Prynne could be thinking of Philip Massinger's *The Renegado*, which was first performed in 1623 and which does indeed include something close to a staged baptism. But the fit is inexact: Vitelli, a Venetian gentleman, throws water onto the face of his lover Donusa with the words "it hath power / To purge those spots that cleave upon the mind."[51] He does not invoke the Trinity, and he does not baptize himself. Whether Prynne is thinking of *The Renegado* or a different play, or whether his example is apocryphal or simply invented, should not distract us from the shared web of assumptions between the Puritan polemic and the official ecclesiastical statutes. For nearly a century, between the 1540s and the 1630s—that is, throughout

Shakespeare's lifetime—English drama was considered, by well-informed contemporaries, to be troublingly liturgical.

Church rites were—as the theologians I have quoted insist—dramatic events: their dramatic form offered an index of their theological content. Where sacraments were dramatic, plays were sacramental, as the same movements and phrases dictated by liturgy appeared on the stage. This was not an effect of a vague echo, a shared cultural vocabulary, for as Prynne insisted the sacraments themselves were specifically performed also on stage. There is a simple reason why dramatists should have chosen to incorporate church rites into their plays, as Prynne acknowledges when he notes that the audience who witnessed the mock baptism greeted the controversial spectacle with "a great laughter." There is little humor in a sincerely performed church rite, but when it appears in a theater, the disjoint between context and subject builds a new dramatic effect. Prynne continues his account of Porphyry:

> But lo the goodness of God to this profane miscreant; it pleased God to show such a demonstration of his power and grace upon him, that this sporting baptism of his, became a serious laver of regeneration to him: in so much that of a graceless Player, he became a gracious Christian, and not long after, a constant martyr.

Porphyry attempted to redirect the cultural power of the rite: to drain it of spiritual effect and replace it with a hollow theatrical gesture. But sacraments were, in early modern England, more than simply forms of words and movements. They held within their formulae tangible connection to the divine. Their phrases, properly performed, promise a terrifying and dramatic power. It might be comfortable, in a modern critical study, to skirt such awkward claims to transcendence. We impoverish our reading if we do so.

THE EXCESSES OF Porphyry, the blasphemous player, make a fine anecdote. Literary scholars love anecdotes, for they can read them like a story. This one suggests the tensions of the age, an ongoing rivalry between theater and church, and the odd logic of absolute Christian judgment. But at heart this is a story about shock: powered by Prynne's outraged indignation that this all is so blatant, that paid actors might perform a liturgy on the public stage. This sentiment recurs in the critical habits of modern Shakespeare scholars. Like sixteenth-century Puritans, twentieth-century literary critics assume separation between drama and liturgy, and are shocked when the border appears too porous. Their surprise at times leads them to miss what is in plain sight.

Let us take a single example. As Macbeth considers the murder of Duncan, he looks down and pleads: "Thou sure and firm-set earth, / Hear not my steps, which way they walk." His turn of phrase is apparently illogical: a voiced appeal to silence? An address to the ground? According to the 1873 Variorum edition of the play, which collects the critical history and responses to each line, in 1788 an anonymous writer in *Gentleman's Magazine* gamely speculated: "Macbeth was treading on a boarded floor up one pair of stairs (probably in a passage or lobby), which made a cracking noise that obliged him, in his alarm, to take long and cautious steps."[52] From the beginning of the scene, when Banquo can apparently see the sky, it would seem that we are outside rather than indoors, but this critical fiction of a Macbeth worried about a creaky floorboard testifies to the strain involved in making this make sense. Our unnamed commentator is trying to find dramatic order in a poetic flourish.

Another approach might be to track this phrase within its time, to use the tools of archival research instead of literary criticism, and to see its legibility as historical. In his Arden edition of the play, Kenneth Muir notes that a very similar phrase—"which way they were to walk"—appears also in the dedicatory epistle by the translators of the 1611 King James Bible, but quickly concludes that the echo is irrelevant. "The resemblance is probably accidental," Muir writes, "though it is not impossible that the writer had seen a performance of *Macbeth*, or that the phrase had been used in a sermon or pamphlet written on the accession of King James." There is no further note to this line in the Norton, Riverside, or New Cambridge editions of the play. A more curious reader might follow further the phrase's provenance; and yet, if you were to turn to Naseeb Shaheen's *Biblical References in Shakespeare's Plays* (1999), which is the standard reference work on Shakespeare's scriptural and liturgical allusions, you would find a disappointing gloss upon these lines. "Most persons would probably agree that the resemblance is accidental and that Shakespeare and the translators were using a common expression," Shaheen insists, and this phrase "cannot be attributed to any particular source."[53]

We need not look far, for the phrase is scriptural. It is Jeremiah 7:23, when God orders "walk ye in all the ways I have commanded you," and 10:23, which pleads "O Lord, I know, that the way of man is not in himself, neither *is it* in man to walk and to direct his steps"; it is Ecclesiastes 11:9, instructing "walk in the ways of thine heart" and again in Deuteronomy 5:33, which allows "walk in the ways." But most of all it is in the psalms. Psalm 1 begins, "Blessed is the man that doeth not walk in the counsel of the wicked, nor stand in the way of sinners," Psalm 143:8 asks, "show me the way, that I should walk in," and Psalm 128 opens, "Blessed is every one that feareth the Lord and walketh in his ways."

The assonance is a reassurance, a fit of right with right, but it is also an instruction to Christian conduct. This, at least, is how it was moralized in Elizabethan and Jacobean England. Abraham Fleming was a London preacher and translator who wrote devotional verse and translated sections of Virgil, a Dutch exposition of Ephesians, and a treatise on hunting dogs. One of his few original texts, *The Footepath to Felicitie, Which everie Christian must walke in* (1581), is a handbook to good behavior, full of set prayers and general confessions of worldliness and sin. Fleming describes the form of proper living:

> In which way, being the right way, the true way, the perfect way, the certain way, the pure way, the clean way, the undefiled way, the Lord give us grace to walk whiles we live and draw breath in

our earthly tabernacle, that we may, when we are called out of the
same, tread the footpath to felicity, enter in at the glorious gate of
heavenly Hierusalem.

These lines internalize the scriptural phrase "walk in the ways." They
turn it inside out while repetition, alliteration—"walk while we
live"—and assonance—"way" / "may"—both point to and expand the
simple line. Exegesis is creative: it draws on the rich and familiar
resource of scriptural language to teach specific lessons, and this same
phrase and its attached moral lesson echo through contemporary
verse. In the anti-Catholic polemicist Robert Crowley's dedicatory
poem to *Pleasure and Payne* (1551)—a plea for the relief of the poor in
England—we are told "That all men should walk / in their calling
upright / Directing their ways / by god's holy love," while for Alexander
Craig in *The Poeticall Recreations* (1609), God's lantern "shows the
way to walk, and march upright, / To do all good, and to decline
from ill."[54]

I am trying here, through repetition, to renew a now-lost cultural
knowledge: to trace the bounces of an echo and to show how deeply
familiar, even conventional, both this phrase and practice once were.
The biblical work of this combination of words was to teach a pious
code of conduct. But the phrase raised, in sixteenth-century literary
culture, a second, more specific context. Psalm 128, which begins
"Blessed are they that fear the Lord; and walk in his ways," is the
first of the cycle of psalms in the Book of Common Prayer's rite for
the solemnization of matrimony, and this liturgical connection to
marriage provided the phrase's dominant association for worshippers
in this time. Following the prayer book, it appears in the Elizabethan
homily "Of the State of Matrimony"—"Blessed is the man which
feareth God, and walketh in his ways"—and in countless handbooks
to marriage. It was a well-worn text for wedding sermons. William
Massie, preaching at a wedding in Lancashire in 1586, took as his
text this psalm and explicates the first line. "The second quality of
the husband," he preached, "is to walk in the ways of the Lord."

Samuel Hieron's *The Bridegroome*, preached at a wedding in 1613, instructed his audience that "All that he requireth is to fear him, *to walk in his ways and to love him.*" Heinrich Bullinger, in his treatise on marriage, describes his own purpose in writing: "that men may walk soberly according to the commandment of the Lord." The Bible teaches general conduct, but the prayer book deepens the lesson by applying these words specifically to marriage.[55]

Let us return to Macbeth in the moment of his plea. "Hear not my steps, which way they walk," he says, and the phrase is deliberate, heavily specific. This was conventional, perhaps a cliché. It anticipates our recognition, and renders the audience momentarily complicit with Macbeth. But now we know the phrase, we should know too its connotation, its simple spiritual teaching: we must be aware of the proper behavior of a Christian within marriage. *Macbeth* is a play built upon the tension of a marriage. Its most famous scenes are those between the husband and the wife, making this, curiously, Shakespeare's most domestic play. But here Macbeth, encouraged by his wife, is considering a murder. His situation literally negates the spiritual hope of the phrase—"Hear *not* my steps," he pleads—in a neat and shocking parody. The holy truths of scripture—thou shalt not kill; you must walk in the ways of the Lord—are absent yet also present in the memory of the phrase. In knowing the echo, we approach and yet are distanced from him. We understand his language in his misunderstanding of it, and these straying, shifting sympathies sound the distinctive note of tragedy.

This is not all, quite yet, for Macbeth inverts the expected line and turns liturgy inside out. The process I have sketched here—the phrases of liturgy, animated on stage—was illegal. Shakespeare should not have been doing this, and slight distortions in what characters say offer a plausible deniability; Macbeth is not *really* invoking the marriage rite. But this is also a larger point about drama as opposed to other literary forms. Plays alone proceed by a patchwork of distorted quotations; actors speak lines that are not their own, and yet give them a unique emphasis. It is always therefore unreliable, and Macbeth's phrase insists upon this necessary uncertainty. "Hear not my steps," he asks, and yet even this is slippery.

Macbeth first appears in the 1623 Folio of Shakespeare's plays, where he asks: "hear not my steps, which *they may* walk." He speaks this version of the phrase in each of the subsequent three Folio versions: 1632, 1663–64, and 1685. It is only in Nicholas Rowe's 1709 edition of the play that he first explicitly conjures the liturgical commonplace. In the Folio version, the clause "which they may walk" is syntactically awkward, as it lacks a subject—who or what may walk?—so the emendation most simply cleans up the grammar; it is also a phrase used elsewhere not only by Shakespeare but widely in the literature of his time, and for both of these reasons this strikes me as an entirely sensible alteration. No editor since has thought to question it. But this is also, surely, built upon nothing firmer than an echo. Rowe heard another phrase beneath the surface of the play. Plays are reinvented in the works of others, their editors and audiences, and Macbeth is not speaking alone.

What we hear is conditioned by our desires, by what we are willing to allow. "Hear not my steps": Macbeth asks us not to track the echo, and as if following his command—for this man is soon to be king of Scotland—nobody has done so. The curious blank around this line stands in contrast to the frequent attempts by scholars, over the past two centuries, to find in Shakespeare's plays the trace of religious sensibility. In 1880 Charles Wordsworth, the bishop of St Andrews in Scotland and the nephew of the poet William Wordsworth, described Shakespeare's plays as "saturated with Divine Wisdom, such as could have been derived only from the very Bible itself," and many have since agreed.[56] From Charles Alfred Swinburne's *Sacred & Shakespearian Affinities* (1890) to Stephen Marx's *Shakespeare and the Bible* (2000), critical studies have stressed the similarities between the plays and scripture. Naseeb Shaheen's *Biblical References in Shakespeare's Plays* notes hundreds of common phrases and motifs; H. R. D. Anders's 1904 study *Shakespeare's Books* and *Shakespeare's Religious Background* by Peter Milward (1973) both offer lists of verbal similarities between the plays and the prayer book. None of these studies mention Macbeth's echo.

This momentary gap is a single sign of a longer history of exclusion: critical attention to the apparent religiosity of Shakespeare's plays has always left out the Book of Common Prayer. The prayer book is a curiously forgotten work, overlooked even by those who might be expected to know it. There are two major traditions of reading Shakespeare religiously. Both agree that his plays allude to scriptural and liturgical ideas but differ on why this might be, and what it may tell us about the plays. The first critical school, now a century old, holds that the apparently devotional inflection of Shakespeare's plays is designed to teach a moral lesson. "Interpretation must be metaphysical," writes G. Wilson Knight in *The Wheel of Fire* (1930), and insists that the "moral attitude" of *Measure for Measure* is shared by the Gospels: "the insistence on the blindness of the world, its habitual disregard of the truth exposed by prophet and teacher." "The play must be read," he argues, "as a parable, like the parables of Jesus." In 1955 Hamilton Coleman in *Shakespeare and the Bible* presented Shakespeare as "a Christian philosopher," and more influentially Roy Battenhouse's *Shakespearean Tragedy: Its Art and Christian Premises* (1969) focuses on the Aristotelian elements of the tragedies to present the plays as thematically Christian. Battenhouse argues, for example, that a biblical notion of hamartia, or error, structures *Hamlet*. Most recently, and continuing the line of argument begun by Battenhouse, Peter Milward's *Biblical Influences in Shakespeare's Great Tragedies* (1987) finds the four great tragedies to express the scriptural themes of damnation, original sin, temptation, and penance.[57]

This is a tradition of faith in literature, as if literary skill equaled moral goodness, and as critical readings these come at a cost. These scholars read Shakespeare thematically. They read for spiritual meanings and lessons, and in doing so they present a transhistorical Shakespeare. There is no sense that Shakespeare's age was one not only of faith but also of religious violence, and that the kinds of abstract values they trace in the plays—forgiveness, repentance—were specifically contested; there is no sense that religious doctrine may divide as much as it may unite. Theirs is a faithful Shakespeare, but a man out of his time, so these readings necessarily leave out the prayer book, which was a document of its moment.

In the last two decades, scholars have returned to Shakespeare's treatment of theological arguments, but in the place of stable, polemical themes, they have focused on the playwright's attention to the theological controversies of his day. Stephen Greenblatt is perhaps the most influential recent critic of Shakespeare, and his work has stressed the presence in the plays of religious debate. In particular his work emphasizes religious rites, as these were the flashpoints of controversy. In his groundbreaking study *Shakespearean Negotiations* (1988)—a manifesto for the critical practice known as New Historicism—he traces the echoes, in *King Lear*, of late sixteenth-century arguments over the practice and possibility of exorcism, and in *Hamlet in Purgatory* (2001) he reads *Hamlet* through contemporary disputes over the fate of souls in purgatory. Largely inspired by Greenblatt's work, Huston Diehl and Jeffrey Knapp have found echoes of the Communion service in *Henry V* specifically and in contemporary drama more broadly. In *Alterations of State: Sacred Kingship in the English Reformation* (2002), Richard McCoy argues that *Hamlet* raises early modern arguments, between traditional Catholics and reformed Protestants, over the propriety and function of burial rites.

These scholars have valuably stressed the dramatic qualities of sacraments and repeatedly insisted upon the controversy, rather than stability, of early modern religious thought; the world they describe is historically grounded. But the actual connections offered in their studies between stage plays and sacramental rites remain frustratingly vague. Huston Diehl observes that performances of plays and the celebration of Communion are "related cultural activities." For Jeffrey Knapp, the Chorus in *Henry V* "recalls" the theology of Communion. What is at stake for the New Historicists is always drama, the feints and gestures of theater, so their readings treat church rites only as dramatic symbols, constantly gesturing elsewhere: to large, abstract questions about the nation or the idea of the individual. "Literary critics have understood it to be their task to translate the elements of the poem or play or novel or story into something else," wrote Susan Sontag in her essay "Against Interpretation"; the New Historicists translate the contents of early modern theological debate into modern, liberal concerns. There is little attention to the particulars of language, to the specific phrases of theological debate, and since the prayer book is a literary artifact, it is once more left out.[58]

The absence is even more profound. Neither the Bible nor the Book of Common Prayer are mentioned in the eight volumes of Geoffrey Bullough's *Narrative and Dramatic Sources of Shakespeare* (1957–75). Rather, for Bullough as for the generations of literary scholars who have relied upon his invaluable resource, the sources of Shakespeare are specifically nondevotional. North's translation of Plutarch, Holinshed's Chronicles, Plautus' *Menaechmi*, Arthur Brooke's *Tragical History of Romeus and Juliet*: all were undoubtedly ingredients in the literary and intellectual culture that formed Shakespeare, but all are also notably removed from the rich field of religious controversy, which dominated the publishing industry of early modern England. In *The Sources of Shakespeare's Plays*, Kenneth Muir gives one paragraph to biblical allusions in the plays, and within that paragraph, half a sentence to the prayer book ("There are some echoes from the Prayer Book"). In his study *Shakespeare's Books: A Dictionary of Shakespeare's Sources*, Stuart Gillespie dismisses the possibility that the prayer book could be a source. Even when such influence is apparent, he argues, "Shakespeare's allusions to Prayer Book material tend to be a way of appealing to shared cultural understandings and assumptions in his audience," and any tension between drama and liturgy is here instantly evacuated. They are walled apart once more, as modern literary critics complete the separatist work of long-dead Puritan polemicists.[59]

Bullough, Muir, and Gillespie—three representatives of a field— share the assumption that what constitutes a source is its literariness, specifically defined: a text exhibiting the conventional literary qualities of drama or narrative. Language is considered chiefly as a conduit for plot and all is premised upon a strictly single-track notion of influence. "The source of *Othello* is Giraldi Cinthio's *Hecatomithi*" writes Muir; and for *Macbeth*, "when all is said, Shakespeare's main source was Holinshed." Plays are not rivers; they can have more than a single source, but source-study is marked by a kind of competitiveness, an exclusivity, as everybody wants the skeleton key. In setting out the materials upon which Shakespeare worked, these studies necessarily present all the activity as Shakespeare's. Here are these old stories, they say, waiting for the magic of his touch. The source not only precedes the play; it is transformed and improved by it.

To account for Shakespeare's relation to the prayer book, we need a more active understanding of literary influence, one that preserves playfulness and does not seek to dampen down the richness of an encounter between two rival works. We need a messier and more engaged definition of a source. This is not to limit Shakespeare's creativity or to diminish the texture of the plays. Instead, it is to acknowledge that Shakespeare did not conjure the tensions of his plays from the dust and from the air. This kind of engagement puts work at the center of our reading and sees the plays as carried out between playwright and source, involved with a local world. This will entail a new conception of literary production, in which the writer is perhaps not alone. "In a way that has not been fully recognized or conceptualized by scholars trained to organize material within post-Enlightenment paradigms of individuality, authorship, and textual property, collaboration was a prevalent mode of textual production in the sixteenth and seventeenth centuries," writes Jeffrey Masten, while Brian Vickers has described "the common and accepted practice of co-authorship in Elizabethan, Jacobean, and Caroline drama." The precise rates for collaborative authorship are unknown, but according to the stage historian G. E. Bentley, "Altogether the evidence suggests that it would be reasonable to guess that as many as half the plays by professional dramatists in the period incorporated the writing at some date of more than one man."[60] If we seek to see Shakespeare in his time—as he was, not how we want him—then we first must learn to see him collaborating, joining, sharing. We must learn to see his plays as common work.

There are a thousand ways to read a play and as many ways to tell a life. We start with the records, with what survived, which we work up as we will. We do not know the day of Shakespeare's birth, but we can trace other dates. He buys land on 1 May 1602, and a half-interest in a lease of tithes on 24 July 1605; we have his deposition in the Belott-Montjoy suit of 1612. We know those things he did that were unusual; we know that the plays were his.

But the records tell too another story. He was baptized on 26 April 1564—the parish record notes, "Gulielmus filius Johannes Shakspere," "William son of John Shakespeare"—and on 28 November 1582 his marriage bond was issued at Worcester. This permitted him to marry after only one asking of the banns, instead of the regulation three; this might be a sign of something out of the ordinary, the evidence of a scandal, but as Samuel Schoenbaum notes, "These licenses were not at all uncommon; in 1582 the Worcester court granted ninety-eight." It is similarly usual to have only the date of baptism, and not a birth. "Childbirth was women's work," as David Cressy has noted: "Women, for the most part, were illiterate, and they rarely set forth their experiences in writing. With a few remarkable exceptions, our sources are confined to the viewpoints of husbands, fathers, ministers, doctors, and scribes." This was not a culture that recorded births, for that is not the important date. Rather, as Cressy has it, "Being born into the world was but a prelude to the social and spiritual ritual of baptism."[61] We have the date of his burial, on 25 April 1616, at Stratford, where he began.

The missing date of Shakespeare's birth and the survival of the date of his baptism is the proof of a life measured in rites. Where we think we have the shape of a biography, what we in fact have is its liturgical record. Sacraments are the architecture of social history; they are what make him common.

PART I *The Form of Solemnization of Matrimony*

O Eternal God, creator and preserver of all mankind, giver of all spiritual grace, the author of everlasting life: send thy blessing upon these thy servants, this man and this woman, whom we bless in thy name, that as Isaac and Rebecca lived faithfully together: So these persons may surely perform and keep the vow and covenant betwixt them made, whereof this ring, given and received, is a token and pledge, and may ever remain in perfect love and peace together, and live according to thy laws, through Jesus Christ our Lord. Amen.

Then shall the Priest join their right hands together and say:

Those whom God hath joined together, let no man put asunder.

The Book of Common Prayer (1559), Cummings, 159.

CHAPTER 2 ❧ *For Better, for Worse*

"D early beloved friends," begins the rite for the solemnization of matrimony in the Book of Common Prayer from
1549 on, "we are gathered together here in the sight of
God, and in the face of this congregation, to join together this man
and this woman in holy matrimony, which is an honorable estate."
This is a public event, a gathering, beholden to an audience; it affirms a social bond and is quick to evoke the spiritual. The marriage
is a metaphor, "signifying unto us the mystical union, that is betwixt
Christ and his Church," explains the priest, and the elements of the
rite are symbols too: the ring is "a token and a pledge" of "the vow
and covenant." "With my body I thee worship," vows the man. "Then
shall the earth bring forth her increase: and God, even our God,
shall give us his blessing," follows the priest. Two people, a couple,
stand right before him and yet all is rendered quickly abstract and a
metaphor. Each priestly gesture invites the onlookers to see a trail of
spiritual signs. This is, the priest repeats at the end of the rite, "an
excellent mystery, that in it is signified and represented the spiritual
marriage betwixt Christ and his Church."[1] We are at a moment of
union, of the meeting of parts: of Christ and the Church, of a man
and woman. The theology of the rite is at once its drama.

The spiritual signification of the ceremony was troubling to some.
Following the Hampton Court Conference, a Puritan petition
addressed to James quoted this line and went on to question *"Whether
these words sound not in the ears of most people, as if Matrimony were*

a sacrament as well as baptism and the Lord Supper [?]"[2] Since 1549, the English church had recognized only the two sacraments named here: baptism and Communion. Where the traditional church had held marriage also as a sacrament, it was in England demoted to a church rite. Its form, however, remained. The Roman rite set out three steps—spousal, delivery of ring and dowry, and church blessing and Mass—that were retained by the Book of Common Prayer with very little variation. The prayer book's exhortation can be found in both Sarum and York primers, as is the homily that declares "the causes for which matrimony was ordained." The changes are slight. The prayer book removes the blessings of the ring and bride-bed, which were included in the Sarum primer; the service is moved from the porch into the body of the church. In the ears of its audiences, then, the solemnization of matrimony in the Book of Common Prayer sounds like precisely what it is *not* supposed to be. For some, the dramatic effect of the rite is at odds with its theological purpose.

A sacrament is in the simplest version a sign that confers grace upon men: it is a delivery mechanism and a meeting-point between the human and the divine. The degree of effect and the agents required; the extent to which agents are even involved; its functioning, form, and process: all are hotly contested throughout this period. Those debates take place, as the petition suggests, over reading and revision—over what is heard, perceived, interpreted as much as what is said. Those words might sound one way in the ears of most people, the petition appeals. The prayer book bears the scars of this debate over whether the marriage rite is a spiritual event. In the 1549 version of the rite, the priest follows immediately the moment of union—"I pronounce that they be man and wife together"—with a blessing:

> God the father bless you. God the son keep you: god the holy ghost lighten your understanding: The lord mercifully with his favour look upon you, and so fill you with all spiritual benediction and grace, that you may have remission of your sins in this life, and in the world to come life everlasting. (Cummings, 67)

Here is the promise of transformation: the remission of sin and in the working of the rite the priest is perhaps directing God's hand. This is close to a traditional Catholic efficacy, so the more Protestant 1552 prayer book—and all editions following—quietly elides this blessing. It now runs:

> God the Father, God the Son, God the holy Ghost bless, preserve, and keep you: the Lord mercifully with his favour look upon you, and so fill you with all his spiritual benediction and grace, that you may so live together in this life, that in the world to come you may have life everlasting. (Cummings, 160)

The promised consequence—the remission of sin—has vanished. Now, the rite wishes for worldly fulfillment: "that you may so live together in this life," here on this ground. Debate over the purpose and function of the marriage rite was not settled by the end of the century. Writing his great anthology of controversies known as *Synopsis Papismi* in 1592, Andrew Willet lists as the first and dominant issue, under his section on marriage, "Whether Matrimony be a sacrament properly so called." He insists, "it is no sacrament," and his need for insistence then tells us now that the ambiguity persisted.[3] For Willet and the people of Elizabethan England, matrimony was marked by ontological uncertainty. The newly married couple was blessed, but perhaps by man and not by God; the ceremony itself sat somewhere between spiritual and worldly.

When scholars have come in recent years to consider this period's literature of marriage, they have too often been blind to the fissures within the union. They find certainty in the place of controversy, and that which once was rough is made smooth. The rite itself is apparently of little interest. As Catherine Bates writes in her essay "Love and Courtship," in the *Cambridge Companion to Shakespearean Comedy*: "Marriage—the endpoint to which courtship stories inevitably as if magnetically tend—is literary shorthand for the control of human sexuality by law." Bates presents marriage as no more than a formality, an event without meanings of its own. In her study of courtship in Shakespeare's

England, Ann Jennalie Cook finds only a set of passive and popularly accepted mechanisms. "Signals like letters, gifts, joined hands, kisses, rings, witnesses, even the casual mention of a wedding torch link up with a whole set of assumptions that were the ordinary furnishings of an Elizabethan mentality," she writes.[4] But there was no single ordinary mentality available in this time, and the elements she mentions were instead the pressure points and objects of disagreement.

In assuming consensus rather than controversy, scholars have tended to see stasis instead of drama. They have learned this sensibility from another discipline. Readings of Shakespeare's treatment of marriage are traditionally phrased within an anthropological vocabulary borrowed from such figures as Victor Turner and Arnold van Gennep. Following them, literary critics such as C. L. Barber, René Girard, and Edward Berry trace within Shakespeare's plays a timeless ritual pattern. Berry writes, for example, that "In the form of rites of passage this structure exists in nearly all cultures, including those of Elizabethan England," which means that there is little specific to Shakespeare or his time.[5] Most strikingly, David Bevington's influential study of ritual in Shakespeare's plays observes, "The wedding ceremony itself is never really performed in its entirety on Shakespeare's stage. One reason may be . . . that the occasion ordinarily lacks dramatic conflict." Bevington adds, "Another factor may have been the governmental strictures against derogation or abuse of the Book of Common Prayer."[6] Putting aside for a moment the acuity of this observation as a reading of the plays—which are dense with precise liturgical echo—we may trace here a whole school of assumptions about the relation of drama to ritual. Bevington's second reason—that it was illegal to perform a marriage onstage—is historically correct but contradicts his first. The notion that marriage was a static formality disregards the testament of early modern liturgical debate.

THE UNCERTAINTY OF the marriage rite is a worry over words: about the relation of love its representation and the strength of language to cement emotional bonds. These are a love poet's worries, and their tensions hum beneath the surface of one of Shakespeare's earliest plays. *The Two Gentlemen of Verona* (1588–1594?) opens with an opposition: between "loving Proteus," who wishes to stay at home and Valentine who seeks the world. "Home-keeping youth have ever homely wits," Valentine tells Proteus:

> Were't not affection chains thy tender days
> To the sweet glances of thy honoured love,
> I rather would entreat thy company
> To see the wonders of the world abroad. (1.1.1–6)

Homely Proteus is in love with Julia; for sixty lines the friends banter in the clunky puns of early Shakespeare ("give me not the boots." / "No, I will not: for it boots thee not"). "Love is your master, for he masters you," teases Valentine. "And he that is so yoked by a fool / Methinks should not be chronicled for wise," he goes on, and strides offstage to Milan: "farewell" (1.1.27–28, 40–41, 62).

As a debate between love and manly adventure, the play has little faith in its own opposition. Valentine, as his name suggests, will soon fall in love, and Proteus likewise will change his mind. But the play as a whole never quite escapes the heckling tone of those opening lines. Its distinctive narrative movement is the disavowal of love; this is what powers the plot, keeps it moving, as love is transfer, not stasis. Valentine, in love with Silvia, is banished from Milan. Proteus abandons Julia, and schemes how he may win Silvia. Proteus not only betrays his friend but specifically denies his love for him: "I love him not as I was wont." The changes continue like a carousel. Thurio, who also courts Silvia, runs when he is threatened—"I hold him but a fool that will endanger / His body for a girl that loves him not"—and Valentine too disowns his love and offers her to Proteus as a gift: "All that was mine in Silvia I give thee." All is sudden, jumpy; nothing sticks or stays. The play is riven by weird contradictions, as if it distrusts the capacities of its characters to plot coherently their own lives (2.4.197; 5.4.130–31, 83).

This is at heart a crisis about language: its use and application, its attachment to truth. For the play takes the expression of love as a proof or product of weakness. Valentine advises the Duke in his courtship that "Dumb jewels often in their silent kind / More than quick words do move a woman's mind" (3.1.90–91). The language of love, the play frequently insists, has no formal power. It is rather, in Valentine's phrase, "a discourse of disability"—a poetry of weakness, of incapacity and humiliation. Love, Valentine describes it, has "punished me / With bitter fasts, with penitential groans, / With nightly tears and daily heart-sore sighs" (2.4.102, 123–25). Proteus is similarly disabled in the face of Silvia. "When I look on her perfection / There is no reason but I shall be blind," he declares (2.4.204–5). Those characters who hold love as a strength are shown to be fools. The Duke extends his trust to the faithless Proteus. "You are already love's firm votary, / And cannot soon revolt, and change your mind" he tells him, but Proteus has by now already changed his mind and is soon to do so again (3.2.58–59).

Contrasting the slippery trickeries of love among the male characters in the play is the constancy of the two loved women, Julia and Silvia. One of the rare moments of love poetry is Julia's declaration to Lucetta of her love for Proteus, and that she will follow him to Milan. The journey is not far, she declares, for "she that hath love's wings to fly, / And when the flight is made to one so dear, / Of such divine perfection as Sir Proteus." She goes on to stress the qualities in him upon which her love depends: "His words are bonds, his oaths are oracles, / His love sincere, his thoughts immaculate" (2.7.11–13, 75–76). The imagery of bonding is not accidental. This scene is located immediately after Proteus, alone on stage and in soliloquy, has disavowed his love for Julia—"I will forget that Julia is alive, / Rememb'ring that my love is dead"—and immediately before he begins plotting with the Duke to separate Valentine from Silvia (2.6.27–28). The play's pessimism is expressed in its arrangement. Love poetry, and the verbal bonds upon which hinge its hope, are weak versions of a harsher reality.

The language of bonding, inaugurated in the opening scene—
Proteus is "yoked by a fool"—runs through the play; at each occasion, bonds are present but fallible, and what the opening lines call
"chains of affection" are made of tin and not of steel. Julia, however,
retains her faith in vowing. His words are bonds, she says, and so he
must be true. Before leaving, Proteus comes to Julia, and she gives
him a ring. "Keep this remembrance for Julia's sake," she offers, and
he replies, "Why, then we'll make exchange. Here take you this."
Even without stage directions, their words specify what their actions
must be. "Seal the bargain with a holy kiss," Julia asks, and Proteus
takes her hand: "Here is my hand for my true constancy" (2.2.5–8).

It is easy to overlook this scene, or merely see it as a prompt to pity
Julia. Proteus will soon lie, and they have done nothing more than
exchange rings, hold hands, and kiss. This was, however, enough. As
Anne Barton has shown in a quietly spoken but groundbreaking
essay called "'Wrying but a little': Marriage, Law, and Sexuality in the
Plays of Shakespeare," the centerpiece of early modern marriage custom was the dramatic performance of consent. A handfast and
exchange of rings and agreement was sufficient to bind a couple.
Consent expressed in the present tense formed an indissoluble
bond; if the contract was conditional, sexual consummation made
it binding. The form of the rite of matrimony was required to solemnize the union, but the order of these three events—consent,
consummation, church rite—was largely irrelevant. Barton's article
relies heavily on an early seventeenth-century handbook of the
forms of verbal consent, *Of Spousals or Matrimonial Contracts* by
Henry Swinburne, and convincingly shows how the essentially
dramatic nature of the spousals recorded by Swinburne influenced
Shakespeare's presentation of marriage contracts.[7] According to one
version of early modern law, Proteus and Julia are now half-married.
Her understanding, then, is neither naïve nor incorrect. His words
are bonds.

Barton reminds us that marriage is a dramatic performance: the
spousal is a piece of minor theater. In closely following Swinburne,

however, Barton's description of early modern marriage is necessarily partial. Henry Swinburne was a church lawyer who also wrote *A Briefe Treatise of Testaments and Last Willes* (1590); he was disqualified from a fellowship at Oxford after he married the daughter of a local gentleman without parental permission, so he knew the tensions of marriage law at firsthand. His purpose in writing the *Treatise of Spousals* was to draw an absolute distinction between spousals—the formal expressions of consent between the two parties—and church solemnization. Swinburne therefore downplays the liturgical aspects of marriage, which he mentions only twice in his book: once to repeat that people too often confuse spousals with marriage, and once to comment that the ring mentioned in the Book of Common Prayer is a further sign of mutual consent. Rather than allowing the spiritual dimension of marriage, he repeatedly describes it in the language of business, comparing it to "other Covenants and Bargains."[8]

In leaving out liturgy, Swinburne considers marriage only as consent and this, as the play insists, is of unreliable quality. Behind the confusions of the characters on stage is uncertainty about script. What binds them is a sense of something absent, a pattern of sad silences and lost words. In teasing Valentine for his love for Silvia, Speed compares him to "a schoolboy that hath lost his ABC," and so cannot know what to say; when Proteus writes a love letter to Julia, she tears it up and throws the pieces to the floor. She repents and tries to read its fragments—"Be calm, good wind, blow not a word away / Till I have found each letter in the letter"—but the phrases vanish (1.2.118–20). These characters are thwarted without a whole vocabulary. When Proteus leaves Julia and Verona in silence, she is forced to justify: "What gone without a word? / Ay, so true love should do. It cannot speak" (2.2.16–17). In the closing scene, silence still reigns. Valentine at the end promises to Proteus "our day of marriage shall be yours, / One feast, one house, one mutual happiness" (5.4.169–70). The marriages are outside the world of the play, eternally off-stage. Silvia, one of the brides to be wed, simply does not speak.

Not only does the play repeatedly show and tell us that love is foolish slavery, "a folly bought with wit," even those relationships that bear within their history the traces of affection, such as between Valentine and Silvia, have no presence. All courtships take place offstage: between Julia and Proteus, before the play begins; between Valentine and Silvia; between the first and second acts. When passion appears, it comes only as damage and humiliation; it has no suasive words. "If the gentle spirit of moving words / Can no way change you to a milder form," boasts Proteus to Silvia, "I'll woo you like a soldier, at arm's end, / And love you 'gainst the nature of love: force ye" (5.4.55–58). This is a play in which the expression of affection may take the form of rape.

For Shakespeare, this early in his career, love provides the dramatic occasion for violence and mockery. Courtship is menacing and false; a trustworthy passion scarcely appears on stage. In *The Taming of the Shrew* (1594) marriage assumes a more visible role in the plot, but the church rite is dramatized as another opportunity for humiliation. Petrucchio approaches his wedding to Katherine with the ceremonial self-consciousness of a court jester. He arrives dressed absurdly—"To me she's married, not unto my clothes"—and proceeds to pantomime the church solemnization (3.2.110). The form of matrimony prescribed by the Book of Common Prayer begins with a declaration of consent. The priest asks, "Wilt thou have this woman to thy wedded wife?," expecting the reply "I will"; the formula is then addressed to the woman (Cummings, 158). Petrucchio disrupts the script. As Gremio reports: "When the priest should ask if Katherine should be his wife, / 'Ay, by Gog's woun's,' quoth he, and swore so loud / That all amazed the priest let fall the book" (3.3.31–34). The prayer book rite culminates when "the new married persons (the same day of their marriage) must receive the Holy Communion," and Petrucchio seizes the opportunity:

He calls for wine. "A health," quoth he, as if
He had been aboard, carousing to his mates

After a storm; quaffed off the muscatel
And threw the sops all in the sexton's face. (164; 3.3.43–46)

From here, the solemnization conventionally proceeded with a wedding feast, followed by the sexual consummation; this "mad marriage" preserves the elements by turning them to farce (3.3.55). Petrucchio and Katherine promptly leave for his country house, where he rejects the mutton that his servants have prepared—"for this night we'll fast for company"—and in a parody of their consummation, tears up their marriage bed ("here I'll fling the pillow, there the bolster") and refuses to let her sleep (4.1.158, 182).

For Petrucchio, the elements of the church rite offer stages for the further education of Katherine. "He that knows better how to tame a shrew, / Now let him speak" he declares, and his call echoes again the prayer book rite, in which the priest calls upon the audience: "if any man can show any just cause, why they may not lawfully be joined together, let him now speak" (4.1.191–92, 157). The church rite is hollowed of its emotional intention, but the elements of its structure—the form of consent, the reception of communion, and the consummation—are retained upon the stage.

In these early comedies, love suffers from a crisis of representation; it lacks a dramatic form. Those characters who love do so either unwillingly or in pain. As Biron exclaims in *Love's Labour's Lost* (1594) "What? I love, I sue, I seek a wife?" (3.1.174). The comedies isolate the emotion of love first from its verbal expression and second from its ceremonial enactment, and nowhere is this crisis more miserably apparent than in *Much Ado About Nothing* (1598–99). Claudio loves Hero, but the quality of his love is never explained. He woos her only through the intermediary of Don Pedro, and their marriage is arranged before the young lovers have spoken a word to each other. Once Leonato, Hero's father, has agreed that the marriage to his daughter may take place, Beatrice turns to Claudio to invite him to articulate his emotion—"Speak, Count, 'tis your cue"—but Claudio declines. "Silence is the perfectest herald of joy," he replies (2.1.266–67).

This love, which lovers refuse to speak, is almost willfully incomplete; it is unconvincing even to Claudio, who is quick to abandon Hero. Although Claudio claims to eagerly anticipate the wedding—"Time goes on crutches till love have all his rites," he declares—he is equally eager to abandon his love at the first hint of impropriety. Once Don John suggests that Hero may be untrue, but before he has given any proof, Claudio decides that "tomorrow, in the congregation where I should wed, there will I shame her," and Don Pedro concurs: "I will join thee to disgrace her" (2.1.310–11; 3.2.104–7). In the church, the presiding friar addresses Claudio—"You come hither, my lord, to marry this lady?"—and Claudio simply replies "No." The friar ignores Claudio and returns to the prayer book rite. "If either of you know any inward impediment why you should not be conjoined, I charge you on your souls to utter it," he intones incongruously, echoing the set clerical address to the congregation. Claudio again refuses the bond. "Take her back again," he tells Leonato: "Give not this rotten orange to your friend" (4.1.4–6, 11–12, 29–30).

As Benedick notes, "this looks not like a nuptial," for the dramatic effect of this scene arises not from its presentation of the phrases and sensibility of the prayer book rite, but from their mocking inversion (4.1.66). Not looking like a nuptial is precisely the intended dramatic effect here, and the phrase—as well as the cruel humor of the scene—assumes the familiarity of Elizabethan audiences with what a nuptial did, or at least should, look like. The drama of Shakespeare's comedies written during the 1590s is about love, but one in which love is only thematically present. Its poetic expression is outweighed by a grinding skepticism, and its ceremonies are askew. These plays find drama, then, in the discord between the commercial stage and formal church rites. The first phase of Shakespeare's apprenticeship to the prayer book was marked by this quality of mockery. Church rites were not supposed to be seen on stage. In this early arc of plays he begins to place them there, although phrased, as yet, only as occasions of hurt.

❧

IN SONNET 23, Shakespeare likens a tongue-tied lover to "an imperfect actor upon the stage, / Who with his fear is put besides his part." The analogy is curious, implying that the expression of love has a set form, a particular script to follow; one text for the whole variety of lovers and occasions, one ideal expression of emotion. He calls this "the perfect ceremony of love's rite," although he apparently cannot say it. "O let my books be then the eloquence / And dumb presagers of my speaking breast," he asks. The sonnets are games of form and articulation: they are about what truth may be boxed in set speech. Here the truest speaker is an actor, straining for the words of his role.

During the mid-1590s, as Shakespeare was writing a series of comedies that dwell on the failure of loving unions, his interest turned to the mechanics of their opposite: the formal structures of sincere bonds. This small but poignant revolution, whose dramatic consequences echo through the plays he writes in the opening years of the seventeenth century—arguably the plays for which he is most celebrated—begins in a tragedy that comes within a breath of being a comedy. In *Romeo and Juliet* (1595), as if weary of the dizzying skepticism of the early plays, Shakespeare for the first time gives the elements of the marriage rite a dramatic purpose larger than parody. The prayer book now shifts from antagonist to ally.

Romeo and Juliet contains a familiar tone: the heckling mockery of the early comedies surfaces in the voice of Mercutio. He is an arbiter of irony and well-read in the poetry of love. He mocks the rhymes of lovers—"Speak but one rhyme and I am satisfied"—and the conventional blazon, a listing of the aspects of the loved one. "I conjure thee by Rosaline's bright eyes, / By her high forehead and her scarlet lip"; as he lists, he names and debunks the poetic forms available to lovers. "Now he is for the numbers that Petrarch flowed in," he teases: "Laura, to his lady, was a kitchen wench" (2.1.9, 17–18; 2.3.34–35). Dante will not do, nor Petrarch, nor any of those old poets.

Rosaline is Romeo's first love, and she never appears on stage; she is the ghost of the silent, formless loves of the early comedies, and like those earlier lovers is soon forgotten by the play. For the play revels gloriously in Romeo's second love, and presents their bond in a new vocabulary. Romeo and Juliet, upon meeting, speak instantly of holiness. "I'll watch her stand," Romeo declares upon sighting Juliet: "And touching hers, make blessed my rude hand." Their exchange, in full, reads as part of another, different type of play:

> ROMEO: If I profane with my unworthiest hand
> This holy shrine, the gentler sin is this:
> My lips, two blushing pilgrims, ready stand
> To smooth that rough touch with a tender kiss.
> JULIET: Good pilgrim, you do wrong your hand too much,
> Which mannerly devotion shows in this.
> For saints have hands that pilgrims' hands too touch,
> And palm to palm is holy palmers' kiss.
> ROMEO: Have not saints lips, and holy palmers, too?
> JULIET: Ay, pilgrim, lips that they must use in prayer.
> ROMEO: O then, dear saint, let lips do what hands do:
> They pray; grant thou, lest faith turn to despair.
> JULIET: Saints do not move, though grant for prayers' sake.
> ROMEO: Then move not while my prayer's effect I take. (1.5.90–103)

This is a formal sonnet: three quatrains, each alternately rhymed, and a closing rhyming couplet. He speaks the first four lines, and she follows; then, in the third quatrain, they speak together; each shares half the final couplet. They are speaking of love and giving it form. This is the lost ABC from *The Two Gentlemen of Verona*, and the eloquent book of Sonnet 23. Our unworthy actors, upon the stage, have found the perfect ceremony of love's rite.

For Romeo and Juliet, love is structure and they tumble into form. We should by now be familiar with each of the dance steps, and watch as they intuit them for themselves. Their spousal is not explicitly uttered on stage, but both characters understand it to be in place. "I have no joy of this contract tonight," says Juliet, and when Romeo leaves her to visit Friar Laurence he agrees. They are, he says, "all combined save what thou must combine / By holy marriage." Now they require the institutional presence of the church, so Romeo returns to the friar to ask: "close our hands with holy words" (2.1.159; 2.2.60–61; 2.5.6). He is following the steps of convention as if they were written only for him.

We are far from *The Two Gentlemen of Verona* here, and yet the setting of *Romeo and Juliet* is the same: "In fair Verona, where we lay our scene" (Prologue, 2). The latter play, like the marriage rite, demands the presence of a priest, and a glance backwards to the earlier play here clarifies the dramatic innovation. In *Two Gentlemen* Silvia agrees to meet Eglamour at the forest cell of a priest: he is named in the play as Friar Patrick, though never appears on stage. This play touches only lightly upon the mechanics of marriage, never needing the services of a priest. Nonetheless when the Folio compositors came to set the scene, they were perhaps thinking of the later play. The Folio twice names the friar in *Two Gentlemen* "Patrick," and then at the third mention, "Friar Laurence" (4.3.43; 5.1.3; 5.2.35). Unconsciously trying to compensate for its lack of the churchly form of love, they left a ghostly trace of the later and more important friar.

Not only the two parts of a vow—its consent, declared in a spousal contract, and its formal solemnization—make a marriage complete. Even as Romeo and Juliet trade the tropes of devotional love, they talk also of sex, for the two—sex and worship—are not contradictory but commensurate. To Romeo's demand, "O wilt thou leave me so unsatisfied?" Juliet replies, "what satisfaction canst thou have tonight?"; his response—"Th'exchange of thy love's faithful vow for mine"—neatly collapses sexual satisfaction onto the formal vows of love, suggesting that the two are parallel phases of a single movement (2.2.125–27). As with Nurse's ceaseless bawdy—"you shall bear the burden soon at night," she tells Juliet (2.5.77)—the play insists not only that the marriage rite finds completion in sexual consummation but also that the sequence of events is predetermined.

The marriage itself must take place offstage, between acts 2 and 3, but the movement of the play follows its logic. The rite is unfinished until consummation, as Juliet acknowledges while she waits for Romeo to come to her after the marriage. "O, I have bought the mansion of a love, / But not possess'd it," she muses, and continues: "and though I am sold, / Not yet enjoy'd" (3.2.26–28). She is as yet only half-married. This conjunction of formal vows and sex echoes the orthodox English theology of marriage. In her eloquent history of literary representations of the married couple, Jean Hagstrum notes the tension, within marriage, between desire and devotion. She attends to the increasingly erotic nature of Renaissance art and the writings of Erasmus, Luther, and Calvin to argue that the Reformation was marked by deliberate attempts to connect eroticism with the ideal of marriage. She calls this innovation "the placing of desire in holy matrimony," and cites examples from Shakespeare's comedies and histories.[9]

Hagstrum does not suggest that this tradition was theologically specific, but she clearly describes an innovation of reformed accounts of marriage. Even as they demoted marriage from sacrament to church rite, Protestant thinkers defended the holiness of the state and specifically praised married sex as an act of devotion. In the early years of the English Reformation, the traditional bishop Edmund Bonner described married sex as "carnal multiplication"; forty years later, toward the end of Elizabeth's reign, a divinity student by the name of Francis Meres (who would later become famous to scholars as one of Shakespeare's first literary critics) used a similar image to describe the same subject in very different terms. "When God had married Adam and Eva together," he wrote, "God said to them both increase, multiple and replenish the earth: this is Gods Arithmetic."[10] The shift from carnal multiplication to God's arithmetic is a shift in sympathy, from the passing and negative suggestion to a joyful defense. That which was carnal is now godly.

There is debate just beneath the surface of *Romeo and Juliet*, and it is invisible to us unless we are sensitive to the currents of theology. The controversy over the sanctity of sex began in the first years of the Reformation within disagreements over clerical marriage. Where ministers had traditionally been forbidden to marry, the reformed English Church permitted them to take wives. In his *Treatise of the Sacraments*, written in the late 1550s, John Jewel—who never married—attacked the traditional position that married sex is in some way unspiritual and therefore unfitting for the priesthood. "What are they that call marriage uncleanness, filthiness, a work of the flesh?" he demands: "That say it defileth a man; and therefore God's ministers may not be married?" Precisely, Jewel here mocks the idea that married sex is unclean. In his subsequent *Defence of the Apology*, the longest section of back and forth between Jewel and his opponent, the traditional theologian Thomas Harding, is over the issue of clerical marriage, but his defense of priestly sex takes the form of a defense of sex as an act of devotion. "God ordained not only the state of matrimony itself, but also the very act of generation" he writes, and continues: "Know ye not that your bodies be the temple of the Holy Ghost? Therefore, if the man and wife keep their faith both between themselves and to the Lord, their bodies are holy."[11] Jewel's defense of clerical marriage hinges upon a defense of married sex, between all men and women.

The reformed treatment of sexual activity is marked by a close consideration of the physical body. The logical consequence of the reformed celebration of married—legitimate—sexual activity is an intense attention to the physical depravities of illegitimate sexual activity. The 1547 Edwardian homily "Of Whoredom and Uncleanness" centers upon the body. It rejects the "carnal delectation, and filthy pleasure" of sexual activity out of wedlock, and demands, "Do ye not know that he, which cleaveth to an whore, is made one body with her?" Disease is the physical manifestation of sin: "Come not the French pocks, with other diverse diseases of whoredom?"[12]

When Queen Mary's Catholic bishops came to write their own homilies, they borrowed heavily from the language of the Edwardian Protestant versions. There is no specific homily on whoredom in Bonner's 1555 *Profitable and necessary doctrine, with certain homilies*, but the exposition of the seventh commandment—"thou shalt not commit adultery"—is largely based on the 1547 Edwardian homily on whoredom. Bonner's version removes each of the lines I quoted earlier and introduces instead a far more metaphorical version of sin. One of the very few original paragraphs in Bonner's book runs:

> Furthermore in this commandment not only the vices before rehearsed, be forbidden and prohibited, but also the virtues contrary to them be required and commanded: That is to say. Fidelity, and true keeping of wedlock, in them that be married, continence in them that be unmarried: And generally in all persons, shamefastness and chasteness, not only of deeds, but of words, and manners, countenance, and thought. And moresoever fasting, temperance, watching, labour, and all lawful things that conduce and help to chastity.

"Shamefastness and chasteness" are the ways to holiness, and the reformed connection between sex and marriage is here severed. Bonner's exposition continues, "consent doth make matrimony, and not the carnal copulation or lying together."[13]

For traditional Catholic theologians, sex was not a sacramental activity. In the reformed imagination, however, sex was a minor sacrament, a devotion of its own. The Puritan divine William Perkins details the parts of marriage in his posthumously published handbook to the devotional life, *Christian Oeconomie* (1609), and he insists that liturgy is made complete in sexual intercourse:

> if the parties betrothed, do lie together before the condition (though honest & appertaining to marriage) be performed; then the contract for time to come is, without further controversy, sure and certain. For where there hath been a carnal use of each others body, it is always pre-supposed, that a mutual consent, as touching Marriage, hath gone before.[14]

Sex makes marriage. There is no contradiction between married sex and godly worship, as must have been clear to the audience who heard William Whately, known as "the roaring boy of Banbury" for his powerful lungs and style, preaching in 1616. In the course of a wedding sermon he gave detailed instructions to the bride and groom as how best to enjoy what he calls "their matrimonial meetings":

> First, it must be cheerful; they must lovingly, willingly, and famil-
> iarly communicate themselves unto themselves. . . . Secondly,
> their meeting must be satisfied. *Paul* saith, meat, drink, and mar-
> riage are good, being satisfied by prayer. Men and women must
> not come together as brute creatures and unreasonable beasts,
> through the heat of desire; To satisfy the marriage-bed, and use it
> reverently with prayer and thanks-giving, will make it moderate,
> and keep them from growing weary each of other.[15]

Sex is both the proof and the articulation of the reformed reinvention of marriage.

It is worth following this detour along the byways of Reformation theological controversy since it lets us see the play as something more than the product of its time; rather, it rests upon the tensions of the period, and tugs to one side of once-vibrant debates. The marriage rite gives *Romeo and Juliet* a dramatic and emotional vocabulary through which to articulate a loving union. Following the larger theological structure, the play insistently connects the elements of love, devotion, and sexual consummation: Romeo arranges not only the marriage rite with the friar but also the rope-ladder up which he will climb to Juliet's bed. Romeo, in meeting with the Nurse, specifies that "Within this hour my man shall be with thee / And bring thee cords made like a tackled stair"; the Nurse, in leaving Juliet, takes her leave "To fetch a ladder"; and Juliet again alludes to the "highway to my bed" (2.3.169–70; 2.4.72; 3.2.134). The play's triple mention of the ladder—on the mechanics by which the couple will consummate their love—is the sign not only of a prurient interest in youthful sex but also the product of its insistence on the specific mechanics of marriage.

The play emphasizes the elements of the church rite. Just as the ladder is noted three times where the demands of plot would have required only one, the characters repeatedly raise the issue of the ring. As the Nurse leaves Juliet's room to visit Romeo, Juliet insists "Give this ring to my true knight"; as she leaves Romeo, the Nurse turns back to him and in passing remembers something she had almost forgotten—"Here sir, a ring she bid me give you"—and in the play's final scene, as Romeo stands over the sleeping body of Juliet, he takes "from her dead finger / A precious ring, a ring that I must use / In dear employment" (3.2.143; 3.3.162; 5.3.30–32). The "dear employment" that Romeo claims is never explicated, for the ring is immaterial to the action of the play; rather, its function is solely relevant in the solemnization of matrimony. The logic of the play is at these moments the logic of the rite.[16]

According to the Book of Common Prayer, "the man shall give unto the woman a ring, laying the same upon the book with the accustomed duty to the Priest and Clerk. And the Priest taking the ring, shall deliver it unto the man, to put it upon the fourth finger of the woman's left hand" (Cummings, 159). This slightly awkward gesture—the man gives the ring to the woman, who gives it to the priest, who gives it back to the man to place upon the woman's finger—is shadowed in the transmission of rings on stage: from Juliet to the Nurse and then the Nurse to Romeo, and later to be taken from Juliet's finger. The conjunction of formal rite and sexual consummation is specific to reformed orthodox doctrine, and the critics of the Anglican settlement opposed the ring. Puritans objected to the ring as a remnant of popish superstition. The ring appears as one of the "matters of Controversy" in an anonymous account of the Hampton Court Conference, and Sir John Harrington noted that during the first day of discussions, "There was much discourse about the ring in marriage."[17] Andrew Willett, who stood on the puritan edge of orthodox Anglican theology, allowed it in the marriage rite "so it be used only as a civil ornament, and token of mutual force"; King James replied to the objection at the conference by suggesting that the ring was, in fact, necessary to the rite. "They would prove to be scarce well married," he declared, "who are not married with the ring."[18]

Romeo and Juliet are married with the greatest degree of formality the stage can allow. The theological version of marriage presented in the play is notably orthodox. Juliet, in describing the "amorous rites" of her marriage to Romeo, raises the crux of English Reformation controversies: the conjunction, within the phrase, of church rite and sexual consummation precisely places the play alongside the prayer book (3.2.8). In these terms, Romeo and Juliet's marriage is properly structured by the church liturgy. But theirs is not the only marriage discussed in the play. As Juliet pleads to Friar Laurence, "O, bid me leap, rather than marry Paris, / From off the battlements of any tower, / Or walk in thievish ways" (4.1.77–79). The phrase "walk in thievish ways" echoes Psalm 128, "Blessed are they that fear the Lord: and walk in his ways," and the citation is not coincidental, for this psalm and phrase were central to the rite of marriage.[19] Juliet negates the image, reversing the humble devotional walking of the psalm into a criminal and desperate suicide. In miniature, she here contrasts her wrong marriage to Paris—an inversion of the liturgy—with her right marriage to Romeo, which enacts the details of the correct rite.

The phrase "walk in the ways," and particularly its keyword "walk," is richly freighted with theological suggestion. I have already surveyed the allusion to marriage suggested by this phrase, but walking, as a devotional image, does not exclusively refer to marriage. When early modern theologians came to instruct the worldly duty of man, they chose this particular phrase. Thomas More, sitting in prison and awaiting execution in 1535, annotated his Book of Hours with a meditation, which describes proper devotion—"To walk the narrow way that leadeth to life"—and the opening declaration of the second session of Council of Trent, on 7 January 1546, exhorts all "in timore Domini ambulare et desideria carnis non perficere."[20] Calvin's exposition of the book of Job instructs that "we must walk in humility"; Hooker's *Laws of Ecclesiastical Polity* suggests that "if we keep not our selves to the ways which he hath appointed for men to walk in is but a self-deceiving vanity."[21] In his exposition of the first epistle to the Thessalonians—which is glossed as a parable of the difficult task of building a new church of correct worship—John Jewel cites this particular scriptural phrase fourteen times.[22]

This was not an obscure phrase. To the people of Elizabethan England, raised on a diet of scriptural exegesis and popular devotion, the simple words "the ways they walk" carried a weighty echo that is since lost to modern readers. The uses of these keywords suggest the cultural competency that Shakespeare's original audiences would implicitly have carried with them in their daily lives. That we do not instinctively hear, in Juliet's words, a specific scriptural echo is a sign of our great distance from the linguistic world that produced *Romeo and Juliet*. While the specific occasions of their use vary, the keywords "walk" and "way" are mobilized, in Reformation religious polemic, to instruct the believer in the form of devotionally correct behavior. They appear in *Romeo and Juliet* advisedly, for the play concerns a civilly disobedient couple who perform a liturgically correct marriage.

In borrowing the structure of liturgy, *Romeo and Juliet* adopts also the theology propounded through that structure. The play is marked by a rage for correctness, shared by all on stage. Their fury is that of those who believe they are following the rules. For the two central characters, this insistence upon propriety takes liturgical form. It insists upon the orthodox stages of the rite, taking the jumble of sixteenth-century marriage law and rendering it as a strict and sequential pattern of steps: from consent to solemnization to consummation. Shakespeare's drama is quite literally walking in older ways, and the play, like the sonnet, aspires toward the perfect ceremony of love's rite. There is drama inside orthodoxy, as *Romeo and Juliet* knows. This realization brings Shakespeare beyond the hollow mockeries of the early comedies and into a new form of liturgical drama.

"WITH THIS RING I thee wed: with my body I thee worship," the man tells the woman as he places the ring upon her finger. This is a double binding, both in word and gesture, and in it he is tutored by the priest standing by. "The man taught by the priest shall say," the prayer book instructs: the priest first speaks the line and is echoed by the man, and both in turn are led by the script of the prayer book (159). This is a curious kind of drama, one deliberately unlearned; each says the words in turn, but they apply to only one. Sincerity rubs against insincerity. The first expression is duplicated, and in being so, made true.

In a Puritan petition against the prayer book, which appeared in late 1605, this phrase is met with particular objection. The petition insists that the prayer book "contains sundry things that are ridiculous and absurd, and such as no reasonable sense can be made of," and goes on to give an example: "It requireth that every husband be taught by the Priest to say to his wife, (in the solemnization of wedlock) *With my body I thee worship*." The phrase mixed the bodily and the devotional into apparent idolatry. According to William Barlow's account of the Hampton Court Conference, the Puritan spokesman "D. *Reyn*[olds] took exceptions to those words," while James, the account continues, acknowledged the possible trouble here. "I was made believe, (saith he,) that the Phrase, did import no less than *Divine worship*," the king noted, and then called for the assembled divines to turn to the prayer book.

What happens next is unexpected, given the otherwise dry proceedings. "By examination I find, that it is a usual English term," says the king, but then

> turning to Doctor *Reyn*[olds] (with smiling, saith his Majestie,) Many a man speaks of *Robin Hood*, who never shot in his bow, if you had a good wife your self, you would think, all the honour and *Worship* you could do her, were well bestowed.[23]

You can almost hear the wink of an easy joke between men. *Well*, James is saying, *I'd worship my wife if I were you*. But beneath the mock literalism is a strain of condescension. Reynolds was here to address the details of liturgy, and that he was unmarried surely irrelevant. But now the laughter—and surely there was laughter, at this joke told by the king—renders all complicit, and ends discussion. According to Barlow and all other accounts of the Hampton Court Conference, the Puritans did not continue to press their objection to this phrase.

This is a flash of minor drama, tucked into the records of long-dead theological debate, but it reveals for us now and with surprising precision how fluid the apparently rigid formulations of the prayer book were. Here, the only means to reconcile a doctrinal contradiction—is marriage an act of worship or not?—lies in an improvisation. The king was no fool: his joke deflates the tension within the rite while the slightly smutty echo of Robin Hood shooting his bow distracts all from the doctrinal controversy. In this moment one liturgical attitude met, and was silenced by, another. The Puritan delegation at Hampton Court shared a hope for the literal sanctity of the prayer book. They believed that its phrases should say precisely what they mean. But this hope was answered by an alternate understanding of liturgy, one in which verbal promises are metaphors, with space for innovation and a little bit of play. This is not to say that the king is being unorthodox, but his defense of orthodoxy rests upon a smile and a laugh.

One may be both sincere to the forms of the prayer book and yet also find humor; one may follow a script and still speak true. *As You Like It* (1599) is a play whose movement is escape but whose logic is reconciliation. In its opening scenes, characters flee from court: first Orlando, followed by Rosalind and Celia. Orlando and Rosalind are in love, although she also fears this; she dresses in disguise as a man. In the forest they come across further lovers, in various states of infatuation. Late in the play, Rosalind is weary of the vacuous Phoebe's continuing rejection of the courting shepherd Silvius. "Look upon him; love him," she commands: "He worships you."

Rosalind is appealing here to the logic and vocabulary of the marriage rite. To achieve its resolution, however, characters must first rehearse their own separate desires. "Good shepherd," Phoebe tormentingly instructs Silvius: "tell this youth what 'tis to love." He responds, "It is to be all made of sighs and tears, / And so I am for Phoebe." He understands love to be particular pain, bound to a personally chosen object of desire, but the problem set by the play's plot is that the many characters in the forest each love at odds. The scene continues:

> PHOEBE: And I for Ganymede.
> ORLANDO: And I for Rosalind.
> ROSALIND: And I for no woman.

Rosalind here is disguised as a fictional male character, under the name of Ganymede. In this guise she is loved by Phoebe, and yet as Rosalind she is loved by Orlando. This is apparently intractable, knotted beyond easy resolution, and yet Silvius continues to list his own understanding of the reconciliations of love. He goes on:

> SILVIUS: It is to be all made of faith and service,
> 　　　And so I am for Phoebe.
> PHOEBE: And I for Ganymede.
> ORLANDO: And I for Rosalind.
> ROSALIND: And I for no woman.

The separate characters voice their own desires in echoing what Silvus has first established. They accept, that is, his verbal expression of love, while disagreeing with its application.

Love is, as he defines it, a pattern of "faith and service," and Silvius goes on to list what this may contain:

> It is to be all made of fantasy,
> All made of passion, and all made of wishes,
> All adoration, duty and observance,
> All humbleness, all patience and impatience,
> All purity, all trial, all obedience,
> And so am I for Phoebe.

Again, the chorus of other characters voice agreement to his words:

PHOEBE: And so am I for Ganymede.

ORLANDO: And so am I for Rosalind.

ROSALIND: And so am I for no woman. (5.2.72–92)

In their responses, Phoebe and Orlando appear to believe they are insisting upon their own individual will: the scene's most frequently repeated word is "I" as each describes his or her own particular desire. But the larger logic of the scene is concord. They follow like proper worshippers. "I take thee," instructs the script of the marriage rite for the woman, "to have and to hold from this day forward, for better, for worse, for richer, for poorer, in sickness, and in health, to love, cherish, and to obey" (159). These various occasions are reconciled into a single structure: a larger obedience guides the individual will, and Silvius's particular promise of "obedience" here concurs with the script of the marriage rite.

The great innovation of *As You Like It* is to reconcile individual wishes with an orthodox structure of consent. It finds continuity between the mockery of *Two Gentlemen of Verona* and the faithfulness of *Romeo and Juliet*; it is both ironic and sincere. The title is a promise: all contradictions may be made true. In arranging the play's climax, Rosalind swears a series of seemingly contradictory promises to each of the play's lovers:

> [To Phoebe] I will marry you if ever I marry woman, and I'll be married tomorrow. [To Orlando] I will satisfy you if ever I satisfy man, and you shall be married tomorrow. [To Silvius] I will content you if what pleases you contents you, and you shall be married tomorrow. (5.2.104–8)

She manages to hold to each of these vows: Phoebe and Silvius shall marry, as shall Orlando and Rosalind. The play finds resolution by allowing the actions promised by simple verbal utterances. In each case, these are marriage vows: the promises implicit to the formal liturgy of marriage are binding.

The laughter and freedom of this play—and the precondition of the characters' happiness—depend upon faith in the logic and order of the prayer book. Where in *Romeo and Juliet* the characters appeared driven by rules they could not quite articulate, here all are deeply conscious of exact liturgical demands. Even those characters presented as foolish are curiously law abiding. As Touchstone woos the illiterate goatherd Audrey, he promises, "I will marry thee." He enters here into a conditional spousal contract, and will require a priest to solemnize the union; as he continues to explain, "to that end I have been with Sir Oliver Martext, the vicar of the next village, who hath promised to meet me in this place in the forest, and to couple us." The country priest appears, and in his first words demands, "Is there none here to give the woman?" According to the prayer book rite, the priest demands before the union, "Who giveth this woman to be married unto this man?" "Truly, she must be given, or the marriage is not lawful," Martext continues, and here Jacques steps forward: "Proceed, proceed, give her," he says (3.3.32–58; Cummings, 158).

They are all so cautious, so correct in the particulars. It looks as though now the wedding may go forward, but these are not the only rules. "Will you, being a man of your breeding, be married under a bush, like a beggar?" demands Jacques, for the rite for the solemnization of matrimony insists that "the persons to be married shall come into the body of the church." This rule was specific to the Book of Common Prayer. The traditional pre-Reformation English marriage rite had taken place ether in the churchyard or, most often, in the porch; the reformed liturgy, beginning with the 1549 prayer book, moved the service indoors. The practice of performing weddings outside the church seems to have persisted. A church proclamation of 1560 specified:

> No Parson, Vicar, or Curate, shall solemnize Matrimony out of his or their Cure, no Parish Church or Chapel; and shall not solemnize the same in private houses, nor lawless or exempt Churches, under the pains of the Law.[24]

Despite the threat of deprivation from the priesthood or imprisonment, this was clearly a continuing problem: the proclamation was reissued in 1575, 1600, and 1605. Yet the play here conforms to the prayer book and law. Touchstone's wedding to Audrey is postponed.

There is a kind of strictness at the heart of this playful play, but this does not preclude humor or the fulfillment of individual desires. We began with an apparent opposition between two ways of handling the Book of Common Prayer: one could mock its rites or follow them. In this play however, both attitudes may simultaneously be true. The mechanisms of consent and concord are the very place of drama as characters appropriate the script of the rite and in it find realization of their own desires. This distinctive dance between freedom and orthodoxy runs deeply through the play's most famous scene, in which Rosalind, still in disguise as Ganymede, instructs Orlando that she will pretend to be his lover so that he may practice his declaration of love. It is a scene built carefully upon a whole skeleton of rules and considerations, and its innovation is most clearly revealed by contrast with its source.

While Shakespeare's play is heavily dependent upon its primary source, Thomas Lodge's overblown pastoral romance *Rosalynde* (1590), certain key moments are advisedly rewritten. In Lodge's version of this scene, Celia (here, Aliena) initiates the action, while the lovers say nothing. The scene runs:

> And thereupon (quoth Aliena) I'll play the priest; and from this day forth Ganimede shall call thee husband, and thou shalt call Ganimede wife, and so we'll have a marriage. Content (quoth Rosader) and laughed.[25]

While Shakespeare borrows the movement of the scene directly from Lodge, he adds a specific attention to the set verbal forms in which the mock-marriage takes place. In the play's revision of this exchange:

ROSALIND [TO Celia]: Come, sister, you shall be the priest and marry us.—Give me your hand, Orlando.—What do you say, sister?

ORLANDO [TO Celia]: Pray thee, marry us.

CELIA: I cannot say the words.

ROSALIND: You must begin, "Will you, Orlando"—

CELIA: Go to. Will you, Orlando, have to wife this Rosalind?

ORLANDO: I will.

ROSALIND: Ay, but when?

ORLANDO: Why now, as fast as she can marry us.

ROSALIND: Then you must say, "I take thee, Rosalind, for wife."

ORLANDO: I take thee, Rosalind, for wife. (4.1.106–16)

The language here is formal. What in Lodge was a mocking joke—"so we'll have a marriage"—becomes sincere: Rosalind insists upon the words themselves. "I cannot say the words," says Celia. "You must," Rosalind commands.

The words spoken by Orlando—and added by Shakespeare—have a double function. First, they bind Orlando and Rosalind to a spousal pre-contract of the kind surveyed by Anne Barton (although Barton surprisingly does not mention this scene). Rosalind is well aware of the legalities of spousals. Orlando first swears to a *de futuro* contract— "I will"—which is conditional upon future renewal. A *de futuro* spousal is not, on its own, legally binding, so Rosalind pushes Orlando further: "Ay, but when?" As he utters the words, "I take thee," he enters into a *de praesenti* contract, which is legally binding as soon as it is reciprocated. In the very next line, Rosalind confirms: "I do take thee, Orlando, for my husband" (4.1.117–18). They are now, according to the widely accepted laws of spousals, married. All that is further required is a church solemnization and sexual consummation.

Second, their words parody the liturgical rite for the solemnization of marriage. According to the Book of Common Prayer, the solemnization has two movements within its liturgy. The priest demands of the man: "Wilt thou have this woman to thy wedded wife?" Rosalind's insistence, which Celia completes—"Will you, Orlando, have to wife this Rosalind?"—is therefore a direct quotation from the prayer book. The man must reply as Orlando does: "I will." Rosalind continues, "Then you must say, 'I take thee, Rosalind, for wife,'" and again she is quoting the liturgy, which instructs the man to begin "I take thee to my wedded wife" (158). Rosalind walks Orlando through the set phrases of liturgy. These lines constitute a liturgical palimpsest: the formal liturgy is disguised under a popular declaration of spousal contract. It is both binding and playful, both pretense and true. And it is what the characters wish.

Promises do not complete the rite; they are not the whole of its logic. *As You Like It* insists, with flirtatious frequency, on the inevitability of sexual consummation. Sex is the end of the liturgy of love: Touchstone replies to Orlando's love-rhymes with a bawdy parody that renders his romantic aspirations sexual. "He that sweetest love will find / Must find love's prick, and Rosalind," he rhymes, and later in the same scene Celia replies to Rosalind—"take the cork out of my mouth, that I may drink thy tidings"—with a similar reduction: "So you may put a man in your belly." This is Rosalind's lesson to Orlando. "He trots hard with a young maid between the contract of her marriage and the day it is solemnized," she teaches, and while the two other dimensions of the wedding rite are here mentioned explicitly, the sexual conclusion is the winking subtext. Marriage must culminate in sex. Celia and Oliver, in love at first sight, "have made a pair of stairs to marriage, which they will climb incontinent, or else be incontinent before marriage." Touchstone, introducing himself to the Duke before the marriage festival that ends the play, declares: "I press in here, sir, among the rest of the country copulatives, to sweat and to forswear, according as marriage binds and blood breaks." The bond of marriage is cemented in the consummation, when "blood breaks." *As You Like It* ties marriage to sex. As the closing couplet has it, "rites" will end "in true delights."[26]

This is not only the loose bawdy of high spirits; it is theologically specific, and dense with precise allusion. Shakespeare found drama in the liturgy of the marriage rite, and as he patterned his plays on its forms he inherited also an arena of controversy, for the very words and objects he adopted were fiercely contested. *Romeo and Juliet* inaugurates a new phase in Shakespeare's drama, in which the staged narrative borrows, at certain key points, the set forms of liturgy. It is precisely because the liturgy was so closely fought over in late Elizabethan England that those moments where plays and rites converge require a dense historical and theological explanation. It is equally due to the controversy generated by the certain moments in liturgy that the plays found in those key elements the possibility of great dramatic effect. *Romeo and Juliet* and *As You Like It* conjoin rites and delights as they render sex sacred and liturgy dramatic; the words and actions performed by the stage characters shadow the key moments of a church rite well-worn into popular familiarity by ceaseless repetition, and contested with great heat. The early comedies make a dramatic virtue of "not look[ing] like a nuptial." With *Romeo and Juliet* and *As You Like It*, Shakespeare discovers the theatrical value of sounding like a rite.

CHAPTER 3 ❧ *Till Death Us Depart*

The marriage rite is a fiction of consequences, each following elegantly one upon the other. Its cautious sequence of consent and devotion build a vision of order and grace. It does this through the promise of a narrative of steps in which the performance of obedience generates fit rewards; where results obey causes, cleanly, clearly: this is a story of satisfaction. Effect follows gesture like soldiers stepping. The priest first speaks an exhortation, setting out "the causes for which matrimony was ordained." There are three:

> One was, the procreation of children to be brought up in the fear and nurture of the Lord, and praise of God. Secondly, it was ordained for a remedy against sin, and to avoid fornication, that such persons as have not the gift of continency might marry, and keep themselves undefiled members of Christ's body. Thirdly, for the mutual society, help, and comfort, that the one ought to have of the other, both in prosperity and adversity. (Cummings, 157)

Here is a comforting structure, of logic and of order. We are imagining the future and what will surely follow: not only children but also how they must be raised over the years to come. This offers also a correction to our own tendencies. We are kept, by married sex, from the temptations of sin.

The bond suggested in the third part of the exhortation—"the mutual society, help, and comfort, that the one ought to have of the other"—is not just the community between the man and the woman. It raises a larger formation. Heinrich Bullinger, defending Christian matrimony in the early years of the Reformation, insisted that those who choose not to marry prefer "to die as unprofitable clods of the earth, than godly to marry and leave behind them such fruit, as in time to come might both profit the common weal and also set forth the glory of God." Peter Martyr Vermigli, professor of Divinity at Oxford and a powerful influence behind the Book of Common Prayer, agreed. Those who do not marry, he recorded in his *Common Places*, "hurt the Common-weal; because they defraud it of good citizens." The provision of children is the family's duty. The marriage rite imagines the community of the church and provides a convenient metaphor; one smaller structure of godly order both builds and implies the larger. The early Jacobean marriage manual *Counsel to the Husband: To the Wife Instruction* suggested that "A family may be compared unto a commonwealth: wherein, there are divers societies and degrees, reciprocally relating, and mutually depending on one another," and the Puritan William Perkins applied the metaphor. "The holy and righteous government" of the family, he wrote, "is a direct mean for the good ordering, both of Church and Commonwealth."[1] A married couple is a symbolically dense unit, bolstered by the interlaced symbols of the prayer book rite.

The rite, however, also imagines rupture. Immediately following the exhortation is a question for the congregation. "Therefore," says the priest, "if any man can show any just cause why they may not lawfully be joined together, let him now speak." The perfectly ordered narrative of steps momentarily pauses, and the rite suspends itself. The prayer book goes on wholly to imagine this crisis. It tells what may happen next:

> if any man do allege and declare any impediment why they may not be coupled together in matrimony, by God's law or the laws of this realm, and will be bound, and sufficient sureties with him, to the parties, or else put in a caution to the full value of such

charges as the persons to be married doth sustain to prove his allegation: then the Solemnization must be deferred unto such time as the truth be tried. (158)

Here we have a junction and are torn between two stories. In one, an interruption in the church, a cry going up from the back—a gasp among the hushed crowd now, the discovery of a scandal—and in the other, all is quiet and no one says a word. "If no impediment be alleged," continues the rite, "then shall the curate say unto the man, Wilt thou have this woman to thy wedded wife." The logic of the marriage rite is in silence restored.

The marriage rite is marked by a double chronology. There is the time within the rite, told in repetition of its phrases, and then the time required for its actual completion. The process began in a vague past with an exchange of consent between a man and woman. Then, once agreed, they publically declare their intent. "First the banns must be asked three several Sundays or holy days," instructs the prayer book: the couple must announce, in their local parish church, their intention to wed, and they must do so repeatedly. Only after this is complete may they proceed to the next step. Matrimony is solemnized within the church but only made perfect in an imagined afterward. The service ends with an instruction of what will immediately happen next: "The new married persons (the same day of their marriage) must receive the Holy Communion" (164). After this will be consummation, the finish to the rite. The marriage rite orders the present to make the past and future continuous. It dreams of reconciling two time schemes and fears that they may ever be held apart.

IN THE OPENING scene of *All's Well That Ends Well*, Helena declares her hopeless love for Bertram. "'Twere all one," she says, "That I should love a bright particular star / And think to wed it, he is so above me." Loving and wedding are for her sequential phases of a single impulse, but here they share only a figure of distance, between an earthbound lover and a starlike love. She continues, "In his bright radiance and collateral light / Must I be comforted, not in his sphere. / Th'ambition in my love thus plagues itself" (1.1.80–84). Helena dwells in the conceit's impossibility and sunders the metaphor's parts: she feels only the light of the far star, not its gravity, its pull. The halves of her fantasy tug against one another, and her awareness of love's plotline is a torment.

The play begins in a flurry of precise allusion. The pompous Paroles enters to Helena, and seeing her lost in thought demands: "Are you meditating upon virginity?" Once she concurs, he goes on, "It is not politic in the commonwealth of nature to preserve virginity." Marriage will, wrote Bullinger, "profit the common weal," and those who refuse, in the phrase of Peter Martyr Vermigli, "hurt the Common-weal"; the image was carefully rendered by theologians of marriage. Its social arrangement, its politics, hinge upon the willingness of individuals to see a larger structure in their own actions. There are three reasons for marriage, explains the priest at the start of the rite: "the procreation of children," "to avoid fornication," and for "mutual society." In *All's Well That Ends Well* Helena imagines Bertram away at the court of France. "There shall your master have a thousand loves, / A mother, a mistress, and a friend," she sadly thinks, and these are precisely the three wifely functions given in the rite. This wistful daydream of orderly Christian marriage recurs in the third scene. The clown Lavatch approaches the Countess to ask that he may marry Isbel, her servant. "Tell me the reason why thou wilt marry," she demands, and he has rehearsed these lines before. "I think I shall never have the blessing of God till I have issue o' my body, for they say bairns are blessings," he begins. Marriage produces children. "I am driven on by the flesh, and he must needs go that the devil drives," he continues. Marriage reduces sexual incontinence. Here are two from the prayer book's exhortation. And then he stumbles. "Is this all your worship's reasons?" she asks; "I have other holy reasons," he begins, and then recalls the third. "I am out o' friends, madam," he says: a spouse is a companion, of mutual society (1.1.105, 119–20, 154–55; 1.3.21–35).

If we begin with the Book of Common Prayer and read through its filter, we see how patterned are the ways in which these characters consider their own desires. Romeo, Rosalind, and legions of reforming theologians established a flexible but powerful narrative of events—from consenting contract to church solemnization and consummation. Upon this sequence their sermons and exegeses built a vast structure of social and devotional meanings. *All's Well That Ends Well* insists that we recall this structure, before it begins to dismantle it; only if we know what is dreamed of as whole can we feel the sadness of its dissolution.

The strained plot of the first half of the play—Helena is the orphan daughter of a great physician and has inherited his cures; with these she treats the sick king of France, in whose court Bertram resides; as a reward the king promises her choice of husband—arranges a set of characters and their divided wills. These characters then collide with the conventions of marriage in the scene in which Helena claims her reward. "I dare not say I take you," says Helena to Bertram, but then turning to the king continues, "This is the man." "Why then, young Bertram, take her, she's thy wife," the king instructs. "I take thee to my wedded wife," the marriage script in the Book of Common Prayer runs, and the king repeats, again to Bertram, "take her hand." Bertram hesitates, so the king once more orders, with increasing precision: "Take her by the hand."

Here in the handfast is the ceremony of a spousal, but the keyword "take" borrowed from the rite elides this also into a formal solemnization. The king, like the Book of Common Prayer, has written a script for Bertram, and he finally concurs: "I take her hand." But the rite depends not only upon the articulation of set phrases; it requires also an exchange of consent, and this is absent from the scene. "I shall beseech your highness," pleads Bertram, "In such a business give me leave to use / The help of mine own eyes"; and again, "I cannot love her, nor will strive to do't." The king refuses to hear:

> Good fortune and the favour of the King
> Smile upon this contract, whose ceremony
> Shall seem expedient on the now-born brief,
> And be performed tonight. (2.3.98–176)

With this authoritarian blessing, all exit the stage, direct to the solemnization.

The words and gestures are here specific, which all the characters know. Bertram returns from his wedding, only seventy lines later, and describes to Paroles: "Although before the solemn priest I have sworn, / I will not bed her" (2.3.254–54). Forced into a handfast and a solemnization, Bertram is still not wholly married to Helena. He vanishes to fight in the Tuscan wars and from there writes to his mother. "I have wedded her, not bedded her," he repeats, as he—like the play at large—insists upon the precise form and meaning of these events. As he writes to Helena: "When thou canst get the ring upon my finger, which never shall come off, and show me a child begotten of thy body that I am father to, then call me husband; but in such a 'then' I write a 'never'" (3.2.20–21, 55–58). He lists the specifics of the form of marriage—the proper rite, with its ring, and consummation—only to deny them. The plot of *All's Well That Ends Well* is built upon the disjunction in Bertram's words. Both proceed by naming, only to suspend, the narrative structure of the marriage rite.

The play finds plot in relation to marriage, and the characters voicing the phrases of the rite demand our recognition. Perhaps this should be unsurprising, for according to the allocation of genres in the first Folio, this play belongs among the comedies. It sits there, in an uneasy catalogue, by *As You Like It* and *The Taming of the Shrew*. Comedies have long been held to be dramas about marriage. One study of Shakespeare's comedies notes in passing that "It is a truism that comedies end in marriage," while another assumes that "His comedies, then, are essentially celebrations of marriage." It is a popular point; a third has more recently asserted that "The most outstanding feature of Shakespearean comedy is its pervading obsession with marriage."[2]

This is one way to explain the repeated motif of the play: that it is required by the rules of genre. But this is a flattened understanding of literary invention. Genres are not simply recipes that dramatists indiscriminately follow. Generic categories may provide a useful vocabulary in which to describe a literary text, but they do not necessarily prescribe the plot. Genre, that is, is a way of reading rather than of writing, as it may tell us what to look for but not what must be there. The plays by Shakespeare conventionally grouped as "comedies" do tend to end in an allusion to marriage, but that single feature does not determine their genre. *Henry V* concludes with a marriage; *Love's Labour's Lost* does not. Aristotle's definition of comedy is unreliable, since his volume on comedy—the apocryphal companion to the *Poetics*—is lost, but he associates the genre with the low status of its characters. Comedy, he writes, is "an imitation of persons worse than the average."[3] The Roman New Comedies— those by Terence and Plautus, for example—whose influence on Shakespeare is widely accepted, culminate not in marriage but by the resolution of disequilibrium between characters. Economic— not sexual or marital—concerns are their defining feature. Contemporaries of Shakespeare did write comedies that reflect contemporary economic anxieties—the so-called "city comedies"—but Shakespeare himself did not. This is not to say that he was not influenced by the New Comedy but instead to suggest that the influence of classical comedy can be seen across his plays, in *Henry IV* as well as *The Comedy of Errors*.[4] Marriage was a theme that interested him promiscuously, and it runs through genres. Among many other things, *Hamlet* is a meditation upon marital propriety.

Those who would read marriage as bound to a genre share a faith that *All's Well That Ends Well* does not: a belief in the resilience of the marriage rite to sustain a dramatic plot. I have traced one arc through Shakespeare's earlier plays, by which the prayer book's liturgy comes to assume a structural role in the unraveling of the play. In specific scenes and moments of *Romeo and Juliet* and *As You Like It*, the marriage rite provides a coherent series of events and a vocabulary in which to consider them; in these plays, liturgy is plot. This is his first level of sophistication. But now he will go farther. As the extraordinary literary critic Frank Kermode has argued in his book *The Sense of an Ending*, "The story that proceeded very simply to its obviously predestined end would be nearer myth than novel or drama," so one of the characteristics of novels or plays is a block or delay in the progress of plot.[5] There is dramatic interest in deranging the smooth and simple route to the end, but only if we know in advance what it will be. We must, in Kermode's terms, have "confidence of the end" before we enjoy the "disconfirmation" of reversal or obstruction. The early comedies teach us, just as the marriage rite taught Shakespeare, of the narrative power of the liturgy, the pleasure and the satisfaction of form, and its resumption after a limited detour.

By the time of writing *All's Well That Ends Well*, Shakespeare's dramatic interest in the flow of plot was succeeded by a heightened concern with obstruction. Nonetheless this is not a departure from liturgy. The marriage rite is haunted by the failure of coherent sequence, and this play exploits its ellipses and fears. In the place of a whole story are now the pieces and the promises, and the plot is not the action of liturgy but its dismantlement. The play performs an autopsy upon the rite. Having fled from Helena, Bertram tries to seduce Diana with the gift of a ring. He has no intention of marrying her. "'Tis not the many oaths that make the truth, / But the plain single vow that is vowed true," she tells him, for he has hollowed out the assurances upon which the marriage rite depends. Diana continues: "your oaths / Are words and poor conditions but unsealed." The fear inside the marriage rite is that words and actions do not cohere into a single demonstrated truth. For its perfect achievement, three registers of attachment must simultaneously be true: the legal, the spiritual, and the emotional, and each guarantees the others. Without this reassurance all is, in Diana's term, "unsealed." A "seal" is the token that authenticates a bond or agreement: it has, according to the Oxford English Dictionary, both a legal and a figurative meaning. It may be "A device (e.g., a heraldic or emblematic design, a letter, word, or sentence) impressed on a piece of wax," or it may instead refer to "A token or symbol of a covenant." Marriage is a legal bond but also a spiritual one; its several dimensions are each shared by this particular term. The completion of marriage is in sexual consummation. A seal too has a sexual resonance, of bringing together, pressing into: in Elegy 19, "To his Mistress Going to Bed," a flirtatious John Donne promises, "To enter in these bonds is to be free; / Then where my hand is set, my seal shall be." The play unseals the marriage rite, exposing it before us now as separate parts.

WE CANNOT READ the plays alone; their concerns are matched elsewhere. The composition of *All's Well* is conventionally dated 1602–3, and scholars place it in a loose grouping known as the "problem plays." The term was first applied by Frederick Boas in 1896. Noting a change in Shakespeare's mood at the start of the seventeenth century—he likened it to "the passage from a sunny charming landscape to a wild mountain-district whose highest peaks are shrouded in thick mist"—he grouped together *All's Well*, *Measure for Measure*, *Hamlet*, and *Troilus and Cressida*. These share a setting, he wrote, in "highly artificial societies, whose civilization is ripe unto rottenness," and, borrowing a term then fashionable in criticism of nineteenth-century drama and particularly Ibsen, he proposed we call them "problem-plays."[6] The title lost the hyphen but retained its currency. In *Shakespeare's Problem Comedies* (1931) William Witherle Lawrence argued that "The essential characteristic of a problem play, I take it, is that a perplexing and distressing complication in human life is presented in a spirit of high seriousness," and included in his category only *All's Well*, *Measure for Measure*, and *Troilus and Cressida*. The group does not remain set or fixed, for different things trouble different ages. In 1961 Ernest Schanzer described *Julius Caesar*, *Measure for Measure*, and *Antony and Cleopatra* as *The Problem Plays of Shakespeare* and argued that the problems they pose are moral, "presented in such a manner that we are unsure of our moral bearings, so that uncertain and divided responses to it in the minds of the audience are possible or even probable."[7]

This is a floating category, uncertain of its contents, but what those who focus on it share is a sense that in this particular moment—in 1602 or 1603—some shade fell upon the plays of Shakespeare. In them he was trying something different or strange, and their family resemblance is their resistance of simple dramatic coherence. Perhaps all of Shakespeare's plays could be described as problem plays for he rarely if ever resolves to absolute satisfaction, but two among the group are particular twins. The cast of characters of *Measure for Measure* includes the following: Isabella, sister to Claudio; Mariana, who was abandoned by Angelo; and Escalus, a Viennese lord. In *All's Well That Ends Well* Isbel is the Countess's servant whom Lavatch wishes to marry. This Isbel does not speak, and nor does another minor but named character: Escalus, one of the soldiers who march past in procession. "That, Escalus," as Diana's mother identifies him, for apparently no reason, and she, too, has a friend called Mariana. The names correspond, for when Shakespeare was writing one of these plays he had either just finished or was just about to begin the other. If we take these plays together, and in the light of liturgical debate, then another family trait emerges. This is not an act of therapy but rather a drawing out of a step in Shakespeare's manipulation of liturgical forms. These two plays share a particular fear inside the marriage rite: of the rupture of narrative, and of incoherence.

In the sinful Vienna of *Measure for Measure*, as Escalus puts it, "Some rise by sin, and some by virtue fall." Devotion is divorced from its conventional guarantees (2.1.38). Sin has overrun the dukedom. The Duke observes, that where in times past the populace would obey civil statute,

> Now, as fond fathers,
> Having bound up the threatening twigs of birch,
> Only to stick it in their children's sight

For terror, not to use, in time the rod
Becomes more mock'd than fear'd: so our decrees,
Dead to infliction, to themselves are dead,
And Liberty plucks Justice by the nose,
The baby beats the nurse, and quite athwart
Goes all decorum. (1.3.23–31)

The central metaphor is of paternal justice, and this fear of a state where old laws are mocked and sin rises to the surface echoes through contemporary conversations about marriage. The Elizabethan homily "Against Whoredom and adultery" finds a world of similarly inverted devotion in contemporary England. "Above other vices, the outrageous seas of adultery or breaking of wedlock, whoredom, fornication & uncleanness, have" the homily worries, "overflowed almost ye whole world." It continues: "through the customable use thereof, this vice is grown unto such an height, that in a manner among many, it is counted no sin at all, but rather a pastime, a dalliance, and but a touch of youth, not rebuked, but winked at: not punished, but laughed at." English whoredom is more mocked than feared, winked at and not punished.

In the promiscuous society imagined by both homily and play, the traditional consequences of sin no longer appear. Where we should be punished for our depravities, we are instead ignored or—worse— permitted. What we do with our bodies should not be taken so lightly. "We should glorify him in our bodies," the homily insists, and continues by asking: "Come not ye French pocks, with other diverse diseases, of Whoredom?"[8] The marriage rite sculpted by the Book of Common Prayer and explicated by orthodox polemicists is a tightly orchestrated structure of consequence, which places a high value on both our promises and our actions. In its precisely calibrated notion of causality, we are able to remake our love as devotion, and to render our words and our bodies to God.

All's Well That Ends Well and *Measure for Measure* shatter this causal structure in their opening scenes, and they do so with specific reference to Reformation notions of marriage. Bertram and Helena are married, according to church rite, but both the consent that the rite assumes and the consummation that would complete it are absent. Angelo has consented to marry Mariana but deferred the rite itself; as a parallel movement, Claudio and Juliet have sworn their consent and consummated their love, but are not married. As Claudio describes,

> upon a true contract
> I got possession of Julietta's bed.
> You know the lady: she is fast my wife,
> Save that we do the denunciation lack
> Of outward order. (1.2.135–38)

Angelo's zealous application of Viennese law—a law which, in this specific, would have contradicted the popular assumption of early modern England—is to deny that the solemnization may take place. The plot hinges on the obstruction: without Angelo's unexpected and liturgically irrelevant denial, the play could here find immediate resolution. In *Much Ado About Nothing*, a similar narrative obstruction is momentarily imagined but immediately dissolved. In the church, when Claudio denies that he may marry Hero, Leonato steps forward: "Dear my lord, if you in your own proof / Have vanquished the resistance of her youth, / And made defeat of her virginity," he begins, but Claudio interrupts him. "I know what you would say," he declares, and goes on: "If I have known her, / You will say she did embrace me as a husband, / And so extenuate the forehand sin" (4.1.43–48). As Claudio correctly understands, consummation following a mutual contract but before the church solemnization is permissible; more than that, it stands as further proof of marriage.[9]

The later play returns to this moment with a transformed understanding. The earlier Claudio, who saw no obstruction, has become a later Claudio, trapped by an impediment; our earlier Juliet, bound to Romeo, has become a problem. As Lucio describes, "Claudio is condemned for untrussing": the consequences of his actions are not commensurate with the actions themselves (3.1.411). Marriage, as defended and described by orthodox polemicists in early modern England, was a narrative, a series of steps—consent to vow to consummation—that redefined human love as pious worship. The premise and the central action that propels the plots of these two plays is that this narrative of events and its concomitant sanctification are not allowed to take place. They are thwarted love stories precisely as the end to which marriage points—sexual and ecclesiastical consummation—has been deferred. Their plots hinge entirely on the suspension of liturgical narrative.

The final scenes of *Measure for Measure* and *All's Well That Ends Well* are self-conscious, rapid, and lack any emotional justification for the marriages toward which they point. Just as in *Measure for Measure* the Duke declares his intention to marry Isabella but does not wait for her response—"What's mine is yours, and what is yours is mine"—the king of France, in the closing lines of *All's Well That Ends Well*, decides that Diana shall be married. "Choose thy husband and I'll pay the dower," he commands, although Diana has not expressed any such desire (5.1.530; 5.3.324). Those characters who do express their consent to marry do so only by radically changing their minds. Bertram, who has spent the entire course of *All's Well That Ends Well* repeating his insistence that he will not marry Helena, meekly demurs. "O, pardon!" he declares, and continues: "If she, my liege, can make me know this clearly / I'll love her dearly, ever ever dearly" (5.3.305, 12–13). This may be heartfelt or it may be pragmatic; he has little choice. Angelo never expresses his consent to marry Mariana, but in accepting his guilt—his final words, "I was, my lord"—he accepts the marriage (5.1.368).

The trouble is the ending: it fails to tie up the strains and strands into a neat single order, and this seems to be a deliberate frustration. As Boas wrote, when he first discussed these as problem plays, "at the close our feeling is neither of simple joy nor pain; we are excited, fascinated, perplexed, for the issues raised preclude a completely satisfactory outcome," while Lawrence agreed that one defining mark of this group was a lack of satisfaction in the close. "The outcome proposed by the dramatist is not the only possible way out of the difficulties," he wrote. A more recent critic of *Measure for Measure* has defended this troubled ending as precisely the play's strength. The ending, he writes, "does not appeal to the vacuous sentimentality that is likely to be pleased by any marriage contrived to finish off a recalcitrant narrative," but rather "Its appeal is primarily intellectual."[10] The only means to defend these plays is to put the mind ahead of the heart. This is a cruel criticism. Like Isabella, Juliet does not at the end of *Measure for Measure* speak; surely if she were to do so she might complain at the extraordinary arbitrariness of the plot and her torment, so her voice must be left out.

Those who acknowledge a problem—that the marriages and endings are unsatisfactory—are fumbling toward a larger acknowledgment here of a precise liturgical pattern wished for by those on stage. "Perfect Consent" wrote Henry Swinburne in his *Treatise of Spousals*, "alone maketh matrimony," and the marriage rite is a public drama of will: both man and woman must specifically answer, "I will." The closing scenes of *Measure for Measure* and *All's Well That Ends Well* lack this consent. The Duke condemns Lucio to marry Kate Keepdown as a punishment for his constant mockery—"The nuptial finished, / Let him be whipped and hanged"—and Lucio twice refuses to concur. "I beseech your highness, do not marry me to a whore," he pleads, and continues: "Marrying a punk, my lord, is pressing to death" (5.1.506–8, 515). The Duke similarly forces marriage upon Angelo:

> DUKE [TO Angelo]: Say, wast thou e'er contracted to this
> woman?
> ANGELO: I was, my lord.
> DUKE: Go take her hence and marry her instantly.
> Do you the office, friar; which consummate. (5.1.367–70)

Even as the three elements that made the marriage rite—contract, solemnization, and consummation—are here specifically named, they are also emptied of their devotional and emotional value. These marriages are hollow ceremonies and grotesque parodies of the reformed ideal of consenting, liturgically proper, and sexually devout matrimony. But this is not to say that they are apart from the reassurance of the Book of Common Prayer, or share a safe ironic distance from liturgy. Rather, these are dramas of precisely the impediment that the marriage rite conjures.

There is one way to solve the problem of impediment, and both plays end with what has become known as a "bed-trick," in which men are fooled into consummation with their own wives. The bed-trick has received much critical attention. The traditional argument concludes that Shakespeare was, here, trapped by his sources. William Lawrence explains the presence of the bed-trick in *Measure for Measure* and *All's Well That Ends Well* by suggesting that Shakespeare did not "make such sweeping changes in the meaning of traditional stories, in situations made familiar to people by centuries of oral narrative" because the audience would be "perplexed and baffled."[11] More recent critics, with a keener sense of the intellectual and dramatic possibilities of bafflement, have found in Shakespeare's treatment of the bed-trick a radical disruption of gender archetypes.[12] Both schools of reading divorce the bed-trick from the liturgical structure in which it most readily would have made sense to contemporary audiences.

The bed-trick is a forced consummation. It solves a narrative challenge but brings with it the further problem of incoherence precisely because it resists the offered coherence of the church rite. *Measure for Measure* and *All's Well That Ends Well* divorce sex from love and rite from promise: they dismantle, with close specificity, the separate elements that make up the structure of marriage. The bed-trick, then, exploits both the hopes and fears implicit to the orthodox structure of marriage. We must read here for what is left out as much as what is put on stage. The marriage rite imagines two parallel dramas but performs only one: the reassuring pattern of true steps, bringing a couple into a whole. The two plays, however, dwell inside the other. "If any man can show any just cause why they may not lawfully be joined together," exhorts the priest: "let him now speak." He is asking for an impediment. The silence here of the marriage rite is a place of tension, and if these two plays are incoherent or problematic, then it is because this is what the marriage rite fears. The saddest line in these tormented, sad plays comes from the unloving Bertram. "Wars is no strife," he declares to Paroles: "To the dark house and the detested wife" (2.3.275–76). That dark house is an imagined state, a counter to the pattern of marriage: it is the nightmare just beneath the clarity of the rite's bounded world.

THE SPACES ENCOURAGE speculation; they force us into fiction. Shakespeare's own marriage was marked by absence. She was older than he, at the solemnization—perhaps twenty-six to his eighteen—and already pregnant, and soon after he went to London while she stayed in Stratford, and while their children grew. He returned perhaps once each year for more than twenty years. He sent money home, as many men do, but he was apart. There is a cool and curious illegibility to his will. "Item, I give unto my wife," it concludes, "my second best bed with furniture." The specificity of this, the apparently redundant detail, might trace some telling gesture; both Anthony Burgess in *Nothing Like the Sun* and James Joyce in *Ulysses* assume that she was unfaithful to him. Each novelist begins with the will as a clue. In Christopher Rush's novel *Will*, Shakespeare confides, "Take it as a dead man's hint that I found a better bed than hers elsewhere, a better woman."[13]

The plays offer themselves to this biographical guess, for there Shakespeare apparently presents married life as a deeply tense state: one soon destroyed by its own violence, quick to dissolve at the first whisper of infidelity. "Shakespeare's imagination did not easily conjure up a couple with long-term prospects for happiness," writes Stephen Greenblatt in his speculative biography *Will in the*

World. When a marriage is represented from the inside—as in *Macbeth* or *The Winter's Tale*—it tends to show the failure of a couple to sympathize. Those pairs presented as mutually loving are either united as the play ends or soon killed off, and more often, as at the close of *Measure for Measure* and *All's Well That Ends Well,* the bonds between those remaining couples are shadowed over by doubt and contradiction. Lavinia in *Titus Andronicus* is raped and her husband killed; Juliet killed, and then Romeo; Demetrius at the end of *A Midsummer Night's Dream* drugged into agreement that he will wed. There are it seems no easy happy marriages. "The greatest lovers in Shakespeare," writes Greenblatt, "are Antony and Cleopatra, the supreme emblems of adultery," and he takes this as a sign of Shakespeare's "deep skepticism about the long-term prospects for happiness in marriage."

Many have taken such absences as proof, and silence as distaste. They have read the plays as coded memoir, as if Shakespeare too were fleeing what Bertram fears, "the dark house and the detested wife." For Greenblatt, "these may have been precisely the feelings evoked in Shakespeare when he looked back upon his own marriage," and this is an entirely plausible if entirely fictional reading. As Germaine Greer has written, Shakespeare's biography has been chiefly written by "commentators determined to interpret any and all evidence as proving that Shakespeare hated his wife," and in her book *Shakespeare's Wife* tries to recover Anne Hathaway. She tells of a willful, independent Anne, making money in Stratford by making lace and brewing. The will, she insists, means little, as "Wills do not account for all the transfers of property that occur at the time of the testator's death," and here is another imagined story of their marriage.[14]

This has been going on for a very long time, this game of guessing, of speculation that sounds more like gossip; of beginning to invent precisely where the evidence leaves off, and of taking the absence of evidence as proof. There is a style of confident bluster that marks this move. "It is evidently intended by Shakespeare that we should find his own early life in this play" declared William Henty in 1882, and went on to explain that in *The Merry Wives of Windsor* Shakespeare is Fenton and Anne Page is Anne Hathaway. Fiction about Mrs. Shakespeare is a small but vibrant subcategory of Shakespeare criticism. In *The Wooing of Anne Hathaway* (1938) by Grace Carlton, Will says to Anne, "This is the haven of my desires, the harbour for my home-coming ships." "William is likely to have felt trapped" after his marriage, writes Katherine Duncan-Jones in her entertaining and cruel *Ungentle Shakespeare* (2001); she continues, "My own suspicion is that conjugal relations between William and Anne ceased sometime in the 1580s." According to Avril Rowlands in *Mrs. Shakespeare . . . The Poet's Wife* (2005) she wrote the plays for him. "All right, Will, so you're not a writer," she comforts her illiterate husband: "But, maybe, I am? And this is where our partnership can really begin!"[15] Greenblatt describes "the strange ineradicable distaste for her that he felt deep within him." Greer describes her as "Shakespeare's oldest, truest love."[16]

We may read the evidence how we will; it may let us find cruelty or devotion, passion or hate. In a poem called simply "Anne Hathaway," Carol Anne Duffy begins again with the will and from it conjures up a romance, remembered by the mourning wife. "The bed we loved in was a spinning world," she writes: "of forests, castles, torchlight, clifftops, seas." This second-best bed was where the married couple slept and made love while "In the other bed, the best, our guests dozed on," and here in Duffy's version that which suggested hate is made to tell of love. The poem fills out the records with imagined emotion. Their passion, Anne recalls, was one of words, of poetry. The bed was "a page beneath his writer's hands," and "Some nights, I dreamed he'd written me." Marriage is here "echo, assonance," a fitting of parts; between them two lovers build a structure and a world; it is something written.[17] There are two stories: one of faithfulness, and one of adultery.

WE CANNOT TELL the moment of marriage. It is by design a multiple structure, of separate moving parts; it coheres not around any simple action but in a pattern of intentions, distributing the performance of accord across an uncertain period. *Othello*, written between or immediately after *Measure for Measure* and *All's Well That Ends Well*, hinges upon a particular crisis: none of the characters know whether or not Othello and Desdemona are married. "Are they married, think you?" Brabanzio asks Roderigo, and the reply is not quite sure: "Truly, I think they are." Later, Montano too is puzzled. "Is your general wived?" he asks Cassio (1.1.168–69; 1.2.11; 2.1.61). Othello and Desdemona are clearly contracted and share consent; perhaps they have too sworn a church solemnization. "It is most true, true I have married her," Othello tells the Duke, while Desdemona describes him as "my husband," and the apparent specificity of these terms is part of a deeper confusion. Shakespeare's characters are expert in the mechanics of the church rite. It is only these two—and it is in their interest to do so—who insist that their union is made. Iago asks Othello:

> Are you fast married? Be assured of this:
> That the magnifico is much beloved,
> And hath in his effect a voice potential
> As double the Duke's. He will divorce you.

Othello does not answer the question. Instead, he claims, "My services which I have done the signory / Shall out-tongue his complaints" (1.2.11–19). The play considers, again and again, what it might take to divide a married couple; it tests the weak points in the structure asserted by the rite. Shortly after Iago's question, Othello leaves the stage. Iago turns to Cassio and they share an odd exchange:

> CASSIO: Ensign, what makes he here?
> IAGO: Faith, he tonight hath boarded a land-carrack.
>   If it prove lawful prize, he's made for ever.
> CASSIO: I do not understand.
> IAGO: He's married.
> CASSIO: To who?

Iago speaks first in bawdy metaphors, in crass allusions; he circles round the theme, in misdirection. But now, with Cassio's question, other characters arrive on stage. "Enter Brabanzio, Roderigo, and officers." Iago begins, "Marry, to—" but is again interrupted as Othello enters. In a turn he now says to Cassio, "Come, captain, will you go?" (1.2.49–52). The timing of this moment might seem a little awkward: just as Iago is about to say, "Othello," Othello enters. This is the action of the play rendered in miniature. It dwells in gaps and insists upon interruption.

"At which day of marriage, if any man do allege and declare any impediment why they may not be coupled together in matrimony," instructs the Book of Common Prayer: "then the Solemnization must be deferred unto such time as the truth be tried." If any know an impediment, "let him now speak." "Now, now," insists Iago, in the opening scene of the play. He has come, with Roderigo, to wake Desdemona's father, and shouts up from the street: "Your heart is burst, you have lost half your soul / Even now, now, very now, an old black ram / Is tupping your white ewe. Arise, arise!" (1.1.87–89). The first line follows perfect pentameter, iambic and smooth; but in the second there is a stutter in the meter, an explosion of stress upon the keyword "now" shared by play and rite. He must prevent the consummation for otherwise the marriage will be complete. Brabanzio, coming before the Duke and senators, wishes to claim an impediment, and he does so specifically. "She is abused, stol'n from me, and corrupted / By spells and medicines bought of mountebanks," he insists, and

> I therefore vouch again
> That with some mixtures powerful o'er the blood,
> Or with some dram conjured to this effect,
> He wrought upon her. (1.3.60–61, 103–6)

This might be simple racism, fearing the evil spirits of those who are foreign, but it is also a precise liturgical objection within the structure of the prayer book. Desdemona did not, Brabanzio insists, give her consent to marry Othello.

But with the exchange of consent, the structure here must hold. Othello calls for Desdemona to testify before the court, and she concurs that she has been what Brabanzio calls "half the wooer"; that her consent was freely given. "Here's my husband," she agrees. "Who giveth this woman to be married unto this man?" asks the Book of Common Prayer, and Brabanzio is now trapped inside its formality; in appealing to the logic of the rite, he is victim to its structure. "Come hither, Moor," Brabanzio commands: "I here do give thee that with all my heart / Which, but thou hast already, with all my heart / I would keep from thee" (1.3.191–94). His agreement is only a formality; he admits they are already bound. It is, however, structurally required by the rite. His grudging, graceless lack of will is liturgically irrelevant, provided that he says the words.

The opening act of *Othello* is strict with time and place. One night, in Venice, Brabanzio is woken by Iago and Roderigo in the street. They hasten to the Duke and the court, and Othello arrives too; Desdemona is summoned, and their union tested there. The reason for its speed and concision lies in the prayer book liturgy. It matters in both the liturgy and law that they have completed a sequence of events: that they have exchanged consent, and married, and consummated that union. The sequence of scenes follows the sequence of prayer book, and yet also suspends it. Othello is called from his bed by the threat of Turkish warships, and he is ordered directly from the court to travel away to war. "Th'affair cries haste," says the Duke, "And speed must answer it." Othello agrees—"With all my heart"—but exits the stage with Desdemona. "Come," he bids: "I have but an hour / Of love, or worldly matter and direction / To spend with thee. We must obey the time" (1.3.275–77, 297–99). They have an hour, alone, apart; in this time they could as an act of obedience consummate their sworn union. But we may only imagine what transpires once they are off stage. The play gives us an absence, a likely space, but shrouds its events in mystery.

Othello has an unusual, broken time scheme. Alone among the major tragedies this is close to observing what classical scholars called the unities of time and place: the setting and timing of the events of a play within a continuous geography and clock. The first act is at Venice, and the events of a single night; but in the pause before act 2 an unknown time passes. On separate ships, Othello, Iago, Desdemona, and others travel to Cyprus, and the second act opens with their arrival. From here, having established and then broken a coherent vision of time and place, the play begins again. The events of the remaining four acts once more follow geographical and temporal logic. The play, then, has two sequences, placed alongside one another. There is Venetian time, and Cypriot time, and it asks but never answers the extent to which these cohere.

We are constantly notified of the passage of time. In act 3, scene 3, Desdemona counts the passing of the days—"Why, then, tomorrow night, or Tuesday morn, / On Tuesday noon, or night, or Wednesday morn"—and working backwards we can calculate that this must now be Sunday (as the day after tomorrow is Tuesday). The third act opens in the morning, and as Cassio and Iago meet in the street, they note they have not been to bed. "You ha' not been abed, then," says Iago, and Cassio replies: "The day had broke before we parted" (3.3.61–62; 3.1.29–30). Still tracking backwards, the previous scene—the last in the second act—takes place just before dawn, as at its end Iago in passing notes, "By the mass, 'tis morning." This was Saturday night, a night broken with interruptions: Cassio is tricked into drinking and into starting a brawl, and Othello is raised from bed by the ringing of the town bells. In act 2, scene 2, a herald enters and announces a feast: "it is the celebration of his nuptial," he tells the audience, for this is Othello's wedding feast. "There is full liberty of feasting from this present hour of five till the bell have told eleven," he declares. This gives us not only the present moment—Saturday, five o'clock—but also the time at which the following scene, at the end of the feast, begins: eleven o'clock. The arrival of the men from Venice had taken place that morning (2.3.351; 2.2.6–9).

Narrative time is set in opposition to liturgical time: the plot proceeds by interrupting the marriage of Othello to Desdemona.

Leaving the feast, at eleven on Saturday night, he beckons her: "Come, my dear love, / The purchase made, the fruits are to ensue. / The profit's yet to come 'tween me and you." They still have not consummated their marriage, and ten lines later Iago informs Cassio, "He hath not yet made wanton the night with her, and she is sport for Jove" (2.3.8–16). Iago now arranges a further interruption. He tricks Cassio into drinking and then into a fight; Othello is summoned from his bed only minutes after leaving. He demands of Iago, "Speak. Who began this?" "I do not know," begins Iago's reply:

> Friends all but now, even now,
> In quarter and in terms like bride and groom
> Devesting them for bed; and then but now—
> As if some plant had unwitted men—
> Swords out, and tilting one at others' breasts
> In opposition bloody. (2.3.161–167)

The play repeatedly exchanges a scene of lovers—a bride and groom, approaching bed—with the act of men brawling, grappling, with their swords out. The private act of consummation is made public and becomes the hinge of the plot.

As many scholars have observed, the play's chronology is faulty. When Lodovico arrives from Venice with a letter from the Duke, he has hardly had time to make the journey, or for news to have reached Venice. Bianca accuses Cassio of keeping away from her a week, but he only arrived yesterday morning in Cyprus. All is over-hasty. Emilia collects the handkerchief dropped by Othello and gives it to Iago, who then decides that he will "in Cassio's lodging lose this napkin" (3.3.325). But Iago then remains on stage until the end of the scene. In the next scene, a little later the same day, he enters with Cassio, who has already found the napkin and given it to Bianca. Somewhere Iago has found the time to go to Cassio's lodging, while Cassio is away; hide the handkerchief; wait for Cassio to return, and find the handkerchief, and give it to Bianca, and then for the two men to meet.

In treating the time-lapses of *Othello* and *Julius Caesar*, Emrys Jones in a classic study called *Scenic Form in Shakespeare* claims that we must rejoice in the artificiality of representation. "We are, after all, experiencing a work of art, with its understood and accepted conventions," he advises, and goes on to insist that we are contemplating a dramatic process "to which such matters are irrelevant."[18] But Montano, Iago, and Brabanzio each demand whether Othello and Desdemona are married. They are questioning here the passing of time, and the sequence of events. They are alerting us to this trouble.

The temporal discontinuities of the play are the by-products of its condensed plot. The major elements of the story line are borrowed directly from Giovanni Battista Giraldi Cinthio's *Gli Hecatommithi* (1566); the major revision Shakespeare undertook was to shrink the span of the narrative from years to days. As Cinthio tells it, Desdemona and Othello were happily married:

> So propitious was their mutual love that, although the lady's relatives did all they could to make her take another husband, they were united in marriage and lived together in such concord and tranquility while they remained in Venice, that never a word passed between them that was not loving.[19]

This is clearly a union conducted over time. Shakespeare, in accordance with the classical unities of time and place he so freely disregards elsewhere, denies Othello and Desdemona this span of happiness. Rather, the stages of their marriage are collapsed onto one another, and the consummation of their contract is thwarted by the intrusions that propel the play forward.

The odd time scheme may be the result of Shakespeare's reworking of his source, but this does not explain why he might have chosen to do so. We cannot naturalize these strange lapses, and the play does not need us to try. As fissures in the passage of time, they suggest a place where all is too quick; they cause us, as an audience, to worry about order and about sequence; to consider what may have been left out. Leaving Venice for Cyprus, Othello admits, "We must obey the time," and later Iago will advise him "keep time in all" (4.1.90). There he is tricked by Iago into the belief that Desdemona is unfaithful, by a story spun from half-shown evidence and often from the absence of alternate proof. "I know not what he did," says Iago, accusing Cassio by omission (4.1.32). He conjures this fantasy from the lack of certain knowledge. "What sense had I of her stol'n hours of lust?" demands Othello: "I saw't not, thought it not; it harmed not me" (3.3.343–44). Later, in challenging Emilia for evidence of his wife's treachery, he finds proof in the very absence of that evidence: "This is a subtle whore, / A closet lock and key of villainous secrets, / And yet she'll kneel and pray" (4.2.22–24). The spaces in the story of a marriage are where fantasies of infidelity may breed.

When Othello comes to strangle Desdemona, he comes as a priest. "Have you prayed tonight, Desdemona?" he asks, and ignores her simple plea: "Will you come to bed my lord?" The logic of the rite stands still behind this scene. Desdemona has earlier commanded Emilia, "Prithee tonight / Lay on my bed my wedding sheets." This is their wedding bed. As he pauses to give her one last chance to pray, Othello returns to the keyword of the solemnization: "I will walk by." The timing of the scene is a kind of torture, oddly now drawn out. She prays, he responds—"I say amen"—and then suddenly attacks her. "Kill me tomorrow," she pleads, and then soon after, "But half an hour"; when he ignores all this she asks that he wait, "while I say one prayer." "It is too late," he replies, and here smothers her. The final prayer, and the finish to the marriage rite, are deferred from the end of the play (4.2.107–8; 5.2.25–92).

Not everyone, as Bianca notes, feels time to pass the same. "Lovers' absent hours," she scolds Cassio, are "More tedious than the dial eightscore times" (3.4.169–70). The marriage rite is an imagination of time. These three plays—*All's Well, Measure for Measure,* and *Othello*—exploit the tensions in the solemnization, the dark places and impediment it fears, and in each the hoped-for sequence is broken. This has felt problematic, to some, as if these were flaws or accidents within the structure of the play. "One standing issue about the rhythm of *Othello*'s plot is that the progress from the completeness of Othello's love to the perfection of his doubt is too precipitous for the fictional time of the play," observes the philosopher Stanley Cavell, who has written much about marriage plots, both in Hollywood movies and this play. He explains the purpose of this. It is, he argues, "the rhythm of skepticism," while he sees the play as a whole as concerned with the impossibility of knowing. "Was she a virgin or not?" Cavell asks, and adds, "We of course have no answer to such questions. But what matters is that Othello has no answer; or rather, he can give none, for any answer to the questions, granted that I am right in taking the questions to be his, is intolerable."[20] Either she was innocent, and he killed her; or she was guilty, and he was shamed.

This is all a liturgical trap. The play and its hero's wretched worry about Desdemona's fidelity is not simply prurience or male anxiety about female sexuality. Each piece is here precise. There is an informing presence behind the structures of these three plays: a deep and specific consciousness of particular liturgical debate. Shakespeare's development from the early comedies of the mid-1590s to three troubling plays written in the opening years of the seventeenth century grows upon a changing, thickening involvement with liturgical form. But this story of dramatic development cannot—and should never be—too cleanly allocated into parts, and nor does it aim for a total coverage. It is one story, one strand, one possibility conjured from the whole field. It would be simple, too, to sketch an alternate story, one in which the liturgy for the solemnization of matrimony does not play a powerful structuring role.

The Merry Wives of Windsor (1597) has two plots: the adultery plot of Falstaff and the two wives, Mistress Page and Mistress Ford; and the marriage plot, of who will marry Anne. The adultery plot dominates. "Thus 'tis to be married," declares Ford, who fears his wife is cheating on him, and this is chiefly how the play considers marriage

(3.5.122). The rites of love are adultery. In attempting to seduce Mistress Ford, Falstaff promises her satisfaction "not only, Mistress Ford, in the simple office of love, but in all the accoutrement, complement, and ceremony of it," but he is here talking about adulterous sex, and the ceremony and office of love is a bawdy joke (4.2.3–5). Fenton's betrothal to Anne is offstage, and while he does give her a ring and orders a vicar "in the lawful name of marrying, / To give our hearts united ceremony," this is without challenge. In the play's closing lines Fenton returns to explain: "The truth is, she and I, long since contracted, / Are now so sure that nothing can dissolve us" (4.6.49–50; 5.5.200–201). The play is interested in sex and marriage, but its tensions are not liturgical.

A sexual relationship is the focus of *Troilus and Cressida* (1602/3), but neither the mechanics of union nor its solemnization feature strongly. At the play's beginning, Troilus loves Cressida, and the play skirts any narrative of courtship; Pandarus brings them together with the ghost of a handfast—"here I hold your hand; here, my cousin's"—and then they go to bed (3.2.185). It might be easy to ascribe this apparent indifference to liturgical form to the play's setting in the ancient world, before Christian rites, but there are two allusions to marriage. "What nearer debt in all humanity / Than wife is to the husband?" asks Hector, and later Aeneas refers to "a bridegroom's fresh alacrity" (2.2.174–75; 4.5.145). But this play rushes to love's limits: to betrayal, and to relationships as political acts, a kind of warfare. Cressida writes to Troilus, but he tears the letter up; the contents are "Words, words, mere words," he says, and Thersites jokes, "I think thy horse will sooner con an oration than thou learn a prayer without book" (5.3.109; 2.1.15–17). Here, the language of love has no set form and nothing is precise in words. Love and marriage are only here a prayer without book.

The Winter's Tale (1609) is a play of wonders and reconciliations between couples, but at heart it attends to the fiction of adultery: not the mechanisms that tie together a couple but those that separate them. There are handfasts here—Leontes suspects Hermione because she apparently takes Polixenes's hand, while at the end he commands Camillo to take Paulina's hand—but little certainty or structure to them. Florizel simply refers to Perdita as "my wife," and we are to assume that they are married but not to worry how (5.1.166). These three plays—*The Winter's Tale, Troilus and Cressida,* and *The Merry Wives of Windsor*—are the counters to the three I have considered at length in this chapter, and their absences might in the end shed a light back over one phase of Shakespeare's twisting, roaming interest. Inside the marriage rite is a junction, and for a moment one fiction is conjured. *All's Well That Ends Well, Measure for Measure,* and *Othello* are the plays of this moment, and he passes through on his way elsewhere.

PART II *The Order for the Administration of the Lord's Supper, or Holy Communion*

And as the son of God did vouchsafe to yield up his soul by death upon the cross for your health, even so it is your duty to receive Communion together, in the remembrance of his death as he himself commanded.

The Book of Common Prayer (1559), Cummings, 130–31.

CHAPTER 4 ❧ *The Quick and the Dead*

Where the marriage rite binds a couple, the Lord's Supper is designed to bind a whole society: so Communion sings a single song, of concord, harmony. We open with the Lord's Prayer—"Our Father which art in heaven"—and the priest goes on to invoke, "Almighty God, unto whom all hearts be open, all desires known, and from whom no secrets are hid." We are escorted by cadence into unity upon this shared ground. The first time the congregation speaks, all together ask: "Lord have mercy upon us, and incline our hearts to keep this law," and then eight times repeat this phrase, following each of the Ten Commandments. The tenth response elaborates our complicity: "Lord have mercy upon us, and write all these laws in our hearts."

In speaking together, all both perform and wish for obedience, and now the community is given further shape. The laws of God, in the Ten Commandments, are followed by a Collect for the queen. "The hearts of kings are in thy rule and governance," the priest begins:

> We humbly beseech thee, so to dispose and govern the heart of Elizabeth, thy servant, our queen and governor, that in all her thoughts, words, and works, she may ever seek thy honor and glory, and study to preserve thy people committed to her charge.

The monarch is both the head and participant of this community; the poor are remembered too. "Lay not up for yourselves treasure upon the earth," beckons the priest, "Blessed be the man who provideth for the sick and needy." Alms are now collected from the congregation. This is a community of the living, both royal and destitute, but earth is only a temporary kingdom. "I look for the resurrection of the dead, and the life of the world to come," the central and repeated prayer known as the Nicene Creed instructs, and all repeat, "he shall come again with glory, to judge both the quick and the dead" (124–26).

Communion rite in the Book of Common Prayer descends from the traditional Roman Catholic Mass. The congregation meets and prays; in celebration of Christ's last supper and sacrifice, they take bread and wine. It arranges around such simple things a great weight of meaning. The *Lay Folks Mass Book*, a popular twelfth-century handbook to the Mass, described the rite as "The worthiest thing, the mast of goodness, / In all the world," and in exile during the Reformation the Catholic polemicist Nicholas Saunders stressed its centrality:

> In this one dish is a composition most delicate of angels, heavens, elements, of herbs, fishes, birds, beasts, of reasonable men, and of God him self. No kind of salt, meat, sauce, fruits, confection, no kind of wine, aqua vita, aqua composita, liquors, syrups can be found in nature, made by art, devised by wit but it is all set upon this table

he wrote, and "that in a small rome."[1] The pun on Rome is perhaps unintentional but it is felicitous. The traditional Mass was at the heart of the late medieval church, its celebration the central devotion, its form the form of faith.

In the early years of the Elizabethan church, and troubled by how to distinguish this new faith from the old, the bishop of Salisbury John Jewel wrote an exegesis upon Paul's epistles to the Thessalonians. "The Mass and God's word cannot dwell in one house together," he insists: "the one is so contrary to the other." Ten years later, Archbishop Whitgift concurred. "How contrary is our communion to theirs" he declared, and "What diversity is there in the celebration of our sacraments and theirs!" There is a kind of fury provoked by affiliation; it arises when the object of love sits troublingly close to the object of hate. Twenty years after Whitgift, the reformed polemicist Andrew Willet described the traditional Mass. In his 1592 *Synopsis Papismi*, that great compendium of reformed theology, he writes:

> it is an epitome and abridgement of Papistry, the marrow, sinews, and bones of their idolatrous profession: yea the very darling of the popish Church: it is the very proper badge and mark of a papist. He that hateth the Mass, hateth the whore of Babylon: he that loveth the Mass, cannot love the truth.[2]

The gesture of separation is dramatic; it effaces all shared ground. The way that we know what we are is by being nothing like that.

Communion promises a way to know and isolate the foreign. It keeps borders on the devotional world and it was long like this. The period I consider here—the sixteenth and early seventeenth centuries—is given the academic title "early modern," as if all were looking toward now, and the name might lead us to forget that Reformation debates over theology and doctrine were nothing new. The oldest and most worn of them all was debate over the Mass. As the medieval historian Paul Strohm observes in *England's Empty Throne*, late fourteenth-century heresy trials of the followers of the renegade theologian John Wycliffe—known as "Lollards"—tended to dwell upon the theology of this rite. "Eucharistic doctrine," he writes, was "a matter of prosecutorial convenience," for the specific points of divergence between Lollard and orthodox theology were trickily slight. The Mass however provides "a ground so argumentatively vexed that no difference could confidently be sustained against the full weight of orthodox institutions."[3] Theology here works as a convenient tool for the isolation—and condemnation—of another group. A century and a half later, in Reformation England, those who invoke the Mass and its cousin the reformed Communion are the heirs of an old paradigm.

Obscure doctrine and its furious invocation may at times be strategic. The Communion rite is no simple expression of community; it also creates that community, performs it into being, and so it is at times of larger social and political crisis that we find it most hotly fought. On 26 November 1559, a little more than a week after the accession of Queen Elizabeth, and in the dawning moments of a Protestant English church and state, John Jewel preached at Paul's Cross in London. He was recently returned from exile in Frankfurt, where he had waited out Queen Mary's reign; he was soon to be ordained as bishop of Salisbury. He chose as his text for the sermon that day a line from Paul's first epistle to the Corinthians: "the Lord Jesus, in the night that he was betrayed, took bread." This is the act marked in all celebration of Communion, but traditional Catholic worship has, he insists, perverted an act of community into one of discord. By speaking the rite in Latin, a language incomprehensible to many; by giving the people only bread; and by allowing Mass to be held in private, they have "made the holy sacrament of love and charity to serve them as an instrument of discord and dissension." He ends with the boast that subsequently gave the nickname of "the Challenge Sermon" to this piece:

> If any learned man of all our adversaries, or of all the learned men that be alive, be able to bring one sufficient sentence out of any old catholic doctor, or father, or out of any general council, or out of the holy scriptures of God, or any one example of the primitive church, whereby it may be clearly and plainly proved that there was any private mass in the whole world at that time, for the space of six hundred years after Christ; Or that there was then any communion ministered unto the people under one kind; Or that the people had their communion prayers then in a strange tongue that they understood not,

he insists, then: "as I have said before, so say I now again, I am content to yield unto him, and to subscribe."[4]

This was high theological gamesmanship, less a sermon than a provocation. In May 1560, Jewel was invited to preach the challenge again, at the Chapel Royal in the presence of the queen; and two weeks after that once more, again at Paul's Cross. Henry Cole, dean of St. Paul's and a leading traditional theologian, soon answered. Their exchange of letters was quickly printed as *The True Copies of the Letters between the reverend father in God John Bishop of Sarum and D.Cole* (1560). The volume is presented as a handbook to controversy. At the end is a careful index of the flashpoints of debate, such as "Communion under one kind great abuse," "Marriage of priests," and "Grounds to build sound doctrine upon," and from here, the quarrel spread. It has become known as the "Great Controversy," and during the 1560s both theologians and their supporters published more than fifty sermons, treatises, and pamphlets. This was, according to one church historian, "wholly without precedent." The extent of publication reveals the depth and intensity of popular care.[5]

In opening, Bishop Jewel allows that he will not cover everything. Of some matters, he says, "I am content to disadvantage myself at this time," adding that he will not "speak either of transubstantiation, either of the real presence, either of the sacrifice, either of the common sale or utterance, either of the superstitious ceremonies of the mass." He will not discuss the particular theologies of the traditional rite, and Dean Cole in his first response questioned why this was so. He raised, "the article of the presence of Christ's body and blood in the sacrament," and goes on to emphasize that the Mass is a "sacrifice acceptable to God indeed, and good both for the quick and dead." The late medieval church held that a transformation took place in the rite, and that the performance of a Mass may improve the condition of the dead in purgatory. The traditional Mass in this way links the quick to the dead; this world and the next are held in elegant relation. Prayer for the dead was a central strand of the Mass, and yet Jewel apparently overlooks it. In response, Jewel explains his omission. "I knew the matters," he admits, "might at least have some colour or shadow of the doctors," that is, among the writings of the early fathers of the church might be found some trace of support for these positions. So, he continues, "I thought it best to make my entry with such things, as wherein I was well assured ye should not be able to find so much as any colour at all."[6] Not all questions are equal in this great debate. There are those in black and white: those where you find "not so much as any colour at all." The language used in administering the rite, for example, was a point of neat division. Traditional theologians held that Latin was proper, while reformers argued for the vernacular. But there are others, too, where we may see "some colour or shadow": where theological distinction is obscure, and the ground troublingly common.

The particular point of controversy was intercessory prayer for the dead during the service of Communion. This is the topic that Jewel sought to avoid, and deliberately so. Before he went into exile in Frankfurt in late 1554 he had signed his name to a set of articles, which embraced the traditional faith. The text of these articles is now lost. Lawrence Humfrey's hagiographic 1573 biography acknowledges that he signed them but passes over the contents, and the essay attached to the 1609 folio of Jewel's *Works*—"The Life of the Worthy Prelate and Faithfull Servant of God John Jewel"—by the popular anti-Catholic preacher Daniel Featley again declines to specify. "The Inquisition caught him, urging upon him subscription under pain of proscription and horrible tortures," Featley recounts, and continues: he "took the pen, and unwillingly and hastily wrote his name, whereby he seemed to approve some articles of Popery."[7] In his 1566 attack, *A Rejoindre to M. Jewels Replie*, the Catholic polemicist Thomas Harding dwells mockingly on the incident:

> Are you not one M. John Jewel that in S. Mary's Church at Oxford, subscribed openly, before the whole University to the Articles by the Catholics maintained, by the Gospellers impugned. . . . Subscribed you not to those Articles, that Christ's true and natural body and blood are verily and really present in the Sacrament of the Alter under the forms of bread and wine? That the Mass is a sacrifice propitiatory for the quick and dead?[8]

Harding specifies two articles to Jewel's confession: acceptance of the real presence, and intercessory prayer for the dead. Jewel had once accepted precisely those elements that the Challenge Sermon denied.

As an anecdote this might tell much of the relation of variable human character to theology and might warn us, perhaps, against any too strict understanding of the differences between faiths. But above all, it can trace for us now one hot place of liturgical debate for worshippers of sixteenth-century England. Communion promises to build a perfect community, and it may be used as a tool to exclude others from that society.

The traditional Mass insists that we are bound to the dead in duty and in obligation as well as in love.[9] Church receipts from the northern parish of Scarborough for the year 1435–36 testify to the traditional presence of the dead in the religion of the living: of 213 special ceremonies, 107 are directly concerned with intercession for departed souls.[10] These high figures exclude the moment at which we most powerfully touch the dead: during the common rite of the Mass. For traditional worshippers, the Mass grew upon intercessory prayer. *Mirk's Festial*—a collection of late fourteenth-century homilies—lists its functions: "the masse maketh joyful all the angels of Heaven, it feedeth and comforteth the souls in purgatory, and succoureth all that lived in earth and charity."[11] The charity of the Mass links living and dead, and as the *Lay Folks Mass Book* explains:

> Father and mother, and brother souls so dear,
> Sister and sibbe men, and others ifere,
> That us good would, or us good do . . .
> And to all though, that in purgatory have pain,
> Lord, this mess be mede and medicine.[12]

All are bound by this. As John Fisher, preaching an exhortation to remember the dead in 1532, noted, "our own profit and our own wealth hangeth thereby."[13] Just as the Mass remembers the dead, so is the centerpiece of a traditional burial the celebration of the Mass.

The English Reformation began to sever the bond between the dead and living that was traditionally organized at the Mass. The burial rite in the 1549 Book of Common Prayer culminates in the reception of Communion. But the 1552 edition eliminates Communion from the burial rite, and 1559, 1604, and all subsequent editions follow this. Further, the Communion rite excises the structures of traditional intercession: there is no prayer for souls in purgatory. This is a theology distinguished by that which it leaves out. The traditional Latin version of the Nicene Creed, as affirmed by the Council of Trent in 1546, included the dead within its powerful verbal formula. "Expecto resurrectionem mortuorum et vitam venturi saeculi," it runs, and ends "Amen." In Cranmer's translation for the first Book of Common Prayer, a silent emendation reveals the wholesale absence of the dead. Cranmer's creed states faith in "The resurrection of the body. And the life to come"; for the traditional "resurrectionem mortuorum," he inserts "resurrection of the body." The dead disappear, replaced by the ever-living Christ.[14] When Harding and Cole remind Jewel of the topics of real presence and intercessory prayer, they are implicitly linking the rites of burial and Communion. When Jewel seeks to ignore the topic of intercession, he is implicitly claiming that the dead have no place in discussion of Communion—as if this were a rite only for the living.

Such clarity is always only fiction; the controversies of the Reformation never divide so neatly in two. It would be elegant and comfortable to typify theology so that Catholics believed they could pray for the dead at the Mass, and Protestants did not. Such a black-and-white schema would scarcely testify to the color of liturgical debate, and the English revision of traditional rites was in the kindest terms fragile and is perhaps better described as a contradictory mess. There are two different creeds in the Book of Common Prayer, and they are largely but not entirely similar. The first—to be said during Morning Prayer and at Confirmation—neglects the dead. But the second—to be said during the Communion rite— remembers them. "I look for the resurrection of the dead, and the life of the world to come," it insists, and the dead are yet in our prayers (Cummings, 127).

The Communion rite sings a single song, but its words are old and with them come deep controversy. We form communities by ceremonies and by how we consider the dead; and each time we trace the limits of our world, we must leave some out. "The quick and the dead" is a simple phrase yet a conjunction that carries a great theological weight. It reminds us of obligations toward the dead and acknowledges their absence.

THE RIVAL VERSIONS of the creed were never meant to be held up side by side. They belong in separate phases: one at the start of the day, in Morning Prayer, and the other at the Communion rite. But taken as alternatives, they reveal fractures in the whole imaginative act that is the Book of Common Prayer, and these fractures are for us now displayed in the intricacies of a turn of phrase. Both creeds invoke "the quick and the dead," "the quick" being of course the living, in contrast to the dead. Translation, however, from one idiom into another dilutes the density of debate. These particular words— the quick, the dead—echoed through all the controversies above; it matters when we link them, and when we think of them apart. When Cole and Jewel return to the vocabulary of the creed, they show how deeply liturgical debate was embedded in turns of phrase. Many were tortured and executed during the Reformation over precisely these questions, and they were at heart arguments in and about language.

In the opening moments of *Titus Andronicus*, one of Shakespeare's earliest plays, the defeated armies of the Goths are led into Rome. Here is a procession, of royal prisoners, soldiers, captives, but in the midst are the bodies of the slain. "Behold the poor remains, alive and dead," announces Titus Andronicus, and demands proper burial for his sons. "Make way to lie them by their brethren," he declares, and as they are laid inside their tomb, commands them, "sleep in peace." This is not the whole ritual. Titus now points to his surviving sons and explains to Tamora, queen of the Goths: "These are their brethren whom your Goths beheld / Alive and dead, and for their brethren slain, / Religiously they ask a sacrifice." He repeats this phrase "alive and dead" for each has demands upon the other. "Alarbus' limbs are lopped, / And entrails feed the sacrificing fire," says Lucius, taking pleasure in propriety: "See, lord and father, how we have performed / Our Roman rites." Titus then speaks over the dead a strange, repetitive prayer:

> In peace and honour rest you here, my sons;
> Rome's readiest champions, repose you here in rest,
> Secure from worldly chances and mishaps.
> Here lurks no treason, here no envy swells,
> Here grow no damned drugs, here are no storms,
> No noise, but silence and eternal sleep.
> In peace and honour rest you here, my sons. (1.1.81–156)

This culminates the imagery echoing through the scene. Death is sleep and rest, and the vocabulary proof of our pomp and courtesy toward the dead.

Such orderly vision of ritual is immediately undone. Tamora calls the sacrifice of her son "cruel irreligious piety," a wrongful ceremony, and then that first burial rite is unraveled by its repetition in another (1.1.130). There is a scuffle between the new emperor and his brother; in intervening, Titus kills Mutius, who is one of his own sons; Titus then refuses to bury him in the family tomb. "My lord, this is impiety in you," says Marcus, echoing Tamora, and Lucius pleads, "let us give him burial as becomes" (1.1.532, 344). But the notion that there is any proper, pious form—"burial as becomes"—is here slipping from view. Although Titus agrees that Mutius must be buried, his rite is an atrophied, shrunken version. "There lie thy bones, sweet Mutius, with thy friends,'" says Lucius as they put him in the tomb; and then all repeat, "No man shed tears for noble Mutius, / He lives in fame, that died in virtue's cause" (1.1.384–87). This is all the ceremony he receives.

The play begins with two burials; we can see them side by side. For those who stand outside its decorum, a rite is a pattern of arbitrary actions, and this is the grand fear of the play. Here Rome is a place of uncertain ceremony, and none know quite how it is proper to mourn. Marcus, upon finding the raped Lavinia, first asks her to speak. "Speak, gentle niece," he asks, and, when she remains silent, "Why dost not speak to me?" and then, confused and frustrated, "Shall I speak for thee?" He warns, "Sorrow concealed, like an oven stopped, / Doth burn the heart to cinders" (2.4.16, 21, 33, 36–37). All words are now futile. "O, could our mourning ease thy misery," wishes Marcus, but it of course cannot; later, Titus kneels, and tells his sorrow to the stones (2.4.57). He curses his own hands. "In bootless prayer have they been held up, / And they have served me to effectless use," he says, and chops one off. He tries to pray with the other—"here I lift this one hand up to heaven"—and demands what he must do. He asks, "shall we bite our tongues?" for words seem to fail, and later, he only laughs: "Ha, ha, ha!" (3.1.75–76, 131, 263). All is hectic, uncertain, and wild with excess. "I have heard my grandsire say full oft," warns Young Lucius, "Extremity of griefs would make men mad" (4.1.18–19). None can conceive a proper form of piety toward the dead. "Oft have I digged up dead men from their graves," boasts Aaron the Moor, "And set them upright at their dear friends' door," neatly reversing the action of a burial; Titus imagines that a fly in grief might "buzz lamenting dirges in the air" (5.1.135–36; 3.2.62).

The play's only answer to uncertainty is violence. Sacrifice leads to revenge, to murder and to rape; children are killed in front of their parents, and a father kills his own daughter; and then in turn, Titus kills the children of the queen and feeds them to her. "Why, there they are, both baked in this pie, / Whereof their mother daintily hath fed," he tells her, and kills her (5.3.59–60). This dizzied, nauseous trail of hurt runs on until the end, and the play closes as it began, in divided ceremony. Marcus stands before the survivors. "You sad-faced men, people and sons of Rome, / By uproars severed, as a flight of fowl / Scattered by winds," he begins, but the community must go on. He continues, "O, let me teach you how to knit again / This scattered corn into one mutual sheaf, / These broken limbs into one body." We form communities in ceremonies, and here is work to be done. Lucius, the new emperor, speaks last in the play. "Some loving friends convey the Emperor hence," he commands: "give him burial in his father's grave. / My father and Lavinia shall forthwith / Be closed in our household monument." Here is a laying to rest, a ceremony of peace and burial, but he goes on:

> As for that ravenous tiger, Tamora,
> No funeral rite nor man in mourning weed,
> No mournful bell shall ring her burial;
> But throw her forth to beasts and birds to prey. (5.3.66–71,
>   190–97)

In the ceremonies of the dead, we tie all together; some are borne up and some cast out.

It is hard and perhaps a foolish thing to read a play for what it does not do, but I am trying here to trace the growing consciousness of a crisis shared among characters on stage. They know not quite what to do in the occasions of grief and mourning. Often in this cruel rushed play the characters reach for the order of old stories, of classical tales, for a comfort told in myths. Lavinia, tongueless, is literally incapable of voicing her own distress, but she finds a way to explain what has happened by reference to a convenient copy of an old book, the *Metamorphoses* by Ovid. This is of course anachronism, a bound book in ancient Rome, but she needs it now. "So busily she turns the leaves," notes Titus: "This is the tragic tale of Philomel, / And treats of Tereus' treason and his rape" (4.1.45–48). Later, Titus writes a line from the *Odes* of Horace and sends it to Tamora's children as a warning; still later, he quotes an old story— "Was it well done of rash Virginius / To slay his daughter with his own right hand / Because she was enforced, stained, and deflowered?"— as rationale for killing Lavinia (5.3.36–38).

Titus calls this "a pattern, precedent, and lively warrant" for his own stumbling actions, as if there were a script to lead us in times of grief and loss. Among these old stories lies another, straining beneath the surface of the play. In the closing lines, Lucius casts Tamora's body out of Rome, offering it those "birds and beasts to prey," and here he links, perhaps without knowing, the play's two great motifs. Here are the birds and beasts that eat, the cruel funeral; the phrase binds an image of eating to a burial rite, and it does so in a single word, which may mean to eat—to prey—but which is also the sound of devotion: to pray. The play, which opened with burials, builds to a bloody feast and then further funerals. Burial and baking, the eating of blood: this is the pattern of the Mass and its tie to burial.

These are only the slightest of allusions. The echoes are loose, nonspecific. In killing Chiron and Demetrius, Titus is assisted by Lavinia, and he instructs her as he cuts their throats, "Receive the blood" (5.2.196). In his Arden edition of the play, Jonathan Bate notes against this line, "a dark parody of the language of the holy eucharist?"[15] The play's tentative use of sacramental imagery has been met with similarly tentative critical recognition; Bate questions rather than concludes, like all the characters here, disbelieving of what is before them. It hints at a very loaded pattern of debate—links funerals to feasts, the living and the dead—but this all as yet is an implicit uncertain scheme.

The critical commonplace is to dismiss the play as simply flawed. Many have done this and even its admirers feel bound to begin with apology. The opening line of the 1994 New Cambridge edition of the play, edited by Alan Hughes, admits, *"Titus Andronicus* is not everyone's favorite play."[16] In the introduction the 1995 Arden edition Bate notes, "it has been reviled by critics and revived infrequently" (Bate, 1). *Titus Andronicus* is traditionally seen as a very early play, written perhaps in the very late 1580s, and then revised in 1592 or '93; Jonathan Bate argues that it was a new work, written in 1593. All agree that what matters here is that it is looking forward. For Bate, "Titus Andronicus emerges as the pivotal play in Shakespeare's early career . . . and paves the way for his later achievements in tragedy" (Bate, 79). The assumption that the play is looking forward corresponds to what we see on stage: an apparent uncertainty between the characters; a reaching for something just beyond their grasp. "Shall we bite our tongues, and in dumb shows / Pass the remainder of our hateful days?" asks Titus in the abyss of grief. "Why dost thou laugh?" asks Marcus: "It fits not with this hour" (3.1.131–32, 264). We have before us, yet unknown, a greater involvement in and dramatic use of the ceremonies of the dead.

THE GHOST, THEY say, came across from the graveyard next door. E. K. Chambers reports a rumor from the late seventeenth century, "that he hath writ the scene of the Ghost in *Hamlet*, at his House which bordered on the Charnel-House and Church-Yard," and by the beginning of the eighteenth century the tale was spookier still. In his "Remarks on the Plays of Shakespeare" of 1710, Charles Gildon claims: "This scene, I have been assured, Sh. wrote in a Charnel-House, in the midst of the Night."[17]

As *Hamlet* (1600) opens, the nervous guards are cold. It is late in the year, or early; it is the middle of the night and the start of a new king's reign. Last night they saw a ghost in armor, and this evening they are feeling shaky. "Well, sit we down, / And let us hear Barnardo speak this," suggests Horatio, but as the guard begins to tell—"Last night of all, / When yon same star"—the ghost interrupts again. "Thou art a scholar—speak to it, Horatio," says Marcellus. "What art thou . . ." Horatio begins, and "By heaven, I charge thee speak." The ghost silently stalks toward the edge of the stage. Horatio repeats: "Speak, speak, I charge thee speak." Marcellus sadly notes, " 'Tis gone, and will not answer," and they begin to fill its silence with speculation. "It would be spoke to," suggests Barnardo and later, as proof of its desire, adds what is perhaps a hopeful embellishment, "It was about to speak when the cock crew." Horatio takes it as a political sign: "This bodes some strange eruption to our state." None is sure how to approach or comprehend this ghost. Horatio is commanding, blunt with questions, while Barnardo is speculative; when Hamlet hears of the ghost from Horatio, he asks, "Did you not speak to it?"[18]

In the earliest version of the burial rite in the Book of Common Prayer, the priest speaks to the dead. At the moment when the body is lowered to the ground, he scatters earth and addresses the corpse:

> I commend thy soul to God the father almighty, and thy body to the ground, earth to earth, ashes to ashes, dust to dust, in sure and certain hope of resurrection to eternal life, through our Lord Jesus Christ. (Cummings, 82–83)

This is the traditional theological claim—that the dead may listen, are still with us—but by the first revision of the prayer book it was dropped. In the 1552 burial rite, the priest says, "we therefore commit his body to the ground, earth to earth, ashes to ashes, dust to dust," and the 1559 and all later versions follow this. As the religious historian Eamon Duffy explains, now "the dead person is spoken not to, but about, as one no longer here, but precisely as departed." In speaking to the dead—"by heaven I charge thee speak"—we conjure them as among us now; in speaking for them we consider only our own needs and place. This ghost will not be spoken for. "Mark me" he says, in his first line; he has a story and demands. "Speak, I am bound to hear," says Hamlet, and each falls here willingly to the rigor of an older pattern. "Funerals in late medieval England," writes Duffy, "were intensely concerned with the notion of community, in which living and dead were not separated, in which the bonds of affection, duty, and blood continued to bind," and in speaking now the ghost and Hamlet are bound to one another.[19] The ghost tells Hamlet of the murder of his father, and then makes two demands. "Revenge his foul and most unnatural murder," he instructs, and "Remember me" (1.5.25, 91).

Late medieval liturgical "remembrance" is something stricter than the passive recollection we take the word to mean today. A "remembrance" is the liturgical term for the set of intercessory prayers given for a departed soul at regular intervals after death. A funeral in the traditional church might be repeated at the "month's mind" and again at the anniversary of the death, when mourners performed a perfect copy: with, as the historian Peter Marshall writes, "the bell-man going forth once more, candles, mass and *dirige*, doles to the poor, and even the presence of a hearse in the parish church." This funeral is living theater around an empty hearse, and mourners might commission cycles of masses to be sung at regular delays. These were called "chantries," after the Latin for "to sing."[20] Each Mass links living to the dead. In the Sarum missal, the "memento," which recalls the living and the dead, is immediately followed by the "communicantes," which describes the community of the saints. "Memento etiam, Domine," the worshippers pray, "animarum famulorum famularomque tuarum [name] qui nos praecesserunt cum signo fidei, et dormiunt in somno pacis."[21] Memory and community are linked in the group rites of commemoration for the dead, the saints, and Christ. During the 1550s, the Roman Catholic Church convened a huge council—known as the Council of Trent—to condemn Protestantism and to clarify doctrine, and defined the Eucharist around its memorial intention:

> Ergo Salvator noster discessums ex hoc mundo as Patrem sacramentum hoc instituit, in quo divitias divini sui erga homines amoris velut effudit memoriam faciens mirabilium suorum, et in illius sumptione colere nos sui memoriam praecepit.
>
> Therefore, our Saviour, about to depart from this world to the Father, instituted this sacrament in which he as it were poured out the riches of his divine love towards humanity, causing his wonderful works to be remembered, and he bade us cherish his memory as we partook of it.[22]

In the 1539 *Manual of Prayers*—one of the Book of Common Prayer's direct ancestors—the prayer that immediately precedes the Mass describes the rite as "that blessed sacrifice of praising which thou thyself commanded to be done for a memorial of thy holy passion, to the intent it might stir up in me a fresh remembrance of thy most blessed death."[23] The action and the word itself—"Remember me"— cannot be separated from the traditional Mass.

The Parisian printers François Regnault and Simon Vostre produced the finest traditional primers. Vellum-bound and engraved, they are an eloquent testament to the medieval cult of the dead. Their liturgies are conventional, according to the Sarum rite.[24] In a typical illustrated primer, printed by Regnault in Paris in 1531, the "Virgilie Mortuorum" begins with two woodcuts—one of a man alive in sin, the other the dance of death—and the opening prayer begs, "Convertere anima mea in requiem tuam" [Return to your rest, my soul"].[25] Here in the requiem the living directly address the dead, and the primer begins with a set of woodcuts that moralize the months as the stages of a life. The penultimate woodcut instructs:

> When man is at lxvi [66] year old
> Which likened is to barren November
> He wereth unwieldy/sickly/and cold
> Then his soul health is time to remember. (Biiii v)

With elegant economy, the keyword connects the preparation of one's own soul to the Passion of Christ and to those who are already dead.

Remembrance is both objective mechanism and subjective action; as the Council of Trent's decree suggests, there are two slightly different forms of memory. Christ's sacrifice forces—"faciens"—and begs—"praecepit"—us to remember. The latter is more familiar to us now: memory as the play between chance recollection and erasure, a subjective tendency, as in the soft unquantifiable memories of childhood. But the former is hard: remembrance as a task or as a series of actions as clearly defined as a ballroom dance or military drill. This was the style of remembrance imagined by traditional liturgies, and these hardened mechanisms of mourning—worn into shape by repetition—had a function. In the memorable phrase of the great French sociologist Philippe Ariès, they "tamed death." Just as the medieval cult of the saints had breached the terrifying barrier between this world and next with familiar and local mechanisms of intercession, so the elaborate technologies of death domesticated wild fears that the dead were forever lost.[26] The formal institutions of medieval remembrance—the chantries and the empty hearse, the bell and dirges, and most of all the strategic repetition of the Mass—shared an intimate and gentle project. They gave comfort in a time of grief.

And then instead of actions, a new church made of words. Peter Marshall has calculated that on tombs in Sussex from the period 1496–1515, the median number of words was thirty-five; for the period 1596–1615 it was eighty-six; and for 1616–1635, it was ninety-four. This is one example of a national trend.[27] The Reformation redefined the memorialization of the dead. In the place of intercession was commemoration, great splashes of powerful language in which early Elizabethan reformers taught worshippers to out-think grief. "There is great error and darkness and ignorance in man's life" insists John Jewel in his explication of the Thessalonian epistles: "We rejoice when we have cause to mourn, and mourn many times when we have cause to rejoice." Our reaction to death is confused since this should be a point of celebration:

> why may not Christians mourn and continue in heaviness? Because it is no new thing for a man to die; because he goeth the way of all flesh. . . . The death of a godly man is nothing else but a sleep. . . . He goeth into his grave as into a bed; he forsaketh this life as if he lay down to sleep. He shall shake off his sleep, rouse himself, and rise again though we know not how.[28]

The first book of homilies, written by Cranmer and issued in 1547, includes an exhortation "Against the fear of death," which shares the biblical image of death as sleep and offers consolation in the same terms as Jewel: "death shall be to him no death at all, but a very deliverance from death, from all pains, cares and sorrows, miseries, and wretchedness of this world." The homily continues, "Therefore let us be always of good comfort: for we know that, so long as we be in the body, we be as it were far from God in a strange country, subject to many perils," and at the start of the burial rite in the Book of Common Prayer the priest promises, "whosoever liveth and believeth in me, shall not die forever."[29]

Hamlet was familiar with this language. It is currency at the court of Denmark where Claudius mixes mirth and dirge—"In equal scale weighing delight and dole"—and Gertrude consoles her son "all that lives must die, / Passing through nature to eternity" (1.2.13, 72–73). Hamlet knows these clichés as every worshipper in the English Church knew them, familiar from a lifetime of repetition, and in the most famous speech in all of Shakespeare's writings, he holds them up as specimens:

> To die—to sleep,
> No more; and by a sleep to say we end
> The heart-ache and the thousand natural shocks
> That flesh is heir to: 'tis a consummation
> Devoutly to be wished. (3.1.62–66)

There is a striking absence of agency in these lines. For Hamlet, the sleep of death is a consolation only in theory. He investigates the conventional images *as* images—"to say"—and finds them insufficient not because they are not Christian, or not true, but because as images they do not work. The reforming insistence that we cannot in our actions touch the dead—that death is an end—is belied by the very imagery used to promote this view, that death is like sleep. The imagery does not work because it is necessarily vague. To return to Jewel: "He shall shake off his sleep, rouse himself, and rise again though we know not how." Our curiosity, our desire to breach the gap between the living and the dead, is not consoled by the acknowledgment that "we know not how." Hamlet, faced with the reformed clichés of a providential insistence upon the absolute will of God, finds them illogical, and he explains why in an image, which strategically reverses the homily. The homily typifies human life as "a strange country," far from God, which we should be happy to leave behind. But it is not strange; if anything, it is too familiar to us, and the insistence that we must forget the duty of the living and consign the dead to their proper realm is incomprehensible: "The undiscover'd country, from whose bourn / No traveller returns, puzzles the will" (3.1.64–65, 79–80).

The logical product of providentialism is a refusal to mourn. For Calvin, in his exegesis of Job, the ceremonies of mourning are proof of a barely sublimated atheism:

> death showeth what we be, and what is our nature: and yet never-theless ye shall see many strive against that necessity. They make them gorgeous Tombs, and they will have triumphant funerals. It should seem that such men could find in their hearts to resist God: but they can not attain to their purpose.[30]

Subsequent reformers were more forgiving. Andrew Willet allowed a degree of ceremonial mourning on the grounds of decorum. "We do also grant, that according to the divers customs of countries, it is not unlawful to use some comely rites and ceremonies in the burial of the dead" he wrote, and went on to specify, "not for religion, but for orders sake."[31] Archbishop Whitgift permitted mourning clothes on the same grounds. "If any man wear such apparel of purpose to pro-voke sorrow, he is not to be excused," he declared; but "if for order and civility, he is to be commended."[32] As part of the larger defense of religious ceremony collected in *Of the laws of Ecclesiastical Polity*, the hugely influential early Anglican theologian Richard Hooker allowed mourning rites:

> Take away this which was ordained to show at burials the peculiar hope of the church of God concerning the dead, and in the manner of those dumb funerals what one thing is there whereby the world may perceive we are Christian men.[33]

Funerals are dramatic events. Royal and aristocratic funerals in Shakespeare's England were carefully graded precisely because they

were occasions of political display. Hooker's theatrical language—
"ordained to show," "whereby the world may perceive"—is not incidental. At a reformed burial, the community of the living was
consolidated in a public performance.

In his first lines in *Hamlet*, Claudius insists that the dead are no
more than memories:

> Though yet of Hamlet our dear brother's death
> The memory be green, and that it us befitted
> To bear our hearts in grief, and our whole kingdom
> To be contracted in one brow of woe,
> Yet so far hath discretion fought with nature
> That we with wisest sorrow think on him
> Together with remembrance of ourselves.

Even as he acknowledges that a degree of formal mourning is politic,
Claudius insists upon the state of the living. "Remembrance" here is
not the traditional rite but a vague "memory," and its object is himself, the living not the dead king. The model of grief that is here
permitted—befitting, discreet, wise—is the decorous mourning
allowed by Willet, Whitgift, and Hooker, and Claudius goes on to
warn that excessive grief "is a course / Of impious stubbornness . . .
most incorrect to heaven" (1.2.1–7, 94–95). The voice of Calvin is
behind these lines: "It should seem that such men could find in their
hearts to resist God."[34] Hamlet precisely rejects such polite allow-
ance of mourning and gestures toward a dangerous excess of grief
that is not constrained by "my inky cloak, good mother, / Nor customary
suits of solemn black" (1.2.77–78). These "trapping and suits of woe"
are not the limit upon his grief: they are only its external signs. Hooker
defended mourning clothes in a coy joke that separated grief from
ceremony. "It doth not come oftentimes to pass that men are fain
to have their mourning gowns pulled off their backs for fear of
killing themselves with sorrow that way nourished," he quipped.[35]
But for Hamlet, the phrases and decorum of reformed mourning
are insufficient. His unruly grief, once tamed by the traditional

technologies of death, overwhelms the ordered rhetoric of reformed memorialization, and surely some of his fury is sheer frustration that there is nothing else he can now do.

In England still we read poems at funerals. On a cold day more than a decade ago, at my uncle's funeral in a redbrick crematorium just to the north of London, I read one by Robert Frost. I wore a dark suit, for this is proper, and thought no more of that, but to ready myself for the reading I first committed the poem to heart, so that I would not stumble; and printed it out, in a large typeface, on a new sheet of paper; and each of these were barriers against the fear that I might during the reading break down and be unable to go on. This behavior is the heir of the reformed consolation of mourning, and it grows upon the belief that a pattern of good enough, rich enough words might count in the place of grief. It is an act of faith in order, in pattern, in proper sequence.

THE REFORMATION OF burial rites was partial and compromised; it stuttered in contradictions and half-done work, a thing of shreds and patches. In the generations between us and then, the cadence of the prayer book has won authority of its own. Perhaps the best metaphor is architectural. The lines of the liturgy are the grooves in a flight of old stone steps, and as we come to that staircase then it is sensible that we should follow upon its memory of footfalls. This sense divides us from the worshippers of Shakespeare's England. They saw flaws in the prayer book and felt the struggle between alternatives; they found it neither perfect nor inevitable.

"An Admonition to the Parliament" (1572) was, according to its modern editors, "the first open manifesto of the puritan party," and it insists that the Book of Common Prayer is insufficiently purified. "This book is an unperfected book, culled & picked out of that popish dunghill, the Mass book full of abominations," the admonition spits, and lists its failings: in the eleventh section, on the burial rite, it notes that "prayer for the dead is maintained."[36] In 1610, a defense of those nonconforming ministers who lost their living after

the Hampton Court Conference, agreed. *"Perfect consummation &*
bliss both in body and soul seemeth to be desired as well for the now
buried brother, and all the other departed in the true faith, whose
souls only (as yet) be in felicity, as for the living," the petition noted
among its list of faults in the ecclesiology of the new church.[37] They
were correct. The Elizabethan *Primer*—a new edition of the 1545
Henrician *Primer*, published in 1559, 1560, and 1568, and intended
for private prayer—openly retained intercessory prayers in the Dirige.
Following the traditional burial psalm "Lauda anima mea Dominum"
is the prayer:

> Lord, give thy people eternal rest,
> And light perpetual shine on them.
> From the gates of hell,
> Lord, deliver their souls

and the Dirige ends with the supplication "be merciful to the souls
of thy servants, being departed from this world in the confession of
thy name."[38] Here is the old promise: that we may still touch the
dead. While the Book of Common Prayer removed the requiem
mass from the burial rite, the Latin prayer book—the *Liber Precum
Publicarum*, published in 1560—retained a Communion service at
the burial: "Celebratio Coenae Domini, in funebribus."[39]

This is a history of words and their relation to faith; these are the
tangled and troubled poetics of theology. The same liturgy that
attempted to remove traditional intercession from the Communion
rite did so by using the word that promised intercession. "Take and
drink ye all of this: do this in remembrance of me" instructs the priest
in the rite for Communion, and he leads the congregation in general
confession. "The remembrance of them is grievous unto us," he says,
and then at the moment of administration we kneel and take bread
"in remembrance that Christ died for thee," and we take wine "in
remembrance that Christ's blood was shed for thee" (Cummings, 131,
134, 137). The Book of Common Prayer held Communion to be an
act conducted in remembrance of Christ's death. Queen Mary I,

after she acceded to the throne in 1553, sought to return traditional Roman worship to the English Church; notoriously, she tried Protestants for heresy, and during their interrogations they returned again and again to this word. "I believe it to be a most necessary remembrance of his glorious sufferings and death," insists Anne Askew, faced with torture, and twice she says: "in remembrance of Christ's death." The debate over Communion was, too, at the heart of Nicholas Ridley's disputation, and he comes back to the key word: "the body of Christ in the remembrance of him and his death." Remembrance is, as defined by Ridley, the proof of absence. "A remembrance is not of a thing present, but of a thing past and absent," he declares: "There is a difference between remembrance and presence."[40]

The struggle over the term "remembrance" was not complete with the publication of the Book of Common Prayer, for each claim and innovation was met with a counter claim: reformation answered in what historians now call the Counter-Reformation. Roman Catholic polemicists did not accept the prayer book's reappropriation of the word. In 1555 Bishop Bonner's Marian homily "Answer to certain objections against the presence of Christ's body in the Sacrament" reclaims the word as proof of Christ's presence in the transformation of the Mass. "The body and blood of our Saviour Christ (as it is in the Sacrament, under the forms of bread and wine)," he insists, "may in that respect also very well be a remembrance of it self." Nicholas Sanders's 1566 treatise *The Supper of our Lord* offers the same carnal version of remembrance:

> If you take from us the making of his body which causeth the vehement remembrance of the death, it is afterward a vain thing to talk of the remembrance of his death by eating bread and drinking wine. For the necessary mean of necessary remembrance of his death, consisteth in the real presence.[41]

The word and its meanings were claimed by both traditional and reformed movements; they are joined in use and divided by meaning.

In *Henry V* (1599) the new young king retains a traditional faith in the ceremonies of mourning. To atone for the usurpation of his father, he has commissioned a cycle of chantries for the soul of the deposed Richard II—

> Five hundred poor have I in yearly pay
> Who twice a day their withered hands hold up
> Toward heaven to pardon blood. And I have built
> Two chantries, where the sad and solemn priests
> Sing still for Richard's soul

—and the most terrifying curse he can invoke upon the French king is that he will "lay these bones in an unworthy urn, / Tombless, with no remembrance over them" (4.1.279–84; 1.2.228–29). In *Twelfth Night* (1602), Olivia will not see Orsino because she is mourning her brother. As Valentine describes,

> like a cloistress she will veiled walk
> And water once a day her chamber round
> With eye-offending brine: all this to season
> A brother's dead love, which she would keep fresh
> And lasting, in her sad remembrance. (1.1.27–31)

This remembrance is traditional mourning: the cloister suggests a convent, and her actions are touching in their formality. Hamlet begs of Ophelia, "Nymph, in thy orisons, / Be all my sins remembered" (3.1.91–92). Each of these moments resonates with a traditional hope that had been half-buried beneath half a century of reformed polemic. Inside this word lies a pattern of linkage that may seem strange or counterintuitive to us now: between feast and funeral, between eating and burying, between Communion and the dead.

Hamlet, having hauled Polonius's corpse off-stage, is asked by Claudius "where's Polonius?," and he replies,

> At supper.
> KING CLAUDIUS: At supper? Where?
> HAMLET: Not where he eats but where is eaten. (4.3.17–20)

I am scarcely the first to hear in this exchange something more than a gruesome joke. The Lord's Supper is where one eats and one— Christ—is eaten. As Stephen Greenblatt has argued, these lines "echo and reinforce the theological and, specifically, the eucharistic subtext" of the play.[42] All contemporary scholarship that traces sacramental controversy through Shakespeare's plays owes a great debt to Greenblatt, whose work has given a vocabulary and direction to a generation of critics. His essay "The Mousetrap" finds echoed within Hamlet the conversations and debates over early modern theology of Communion, and he has written also about the late medieval customs of burial. His book *Hamlet in Purgatory* elegantly surveys traditional structures of mourning and intercession: specifically, the popular belief in an intermediate realm after death, neither heaven nor hell, where the fate of the recently departed souls might be aided by prayer among the living. These are fine, elegant works, and valuable; what is odd about them is that they are separate.

To anyone familiar with the 1549 Book of Common Prayer, the Latin prayer book, or the petitions of the Puritan opponents against the late Elizabethan liturgy, the clean division of burial and Mass must appear unfamiliar. Greenblatt describes the special intercessory prayers of the late medieval church, and the requiems directed toward purgatory and the souls of the departed. He notes that "Masses lovingly paid for and performed in memory of the dead were particularly efficacious," yet all masses were performed in memory of the dead.[43] And even as he traces what he calls "the language of Eucharistic anxiety" through Hamlet's bundling of Polonius, he does not note why Hamlet might invoke the Mass at this particular moment: he is attempting a kind of rough burial. To isolate the common Mass from the dead and to assume that reformed rites abandoned the promise of intercession is in itself a polemical, partial claim. It is to assume that reformed theology was better defined than either its critics or its proponents ever claimed, and by extension to imagine the perfection of the Book of Common Prayer. In an essay in the *New York Review of Books*, on the death of Shakespeare's son Hamnet, Greenblatt describes the rich formalities of traditional mourning and observes that after the Reformation "everything had been scaled back, forced underground, or eliminated outright. Above all, it was now illegal to pray for the dead."[44] It should now be apparent that I am more than in agreement with Greenblatt's larger story—that Shakespeare's imagination was provoked by the revision of church rites. But his claim that prayer for the dead was made illegal and vanished would surely surprise those Puritan petitioners who insisted that "prayer for the dead is maintained," and still more any who at Morning Prayer invoked the fate of all the quick and the dead.

There is no perfect pattern, here. What we see in prayer book and play are moments, echoes, flashes of desire. These are legible only by reference to traditional practice. Gertrude describes the mourning Ophelia as incoherent in grief:

> She speaks much of her father, says she hears
> There's tricks i'th'world, and hems, and beats her heart,
> Spurns enviously at straws, speaks things in doubt,
> That carry but half sense. Her speech is nothing

she declares. Yet when she enters, this is not all we see. Ophelia's song movingly dwells upon his death in a half-mad formality, and ends, "God a mercy on his soul. / And of all Christian souls, I pray God" (4.5.4–7, 194–95). Her plea is a conventional declaration. Henry Machyn's diary of 1550s London records a strikingly similar prayer offered twice by local parishioners at funerals: "I beseech [God] have mercy on his soul, amen!" and "I pray God have mercy!"[45] This conventionality is precisely what makes it controversial. Ophelia's plea rephrases the traditional suffrage for the souls of the dead, banished from the reformed burial rite, and in its spirit and image returns us to the closing prayer of the funeral service of the 1599 Counter-Reformation primer, the *Office of the Blessed Virgin Marie*, which pleads: "God the creator, and redeemer of all the faithful, give unto the souls of thy servants, men, and women, remission of their sins."[46] The same sentiment reappears in the Marian suffrage "For the Souls Departed":

> God that art creator and redeemer of all faithful people, grant unto the souls of al their sins, that through devout prayers they may attain the gracious pardon, which they have always desired.[47]

When Laertes comes to witness the grief of his sister, his response is strikingly different from Gertrude. "A document in madness— thoughts and remembrance fitted," he declares (4.5.175–76). This is surely half a chaos, the wild voicing of grief. It also half remembrance, fitted to proper order.

Shakespeare probably did not know the specifics of the Counter-Reformation rite, but he knew that there is no single way to mourn the dead. In drowning, as Gertrude describes it, Ophelia "chanted snatches of old tunes / As one incapable of her own distress," and this is true too of all expressions of grief in Elizabethan England. The burial rite proposed by the Book of Common Prayer is a palimpsest of rival theologies; it is a work of older tunes bound into new form, and in deferring to it we all show ourselves incapable of our own subjective distress. Many who have read *Hamlet* have assumed that behind its many burials, in the culture of its time, there must have been some single correct form. But that form was the product of its own construction, in pieces and in rival claims.

In the graveyard, Hamlet sees a funeral procession. "Here comes the King, / The Queen, the courtiers," he notes, and asks: "but who is that they follow / And with such maimed rites?" (5.1.200–202). This is Ophelia's funeral, and Hamlet's sense that something is lacking is in turn echoed by Laertes, who demands of the priest, "What ceremony else?" (5.1.218). As the priest insists when challenged by Laertes, "We should profane the service of the dead / To sing sage requiem and such rest to her / As to peace-parted souls" (5.1.229–31). He is defending the formality of proper burial rites by not allowing them to a suicide.[48] Critics disagree over the implications of this decision. Where Roland Mushat Frye insisted that audiences in the Globe Theatre would have shared Laertes's disgust that Ophelia was denied full rites, Michael Mac-Donald has more recently shown that contemporary coroners' juries tended to apply church law rigorously in cases such as these.[49] There is however a larger point here, an assumption shared among the disagreeing characters. Neither the priest nor Laertes would have insisted upon the importance of the set form of burial had they not agreed both that the form had a logic to it greater than mere decorum and that the form itself was undecided. Here we are split not between sympathy and disregard for Ophelia but between rival conceptions of propriety.

Many scholars have been struck—like Hamlet, like Laertes—by these "maimed rites." David Bevington, in his great study of gesture and ritual in Shakespeare's plays, describes the central presence of broken ceremony in *Hamlet*—"a pattern of 'maimed rites' that extends from the very first scene, with its inversions of precedence on the guard platform, to the very last"—and Stephen Greenblatt echoes Bevington in suggesting that this is "an instance of an overarching phenomenon in *Hamlet*: the disruption or poisoning of virtually all rituals for managing grief, allaying personal and collective anxiety, and restoring order."[50] They share the notion that a complete burial was available and that some rites might be whole. But stage rites were always necessarily maimed. Since it was illegal to perform church rites on stage, *Hamlet* is incapable of presenting anything other than a disrupted, inverted rite. Even beyond this ruling, no burial rite would be greeted as "full and proper" by the whole population. If you performed a funeral rite without the Mass, following the Book of Common Prayer, you had maimed the traditional rite; if you performed it with the Mass, then you were parodying Christ.

All notions of propriety are historically constructed. Laertes, the priest, and countless twentieth-century critics of the play have insisted that Ophelia's burial is lacking, but it is complete according to at least one early modern liturgy. A radical Protestant liturgy called *A Booke of the Forme of common prayers, administration of the Sacraments, & c. agreeable to Gods Worde* was first printed at Middleburgh in 1584, and reprinted in 1587 and 1602, and it prescribes a stripped-down burial rite. "The corpse is reverently to be brought to the grave, accompanied with the neighbours in comely manner," it insists: "without any further ceremony."[51] "What ceremony else?" demands Laertes. None. As the Anglican polemicist Thomas Hutton explains, Puritan burials follow such a strict form: "only the neighbours following the corps to the grave, and there with a dumb show turning it to the earth to leave it without any admonition and consolation to the living, or comfortable remembrance of ye dead."[52] Ophelia is buried in sanctified ground, but there is no address over her. Such rites were not considered "maimed" by all. What matters is that the play, in the voices of Laertes and Hamlet, actively encourages us to consider this burial to be insufficient.

And something more than this. The 2010 production of *Hamlet* at the National Theatre in London inserted a couple of lines of hasty Latin to Ophelia's burial; the priest denies "sage requiem" but this particular production apparently could not bear his strictness here, and wished to give something more to the dead. In 1539 Bishop Hilsey's *Manual of Prayers* insisted that funeral rites "are more for the comfort of the live, then the help of the dead," and fifty years later Andrew Willet followed this. In *Synopsis Papismi*, he quotes Augustine on early Christian burial:

> *Curatio funeris, pompae exequiarum, vivorum sunt solatia magis, quam subsida mortuorum*: This great provision for funerals, this great pomp of burials, they are comforts for the living, not helps to the dead.[53]

The phrase and its gesture were a commonplace of reformed theology, which held that funerals were ceremonies for the living at which we do not touch the dead. When the prayer book at the Communion rite invokes "both the quick and the dead," this is perhaps best seen as a strategic ambiguity, a blurring of the particular trope that divided theologies. But Hamlet, in the graveyard, is for a moment clear. Standing above the half-dug grave, he declares: "'Tis for the dead, not the quick" (5.1.115–16). He insists that we recall liturgical debate. He takes words seriously, and he traces now a traditional and reciprocal bond between the living and the dead.

In the Book of Common Prayer Shakespeare found a body of contested speech: a pattern and a music of mourning, what Wallace Stevens called in a different context "a literate despair." The rites are at times contradictory, at odds with their own theology, but he borrowed all this roughness and put it here on stage. If the play at times tugs toward traditional rites—in Ophelia's prayers for the dead, in Hamlet's connection between eating and burying—then this is the product of the English liturgy's own fissures and tendencies, its stubborn retention of the old habits. "'Tis for the dead, not the quick" declares Hamlet, and here Shakespeare is working perfectly within a structure discovered in the prayer book. This was the lesson learned in the comedies: that liturgical form has dramatic echo, in both its strengths and troubles. He is standing inside the cathedral now, listening to the whispers of all its ghosts.

MUCH OF WHAT I have written so far has been premised upon a sentimental fiction: that there is or could ever be any single *Hamlet*. In trying to build an argument about the play, I have implied the existence of a discrete object, one that may be spoken for and about, one that may be quoted and its patterns sketched. This is a habit common to much literary criticism, but *Hamlet*, as is made newly visible by recent textual scholarship, exists only in a tangle of revisions. The three chief versions are the 1603 quarto, known as Q1; a rival quarto known as Q2; and the play as published in the first folio of Shakespeare's works of 1623 (F). Their relation is contested, but recent textual scholars broadly agree that Q2 represents a version written by Shakespeare for readers, which was subsequently partially abridged for theatrical performance into what we now have as

F; Q1 seems to represent a further theatrical abridgment, which was assembled by actors from what they remembered of the play. Each is different, subtly and grandly, and as the editors of the most recent Arden edition note, "almost all editors seek to justify what they print by claiming that it represents either a lost text (a manuscript in Shakespeare's handwriting or an early performance of his play) or an ideal text (Shakespeare's intended definitive text or what he would or should have written if it hadn't gone wrong)."[54] They are wary of the pursuit of such ideals and abstractions, and print the play as three separate texts.

At the start of Q2, out on the battlements, Marcellus suggests, "Speak to it, Horatio," but in Q1 and F he is a little more direct: "Question it, Horatio."[55] In Q2 the dying Ophelia chants not "old tunes" but "old lauds," and the versions slightly disagree over how she may be buried.[56] In F and Q2 she is allowed "her virgin crants, / Her maiden strewments," but is denied a requiem; but the first quarto, in sympathy with Laertes, allows a little more. "She hath a dirge sung for her maiden soul," explains the priest there, and Q1 tightens Hamlet's punning allusion to Communion.[57] In F and Q2 Hamlet describes the body of Polonius: "Your fat king and your lean beggar is but variable service, two dishes to one table." In Q1 that king and beggar are "variable services—two dishes to one mess."[58] In Q1 alone Claudius tells Hamlet directly, "None lives on earth but he is born to die," and here something closer to an echo. "Man that is born of woman hath but a short time to live," promises the priest in the burial rite of the Book of Common Prayer.[59]

We cannot establish any perfect rule to explain the differing degrees of liturgy within the various texts. Q1 gives Ophelia a more formal burial rite and deepens Hamlet's allusion to the Mass, and yet in this version as in F—and unlike Q2—Ophelia sings "tunes" in the place of the more liturgically specific "lauds." This is always a play of competing voices and of competing liturgies, and this failure of any clean rule is most deeply true of the play's final and powerful involvement with the whole mixed terrain of funeral rites. We have one more burial yet. Hamlet in his fading moments forces Claudius to drink wine: "Here, thou incestuous, murd'rous, damned Dane, / Drink off this potion," he curses, and by now we surely are familiar with this pattern (5.2.267–68). Hamlet, too, is poisoned, dies, and above him in F and Q2 Horatio declares, "Good night, sweet prince, / And flights of angels sing thee to thy rest" (5.2.302–3). Q1 does not include this line.

Those flights of angels sing the song of an older pattern. In the medieval management of death, two commendations, repeated after death and during the preparation of the body for burial—known as the "Subvenite" and the "Suscipiat" after their opening words— invoke angelic transport, as does the antiphon, "In Paradisum" from the Sarum rite:

> In paradisum deducant te angeli in suum conventum, suscipiant te martyres et perducant te in civitatem sanctam Hierusalem. Chorus angelorum te suscipiat, et in sinu Abrahae collocet, ut cum Lazaro quondam paupere aeternam habeas requiem.

Horatio's blessing over Hamlet's corpse is a jumbled translation of this:

> May the angels lead you into Paradise in their assembley, may the martyrs receive you, and bring you into the holy city, Jerusalem. May the choir of angels receive you, and care for you in Abraham's bosom, and with Lazarus, once a beggar, may you have eternal rest.

Angels appear in engravings, in Books of Hours, and scattered through the great cycles of late medieval mourning and burial, and here they surface as one more echo of traditional devotion.[60]

This prayer is a promise that our words may aid the dead, and the administering angels were soon removed from the reformed English Church. From its first edition in 1549 the burial rite makes no mention of angelic transport, but this does not mean they are wholly gone. There are no angels in the burial rite of the Book of Common

Prayer, but they are remembered in the rite for Communion. In the moments before the administration of the bread and wine, the priest beckons to the congregations and now looks above. "Therefore with angels and archangels, and with all the company of heaven," he says, "we laud and magnify thy glorious name, evermore praising thee."[61] "O God, Horatio, what a wounded name," worries Hamlet, "shall live behind me," but in the moments after death he is praised and then raised up (5.2.286–87).

As the 1560 "Homily of Prayer" instructs:

> neither let us dream any more that the souls of the dead are anything at all holpen by our prayers; but, as the Scripture teacheth us, let us think that the soul of man, passing out of the body, goeth straightaway either to heaven or else to hell, whereof the one needeth no prayer, and the other is without redemption.[62]

This is the old dream of traditional structures of intercession and mourning. Its direct expression was deferred by the Book of Common Prayer, but its phrases remain, suspended in the vocabulary, echoed in the lines; it is held close when Ophelia dreams for her dead father, when Horatio dreams for his dead friend. The marriage rite taught Shakespeare the power of a single structure. But in the broken music and troubled twinning of the rites for Communion and burial, he found a narrative and dramatic form of mourning, of reaching out and touching the living and the dead.

CHAPTER 5 ❧ *A Gap in Our Great Feast*

S o many as do intend to be partakers of the Holy Communion," the prayer book instructs at the beginning of the rite, "shall signify their names to the curate overnight, or else in the morning." Before the rite we must be willing, and signal that will. "If any of those be an open and notorious evil liver," the instructions continue, then "the curate having knowledge thereof, shall call him, and advertise him, in any wise not to presume to the Lord's Table, until he have openly declared himself to have truly repented and amended his former naughty life." Mark the ruling: it is not the repentance that matters here but its show. Considered next are those among the congregation who have fallen to "malice and hatred," and they must before participation "be persuaded to a godly unity." If one will not be reconciled, preferring instead to "remain still in his frowardness and malice," then he shall be excluded (Cummings, 124). This is the rite that renews the community, that cleans and polices it.

"Here's our chief guest," declares the new king Macbeth as he enters to Banquo. His wife agrees. "If he had been forgotten / It had been a gap in our great feast / And all thing unbecoming," she says, and Macbeth repeats, "Tonight we hold a solemn supper, sir, / And I'll request your presence." Now Banquo makes to leave, and Macbeth presses him. "Ride you this afternoon?" he asks, and Banquo replies, "Ay, my good lord." Macbeth goes on, "Is't far you ride?" Banquo promises to return in time, and Macbeth once more repeats: "Fail not our feast." Banquo leaves and Macbeth turns to an attendant. There are two men waiting for him "without the gate"—men who the speech headings will identify as "murderers"—and Macbeth instructs: "Bring them before us."[1]

"Why were the sacraments ordained?" asks John Jewel in his *Treatise of the Sacraments*, and answers: "The first cause why they were ordained is, that thereby one should acknowledge another, as friends of one household, and members of one body."[2] The trouble is that not all agree. "The massmonger doth so handle his mass that it may worthily and justly seem to be an occasion of enmity than amity, of discord rather than concord," writes Thomas Becon in *A Comparison between the Lord's Supper and the Pope's Mass* (1559–63), and goes on to detail the inhospitality of traditional Roman practice:

> For he standeth alone at the altar, he playeth the whole pageant alone, he speaketh alone with himself, yea, and that in a strange tongue, he eateth and drinketh alone, he is merry alone. There is no sign of love, no token of Christian, no, not of heathen-like charity, no show of human fellowship.[3]

Becon is here describing private Mass in cartoonish outline—a Mass at which others might be but were not necessarily present, and only the priest took bread and wine. Private Mass was disallowed in the English Church, as in all reformed churches, but Becon is drawing a larger analogy to all traditional Masses. These were conducted "in a strange tongue," Latin, and the claim that the Mass was inhospitable, divisive, was a cliché of reformed polemic. "Oh! Wicked step-mothers, that so divide Christ, his sacraments, and his people," declared Thomas Cranmer in 1551. This did not, as a trope, belong only to Protestants. In Jewel's controversy with the Catholic Thomas Harding in the formative years of the Anglican Church, both men fall upon this same rhetorical claim. Harding insists of the traditional Mass that "the feast is common; all be invited," and Jewel replies, "if this feast be common, it must needs be common to very few; for the provision is very little to serve so many." A decade later, the traditional polemicist John Rastell advised: "the Ave Maria is a common prayer."[4] All claim that their own vision of prayer is the common one.

As the groundbreaking historian of Reformation religion Peter Lake has argued, "from the first English protestantism had been beset by a tension between a view of the true church as an embattled minority of true believers and the idea or ideal of a genuinely national church."[5] This may be a true church, or an English church; a church of some, or a church for all; the two scenarios in the opening rubric are troubled by this. All should be included but not everyone belongs. "Fail not our feast," Macbeth instructs Banquo, and invites his murderers in.

There is a necessary fiction in this rite: that all among the congregation both wish and deserve to be there. "Let disputes and questions, enemies to piety, abatements to true devotion and hitherto in this cause but over patently heard, let them take their rest," wrote Richard Hooker in the mid-1590s, for he saw the church's community as turned against itself. He goes on to describe the path to unity through participation at Communion:

> in the wounds of our redeemer we there dip our tongues, we are dyed red both within and without, our hunger is satisfied and our thirst for ever quenched, they are things wonderful which he feeleth, great which he seeth and unheard of which he uttereth.[6]

The power of this image arises from its mixing of the sexual and the pious: it is a wild and bloodthirsty scene, physical and almost depraved. As the great scholar of early modern theology Debora Shuger has argued, for Hooker "the utterly private experience of transcendent communion . . . *is* the basis of community," and there is a violent mingling here, of "we," and "wounds," and "our."[7] But the image also exposes the tension in the theology. The communal "we" is built upon a single worshipper and his single experience. "He feeleth," "he seeth," Hooker imagines, and now in the syntax of the sentence one stands slightly apart from the rest.

The dinner begins well. The guests arrive and are welcomed by a beneficent Macbeth. "Ourself will mingle with society, / And play the humble host," he declares: "here I'll sit i'th'midst," and all is ordered, decorous, hospitable. This is his meal, as king; this is his castle. The murderer enters to him, to report Banquo's death. Macbeth stands, confers, and his wife calls him back. "My royal lord, / You do not give the cheer," she chides him, and as he turns to take his seat he finds:

MACBETH: The table's full.

LENNOX: Here is a place reserved, sir.

MACBETH: Where?

LENNOX: Here, my good lord.

He will not sit. "Shame itself! / Why do you make such faces?" Lady Macbeth demands: and "Fie, for shame." He paces the room, apart, and she now exhorts him, "My worthy lord, / Your noble friends do lack you" (3.4.4–84).

The "exhortation at certain times when the curate shall see the people negligent to come to the Holy Communion" was added to the prayer book in 1552. It imagines a scene: a church, a calling to worship, and one or more in the congregation standing back, aloof. Upon this occasion, the priest is instructed to address first the congregation:

> Ye know how grievous and unkind a thing it is, when a man hath prepared a rich feast, decked his table with all kind of provision, so that there lacketh nothing but the guests to sit down; and yet they which be called without any cause most unthankfully refuse to come.

The rich feast is a metaphor for the simple bread and wine offered at Communion, and now the priest turns directly to those who refuse to participate. "I call you in Christ's behalf, I exhort you," he says, "as you love your own salvation, that ye will be partakers of this Holy Communion" (Cummings, 130). All must sit.

The exhortation is no simple telling-off; it begins to describe a character and a motive. "It is an easy matter for a man to say, I will not communicate, because I am otherwise letted with worldly business," observes the priest, "but such excuses be not so easily accepted and allowed before God." The exhortation imagines one who refuses, and although he has not spoken it begins to tell his story. "They that refused the feast in the Gospel, because they had bought a farm, or would try their yokes of oxen, or because they were married, were not so excused," continues the priest, embellishing, improvising a pattern of motives around a silent refusal, some tale of "worldly business." It begins to narrate the opposite of prayer, and this imagination of some humble human thing and its keyword "business" caught Shakespeare's imagination. The word rattles through the play. Macbeth summons Banquo: "When we can entreat an hour to serve, / We would spend it in some word upon that business," and then when faced with a phantom dagger knows "It is the bloody business which informs / Thus to mine eyes." Lady Macbeth asks why the bell has raised the sleepers of Dunsinane—"What's the business, / That such a hideous trumpet calls to parley?"—and Macbeth instructs the murderer to mask "the business from the common eye." The witches promise that "Great business must be wrought ere noon," and in each case this business is murder.[8]

"Business" was a word conventionally opposed to proper Christian activity. The 1531 Sarum primer printed by Regnault includes a short English preface on "The manner to live well," which instructs "go to the church or do ye any worldly works if ye have no needful business," and when Thomas More sat in the Tower of London in 1535 awaiting his execution, he annotated his Book of Hours with a brief prayer:

Not to long for worldly company.
Little & little utterly to cast off ye world.
And rid my mind of all the business thereof.[9]

Business is a distraction from faith, a wrong path. It is a weighted word, and it struck Thomas Cranmer just as it struck Shakespeare. The exhortation is one of the few moments of original writing in the prayer book. Cranmer invited Peter Martyr Vermigli to write it, and his original Latin runs, "Facile est dicere hominibus, Non communico quia non possum." Cranmer's translation for the prayer book extends this. "It is an easy matter, for a man to say, I will not communicate," it begins, and until this point it follows the Latin original, but he then broadens out into the following phrase, "because I am otherwise letted with worldly business."[10] Cranmer embellishes the Latin "non possum" out into the dramatic structure at play in *Macbeth*.

The suggestions of words bring us into the heart of history. The Reformation forced new emphasis upon the proprieties of church rites, and so the word "business"—traditionally the opposite of a vague Christian spirituality—acquired liturgical resonance. As the Elizabethan "Homily of the Place and Time of Prayer" insists, business is what leads us away from the sacraments: "God's obedient people should use the Sunday holily, and rest from their common and daily business, and also give themselves wholly to heavenly exercises of God's true religion and service." This phrase is repeated twice in the homily.[11] Andrew Willet's *Ecclesia Triumphans*, written to welcome James to his new throne, similarly instructs "let not any worldly business draw us from the house of prayer."[12] One of the first court sermons preached to James after his accession fully lays out the sacramental character of reformed business. On Tuesday, 10 May 1603, Thomas Blague defined the grounds for exclusion from Communion. "If any that is called a brother, be a whore, master, a drunkard, or a covetous person: with such do not eat or drink, receive him not into thy house, say not, God speed, lend him no countenance," he instructed, "beware of busy heads." He repeats the phrase, "Blessed therefore is the man, which walketh not after the counsel of such pragmatical and busy heads."[13] While Blague's advice seems vague in its dismissal of business, the linkage of eating and drinking with "receive him not" specifies the Communion rite.

At the royal feast, Macbeth raves and paces. "Unreal mock'ry, hence," he declares. "What will this be else but a neglecting, a despising, and mocking of the testament of Christ?" asks the priest in the exhortation. "You have displaced the mirth, broke the good meeting / With most admired disorder," Lady Macbeth tells her husband, and she sends all home. "At once, good night. / Stand not upon the order of your going, / But go at once," she declares, and here the play inverts the prayer book. "Wherefore, rather than you should do so," now continues the priest, "depart you hence, and give place to them that be godly disposed."[14] Lady Macbeth sends away all except he who refused to sit; the priest sends away only he who would not sit. But for both, one missing is a rebuke to all. One standing back starts to unravel the fabric of community.

A REAL HISTORY stands behind the exhortation's fiction—a priest who waits, and calls, and yet some will not come.

On 5 May 1606 twenty-one people at Stratford were charged with not having received Communion at Easter, two weeks before. Among them were Susannah, Shakespeare's oldest daughter, and Hamnet and Judith Sadler, godparents to his two younger children. This is the record kept in the act book of the local ecclesiastical court:

> Officium domini contra
> Susannam Shakespeere   similiter similiter
> dismissa.

As the *Times Literary Supplement* explained in 1964, when this document was discovered, Susanna's offence was double. She was reported for not taking Communion and then "she did not appear although cited personally by the apparitor and her penalty was reserved until the next court." She was summoned; she did not come. The word "dismissa" here reveals that she must have later appeared before and satisfied the judge. All of the twenty-one were similarly dismissed although "there is no indication that they in fact consented to receive the sacrament."[15]

She was summoned and she did not come, for a time; in the end, she had to. She was reluctant and pragmatic. As Alexandra Walsham has argued in her groundbreaking study of confessional identities in sixteenth-century England, the simple categories of enthusiastic churchgoing Protestant and recusant Catholic hardly describe the range of devotional positions. Recusants were those who refused to attend common prayer, but this was a radical, visible gesture, for "churchgoing was the cornerstone of Elizabethan religious policy, the minimum, minimal commitment the Church of England required of most lay people." She continues, "One appealing alternative to insolent refusal to attend weekly service was deliberate abstention from holy communion." It was enough in the Elizabethan church to attend the service. Once you were inside the church nothing more was legally required. "Symbolic of Elizabeth's vaunted reluctance to molest consciences, to make windows into men's souls, the eucharist never became the legal standard for creedal consent in her reign," Walsham writes, and quotes an epigram from an anonymous sixteenth-century notebook: "If any man will but yield to go to Church all treasons are remitted."[16]

The exhortation is rich evidence, both itself a dramatic story and the beginnings of one larger. It tells us first that there were some in churches who only looked on, who neither refused nor participated in Communion. We might read it too as a sign of liturgical feebleness. The priest harangues his congregation for this is all he can do. "I call you in Christ's behalf, I exhort you, as you love your own salvation," he says: "I admonish, exhort, and beseech you." The speech was retained in the prayer book in 1559 and 1604 because this was an ongoing problem: that some within the community were only partly present. It exposes both the history and the fears of the Elizabethan church.

The reign of King James I began with the possibility of toleration for Catholics. In August 1604 his ministers signed the Treaty of

London, which ended the fluctuating twenty-year series of campaigns and subterfuges of the Anglo-Spanish War. Then in early November 1605 a small group of English Catholics attempted to assassinate the king and blow up the Houses of Parliament in London. This soon became known as the Gunpowder Plot and was followed by more stringent laws. According to new articles for the visitations of far-flung dioceses, issued in late 1605, the church wished to know "How long the popish recusants have obstinately abstained either from divine service, or from the communion," and in late May 1606 Parliament endorsed "An Act for the better discovering and repressing of Popish Recusants," which included the Oath of Allegiance. Fines for those who refused to participate in Communion were set at the huge sum of £20 per year, and the Crown claimed the right to two-thirds of recusants' lands. A man whose wife refused to attend Communion could now be denied civil promotion or appointment.[17]

Here is a catalogue of different strategies within one pattern of concern. "The premodern state was, in many crucial respects, partially blind," writes the political scientist James Scott: "it knew precious little about its subjects." His study *Seeing Like a State* tracks how states have sought to make "legible" their cities and their forests and most of all the behaviors of their citizens, through projects of "simplification": grids, charts, standardization, a fondness for the straight street and census form, and the suppression of variation. "Of all state simplifications," writes Scott, "the imposition of a single official language may be the most powerful, and it is the precondition of many other simplifications."[18] The Book of Common Prayer is a grand simplification: it seeks to make uniform all devotion and in so doing to render legible the habits of worshippers. Either they are or are not obedient; either they do or do not worship in the proper way; the set liturgy throws a harsh light upon variation. However, devotional practice shrugs off the narrows of any such binary. Those who participate at Communion and those who refuse to enter the church are equally legible; those who attend the service and do not participate are opaque. They are speaking one language but meaning in another.

During the exhortation the priest speculates. He offers three hypothetical reasons why some might be unwilling to participate—"because they had bought a farm, or would try their yokes of oxen, or because they were married"—and goes on to demand, "I pray you what can this be else, but even to have the mysteries of Christ in derision?" He is imagining the meaning of their behavior. He is trying to render legible a troubling, confusing absence. When her husband refuses to sit, Lady Macbeth invents a story. "My lord is often thus," she explains, "And hath been from his youth. Pray you, keep seat. / The fit is momentary" (3.4.52–54). This fit is indeed momentary: it is of a time of tightening around the variety of devotional practice. But it takes part, too, in a longer catalogue of worry over absence from Communion, and here the scene acquires a different legibility.

After the Gunpowder Plot the church tightened restrictions around those who refused to participate in Communion. In May of the following year, 1606, Shakespeare's daughter was charged with precisely this. The composition of *Macbeth* is conventionally dated in this period—after the Gunpowder Plot but before the end of the following year. Almost all the chronologies concur: this was a play of late 1605 or 1606. This was, then, a moment of particular attention to the Communion rite and to its absentees. Shakespeare, as I have tried to show, apprenticed by the Book of Common Prayer. He picked up its habits and riffed upon its promises; he embellished its fears and scenarios out into great dramas. But until now this has always been an Elizabethan Shakespeare. Written under King James and, perhaps more importantly, written after the Hampton Court Conference and its particular intensification of liturgical debate, *Macbeth* presents a shift in that apprenticeship. Play and prayer book enter a new relation. One engages the other with a new and harder intensity, beginning with the move to a feast, and its collapse. This play is the perfect product of Shakespeare's own learning, the arc I traced in the first half of this book. The second half will stick closely with this one play, for it is only in a slow reading that we may discover the splendid intricacy of Shakespeare's use of the Book of Common Prayer.

MACBETH SENDS TWO murderers, and then a third arrives. "But who did bid thee join us?" one puzzled murderer asks, and the answer comes, "Macbeth." This play is rippled with oddly precise excess. Its distinctive habit is the addition of a little more, one further element. Duncan has two attendants, and each has a dagger, so Macbeth returns from killing the king with two blood-covered daggers. Macbeth and Banquo, described in fighting, "doubly redoubled strokes upon the foe," and Lady Macbeth promises to Duncan, "All our service, / In every point twice done and then done double." Duncan visits Dunsinane "in double trust"—Macbeth is both "his kinsman and his subject" and also his host—and later when the witches chant they sing the following catch three times: "Double, double toil and trouble." It is hard to keep track of such profusion. "Who lies i'th' second chamber?" asks Macbeth, and late one night Banquo turns to Fleance. "Hold, take my sword," he says to his son, and then a pause—"There's husbandry in heaven," he says, for it is a dark night—and then, "Take thee that too." The father hands his son something extra, unnamed in the play.[19]

The lords and attendants at the feast experience Macbeth's behavior as an absence. "Here is a place reserved, sir," offers Lennox, for he sees an empty seat, but Macbeth replies, "where?" In the place of a gap he finds a troubling presence: the ghost of Banquo, shaking his gory locks, glaring with sightless eyes. Macbeth first addresses the ghost—"If thou canst nod, speak, too!"—but then overcome with fear and revulsion he says:

> If charnel houses and our graves must send
> Those that we bury back, our monuments
> Shall be the maws of kites (3.4.45–46, 69–72).

Kites feed upon carrion, and they shall be our tombs when they feed upon human remains; like all carnivorous birds they regurgitate pellets—the bones and fur, the undigested traces of their prey—so the image of returning corpses is doubly precise. "Let the earth hide thee!" wishes Macbeth, but in the place of a burial here is a bloody feast (3.4.92).

The body of the dead should not be present at the supper, but he will not leave quietly. "Hence" implores Macbeth, and more feebly, "hence." He wishes it to leave. Traditional Roman Catholic theology had since 1215 held that during the rite the actual bread and wine transformed into the body and blood of Christ, a miracle known as "transubstantiation." While the reformed English Church denied full sacramental presence, the 1549 prayer book attempted some conciliation with the theology of the traditional rite. As the title for Communion notes, this rite is "commonly called the Mass," and the moment of administration is carefully blurred. "The body of our Lord Jesus Christ which was given for thee, preserve thy body and soul unto everlasting life," the priest instructs, and "The blood of our Lord Jesus Christ which was shed for thee, preserve thy body and soul unto everlasting life" (Cummings, 34). There is no mention of transformation, but the elements of the real presence are named at the administration, and here inside the language wait the traces of body and blood.

The more Protestant 1552 edition sheds any such conciliation. It proposes instead a strict theology of absence. A brief explanatory comment, known as the "Black Rubric," was added to the service, which stresses: "as concerning the Sacramental bread and wine, they remain still in their very natural substances, and therefore may not be adored, for that were Idolatry to be abhorred of all faithful christians." In administering the bread and wine the priest now says, "Take and eat this, in remembrance that Christ died for thee, and feed on him in thy heart by faith, with thanksgiving" and "Drink this in remembrance that Christ's blood was shed for thee, and be thankful."[20] The rite is now the memorial of a historical episode, and the verb tenses distinguish our own actions from Christ's: his in the past, ours in the present. The literal is succeeded by a figurative interpretation.

These are apparently alternatives; we may have one or the other. The third version of the Book of Common Prayer, however, refused to choose. At the moment of administration, in the 1559 and subsequent editions, the priest says: "The body of our Lord Jesus Christ which was given for thee, preserve thy body and soul into everlasting life: and take and eat this, in remembrance that Christ died for thee, and feed on him in thy heart by faith" and "The blood of our Lord Jesus Christ, which was shed for thee, preserve thy body and soul into everlasting life: and drink this in remembrance that Christ's blood was shed for thee, and be thankful" (Cummings, 137). 1559 adds 1552 to 1549 and gives us both together. We may have presence and absence at a single moment. This is of course a pragmatic move, intended to include many varieties of devotion within a single form; the theology was deliberately blurred, and taken as a single form, this ambiguity is reasonable. But read from the perspective of its genealogy, such accommodation might appear only half-digested. The awkward meeting of two different theologies might suggest not the achievement of community but the point of its rupture.

Beginning with the murder of Duncan the play banishes Macbeth: he is exiled from the community of shared experience. Returning to his wife after killing the king, he describes himself standing above the sleeping grooms:

> One cried, "God bless us!" and, "Amen," the other,
> As they had seen me with these hangman's hands.
> List'ning their fear, I could not say, "Amen,"
> When they did say "God bless us." (2.2.24–27)

They are of one rite and he, another; this is a drama of isolation and the image is loaded. "Before the church grew to corruption, all christian men throughout the world made their common prayers, and had the holy communion, in their own common and known tongue," recounts John Jewel in his Challenge Sermon, and continues:

> But in the mass, as it has been used in this latter age of the world, the priest uttereth the holy mysteries in such a language, as neither the people nor oftentimes himself understandeth the meaning. And thus the death of Christ and his passion is set forth in such sort as the poor people can have no comfort or fruit thereby; nor give thanks unto God, nor say, Amen.[21]

As Andrew Willett wrote in 1600, "the people cannot be edified by a language which they understand not: nor yet can any say Amen to strange prayers." In 1633 an anonymous worshipper considered Jewel's description of Latin worship printed in the volume *Certain Sermons preached before the Queens Majesty* (1603), in a copy now in the British Library. When he came to the following lines—"All things were done in a strange tongue: the priest spake, and the people heard they knew not what. No man could say Amen to their prayer"— he marked them with three little crosses and a marginal note: "The popish worship."[22] Incomprehension and the consequent inability to say Amen were in the English Church common metaphors for the traditional Mass.

As Timothy Rosendale has observed, "Part of the power of the Latin Mass was precisely its incomprehensibility, its expression of the gulf between God and humanity."[23] The traditional rite did not depend upon understanding but rather faith in presence. Reformers, however, stress language as a function of their emphasis upon comprehension: nothing was eaten but all understood, and understanding the new type of feeding. For Jewel, the two are synonymous. He describes a traditional rite at which "The poor people heareth nothing, understandeth nothing, eateth nothing, drinketh nothing, tasteth nothing." Macbeth's thwarted feast dramatizes the collapse of shared comprehension. He sees a body, shaking and nodding, but this divides him from the others. "Here, my good lord," says Lennox, and he points to a space at the table; and Lady Macbeth chides him, "you look but on a stool" (3.4.47, 60). A stool; a body; one or the other, but surely never both.

The play is a creature of the fractured landscape of post-Reformation England. "This is the very painting of your fear," insists Lady Macbeth at the feast, but he sees it only as real. Haunted by images, by things misunderstood, he cannot interpret it safely away. Her words recapitulate a phrase she has used before, at an earlier moment, when he was frozen by a similar confusion after he returned from killing Duncan and was too scared to leave the daggers. "Infirm of purpose!" she declares: "The sleeping and the dead / Are but as pictures; 'tis the eye of childhood / That fears a painted devil." He still will not go so she returns to Duncan's chamber to "gild the faces of the grooms" with the king's blood (2.2.50–54).

We may read this image literally. Traditional English churches were filled with painted devils. The best surviving example of medieval English stained glass is in St. Mary's church at Fairford in Gloucestershire. The church has twenty separate windows, each with three or four panels that illustrate biblical scenes, the apostles, saints, and prophets, installed in the first two decades of the sixteenth century by a Dutch glazier. The entire set is spectacular, for its bright colors and tiny details of faces and clothing are painted on. But the most striking and largest window is at the west end of the church, depicting the Last Judgment. This window is twice as high as any other in the church. The top half shows Christ in heaven, while at the bottom a chaos of souls rise and descend. Of the fourteen main panels that make up the window, the two at the bottom right corner show hell. Collecting the fallen souls are two devils: one blue, with a mournful human face, and the other red, with two heads and a great mouth into which white human bodies pour. The early seventeenth-century poet and chaplain William Strode celebrated the stained glass in his poem "On Fayrford Windows." He begins, "I know no paint of poetry / Can mend such coloured Imag'ry / In sullen ink," and goes on to give a calm catalogue of the biblical stories, broken by the expostulation: "Look there! The Divell!"[24] Strode was not alone in his focus on the painted devils. A visitor to St. Mary's in 1715 noted alone of all the details in the church "the great Devill, with large red and white teeth."[25]

The Fairford stained glass is not a source for *Macbeth*. The windows of St. Mary's are exceptional solely in that they are complete and extant. Read figuratively, these same windows suggest a second story, one concerned with failure, and compromise, and the fractures in the church. The fourteenth-century proto-reformer Wycliffe had condemned stained glass, and during the 1530s monastic churches across England were stripped of their glass during the Henrician Reformation. The iconoclasm intensified under the Protestant King Edward. Injunction 28, issued in 1547, instructed that clergy must "take away, utterly extinct and destroy all shrines, covering of shrines, all tables and candlesticks, trundles or rolls of ware, pictures, paintings and all other monuments of feigned miracles, pilgrimages, idolatry and superstition," and went on to specify: "so that there remain no memory of the same in walls, glasses, windows, or elsewhere." No memory: you must forget this. The same ruling was reissued by Elizabeth upon her accession in 1559.[26] In the late 1580s, the Cheshire Puritan John Bruen listed the church decorations he had removed from his parish church. "Many superstitious images and idolatrous pictures in the painted windows," he noted: "the dumb and dark images by their painted coats and colours, did both darken the light of the Church, and obscure the brightness of the Gospel."[27]

However, the iconoclastic impulse was often limited by practical considerations; absence may come at a cost. Crucifixes, statues, and shrines may be removed or destroyed without changing the structure of a church, but the glass in the windows serves a function—it keeps out rain and cold—and is very expensive to replace. According to Duffy, "stained glass remained everywhere, therefore, and was a potential focus of intense ideological feeling."[28] For worshippers of later Elizabethan England, stained glass was a reminder of the limitations upon the Reformation. Within the architecture and the structures of the post-Reformation English Church remained the traces and the designs of an older theology.

In presenting painted devils as a childhood memory, Lady Macbeth reminds both her husband and the audience of church decorations that have been lost. But the power of the image is not simply nostalgic, for even as there should be no more painted devils—they should belong solely in the landscape of infant memory—the images remained. "'Tis the eye of childhood / That fears a painted devil," she tells him, and the fear is in the present tense. There are still painted devils among us. The old elements continued to haunt new believers, and within a decade of Shakespeare's play two other English dramatists echoed this line. In John Webster's *The White Devil* (1612), Cardinal Monticelso slanders Vittoria. "Terrify babes, my lord, with painted devils, / I am past such needless palsy," she retorts:

> your names
> Of Whore and Murdress, they proceed from you,
> As if a man should spit against the wind,
> The filth returns in's face.

In Elizabeth Cary's *The tragedy of Mariam* (1613), another saintly woman is faced with another bullying, hypocritical man: "painted devil / Thou white enchantress," Herod names Mariam.[29]

For both Webster and Cary, painted devils are meaningless abstractions: "needless palsy" or spittle in the wind. They are constituted solely of abusive words, and painting is naming, an effect of language. Lady Macbeth, however, uses the image in a categorically different mode. These lines allude specifically to the activity of painting. "I'll gild the faces of the grooms," she says, and "gild"—which means to cover with gold—puns on "guilt" but has a literal referent: Lady Macbeth paints the faces of the grooms with blood. And while she appears to mock her husband, the object of her ridicule is his fear rather than the painted images. It is the "eye of childhood" that is mistaken; the painted devils themselves are real, but they need not be feared. In these lines, that is, the image of a painted devil may be working as a metaphor, but it refers to something real.

A. R. Braunmuller's New Cambridge edition of *Macbeth* (1997) footnotes the painted devil image as follows: "Bugbears to scare babes is proverbial; a 'bugbear' (or 'bogey man') was an imaginary figure used to scare children into obedience."[30] In glossing this painted devil as "proverbial" and "imaginary," Braunmuller keeps Shakespeare's allusion within the realm of the strictly literary. His reading dissolves the historical object and its contemporary controversy; but sometimes, surely, a painted devil may be simply that. We may wish to interpret such things away, but they troublingly remain, studding the surface of the play like rivets in old steel, nodding and shaking at us now.

AT THE FIRST meeting with the witches, Banquo opens with a question. "How far is't called to Forres?" he addresses them; he wants directions for the way. Something here is not right, and it takes him a moment to realize—a stumble in time as sense catches up with perception—and as he does he turns to Macbeth without waiting for an answer. Now he asks:

> What are these
> So withered and so wild in their attire,
> That look not like th'inhabitants o'th'earth,
> And yet are on't?

This is the only account in the play of how the witches look, and really it is an evaluation passing as description—their clothes are withered, wild, he notes—for Banquo is struggling now, troubled by their failure to resemble things he already knows. Their presence is a challenge. "Live you," he now asks, "or are you aught / That man may question?" (1.3.37–41). This is a curiously redundant pair of demands, each packaged with its own answer—he is asking if he may question them in a question—but taken together these two halves suggest a particular distinction: between living things, with their own purposes and existence, and symbolic things, which exist to gesture elsewhere. He is asking whether they are there for him or for themselves.

There is a curious motion back and forth within Banquo's speech. He speaks to them and then for them, and even in his questions he begins to narrate. Macbeth is silent but Banquo goes on, and now the witches make one gesture. "You seem to understand me," he notes, "By each at once her choppy finger laying / Upon her skinny lips," and he moves once more from address to description: the choppy fingers, those skinny lips, all this is evidence. He takes their resistance—their gesture of silencing—as proof of their understanding, but each certainty—that feminine pronoun, "her choppy finger"—in turn raises new doubt. He corrects himself. "You should be women," he starts to insist, "And yet your beards forbid me to interpret / That you are so" (1.3.41–45). The beards do not prove that these are men; they are only an impediment. Proof here does not work, and evidence cannot build up to a comprehensive interpretation.

Here is something foreign and apart, something not quite of this world; and here, too, is the struggle of trying to comprehend it. Banquo strains to make the witches legible by asking, speaking for them, about them, by treating them as signs, but in each of these is thwarted. First he asks a direct question; then he asks Macbeth about them; he turns back to them but now his question is rhetorical—"Live you?"—and on to speculation—"You seem to understand me"—and on to the collapse. We may think of this as a stage movement. He is approaching them now, tentative, curious, yet at each question they become more opaque to him; at each step closer they are farther removed. In speaking about them he is speaking for them; he is excluding them. It is only when Banquo finally pauses that Macbeth for the first time speaks. He is untroubled by such ontological crisis. He asks, "Speak if you can: what are you?" and they answer. Their message was for him.

The prayer book has been spoken for, and often spoken about, but it is almost never allowed to speak. Stephen Greenblatt neither quotes nor cites the Book of Common Prayer in his essay "The Mousetrap." The essay is about eucharistic controversies in sixteenth-century England, and the prayer book was where those took place.

Another example is Michael Neill's *Issues of Death*, a serious consideration of the Reformation imagination of death; it also does not quote or cite the Book of Common Prayer even though the funeral rite—as set out only in this book—was the most influential literary narrative of death in England in this period. This is attempting to describe a wave without considering the water. Many assume that the Book of Common Prayer is not worth discussion because everybody surely already knows what it says, and that liturgy is a stable familiar monolith. Two further examples of this widespread scholarly habit: Huston Diehl in *Staging Reform, Reforming the Stage* and Jeffrey Knapp in *Shakespeare's Tribe* both argue for a deep relation between drama and church rites. The Chorus in *Henry V*, Knapp notes, "recalls standard Protestant explications of the Lord's Supper" while for Diehl one of the central "cultural performances" of the age was "the reformed sacrament of the Lord's Supper." Both assume this was a simple, single thing, and the only way to maintain this faith is by avoiding quotation. Quotation would involve selecting one edition from several, so neither Knapp nor Diehl quote. This is attempting to study a wave without acknowledging its movement.[31]

What these works of scholarship share is the belief that church rites are essentially insincere. Timothy Rosendale has noted "criticism's impulse to translate religious belief into *something else*— psychology, ideology, economics, politics—before it can be talked about," and in this understanding the prayer book can only ever be symbolic. Of real interest is not its form but what it implies: for the literary critics, the prayer book is about nationalism, or theater, or broad philosophical debates over meaning. As the anthropologist Talal Asad observes in *Genealogies of Religion*, the meaning of the word "ritual" shifted at the Enlightenment. During the Reformation, a ritual was a manual—such as the *Rituale Romanorum*, the standard Counter-Reformation primer—which set out the ways rites should properly be performed. Under this definition, the Book of Common Prayer itself is correctly considered a "ritual." But this prior meaning has been replaced by "the modern conception of ritual as enacted symbols," and this shift in usage—"from what is literally a script . . . to behavior"—reinforces a modern notion of religion as a set of evocative ideas and performances which offer themselves for interpretation.[32] It is possible to look too quickly beyond the material traces. Faced with the witches, Banquo sees a choice. "Live you, or are you aught / That man may question?" he asks, uncertain of whether the witches are present or are really only symbols: whether they are for themselves or available only for his reading. He is asking if they need him, too.

The tension of the scene repeats a theological tension, and this wish among critics to translate is in turn doctrinally specific. This is precisely the challenge of the play. Banquo's struggle to understand what is before him is in turn a struggle between literal and figurative ways of reading, between a faith in presence as against the desire to interpret. It is the difference between an empty chair at the table or a bloody ghost. It is also a tension for us, as readers who return to these plays in a world so different from theirs. Where are you now, as you read this? What does that air feel like? I am in a cubicle, in a rented office, in lower Manhattan. Outside the city is cold and bright, and I know this: by looking up I can see a skylight; through it, a deep blue of the winter New York sky; I am thirty-three years old as I write this. Perhaps these things should not matter, but the grounds for all our interpretations are cultural; we are readers of a moment. *Macbeth* even more than *Hamlet* is the great drama of uncertain presence. Is it a dagger or not? A ghost or not? In reading we too must make decisions about what it is before us: about what we are willing and capable of seeing in this moment.

"There is something about the notion of Protestantism," notes the scholar of Catholic literature Alison Shell, "which makes it especially attractive to the academic mind: the skeptical, the enquiring, as against the authoritarian, the dogmatic and the superstitious." If we are readers of complex poetry then it is likely we might come to admire the characters who wonder, who pause and ask questions— the characters, that is, who believe in interpretation, who believe that there might lie some little magic in figurative reading. Banquo is skeptical and inquisitive; Macbeth thuggishly direct. We might prefer Banquo's delicate contradictions; soon he will be dead. These may seem matters of personal taste, but they accumulate, and as Allison Shell argues, this affection may explain why scholars and critics have neglected English Catholic imaginative literature. The whole academic study of this period is immersed in bias; even that we call it "early modern" implies the Protestant church's clean succession from its Catholic past. As Eamon Duffy has stated, the conventional account of the Reformation and the religious culture of sixteenth-century England is built upon "a widely shared historiography which was culturally if not confessionally Protestant in its terms of reference," and when literary critics celebrate their heroes they often find them to be pleasingly reformed.[33] Stephen Greenblatt has noted what he calls Hamlet's "distinctly Protestant temperament," while Roland Mushat Frye simply describes him as "Protestant."[34] Each are simply following the great critic J. Dover Wilson, who in his classic *What Happens in Hamlet* (1935) observes that Hamlet and Horatio "are Protestants, and share the Protestant philosophy of spiritualism," and all in turn are heirs of what the historian Herbert Butterfield famously described as "the Whig interpretation of history." This is a self-congratulatory historiography, defined by what Butterfield called "the tendency in many historians to write on the side of Protestants and Whigs, to praise revolutions provided they have been successful, to emphasize certain principles of progress in the past and to produce a story which is the ratification if not the glorification of the present."[35] Here history is always looking toward us.

Shakespeare knew and learned from the English prayer book, but this does not mean I am arguing for an Anglican Shakespeare. Every Elizabethan, Catholic or Protestant, knew the Book of Common Prayer with an intimacy we can scarcely recapture now. My Shakespeare is a man of his time, of an age awash with liturgy; he put it on stage. At the supper Macbeth sees a bloody ghost, and others see only delusion.

"Think of this, good peers, / But as a thing of custom" says Lady Macbeth, but beneath the cool of her interpretation waits a web of fears, about the limits of reason and the ways a story may be thwarted. "Prithee, see there!" shouts Macbeth: "Behold, look, lo!" He sees a ghost. After they have delivered their cryptic, riddling message to Macbeth and then to Banquo, the witches begin to leave. "Stay, you imperfect speakers. Tell me more," Macbeth demands, and "Speak, I charge you," but now they vanish. "What seemed corporal, / Melted, as breath into the wind" notes Macbeth sadly, and nothing can be known. This was, perhaps, a fantasy: "have we eaten on the insane root, / That takes the reason prisoner?" asks Banquo. There are no witches; there are no ghosts.

THERE IS NO single *Hamlet*; the same is true, in a different sense, for *Macbeth*. *Macbeth* marks the moment when Shakespeare's dramatic imagination is so centrally formed by interaction with liturgy—by the adoption of its motifs, by the explosion of its tropes and tensions—that the play is a kind of parasite. This determination is first of all a quality of language. The witches promise that Macbeth may "laugh to scorn / The power of man, for none of woman born / Shall harm Macbeth," and he quotes this like a prayer. "Where's the boy Malcolm?" he asks:

> Was he not born of woman? The spirits that know
> All mortal consequences have pronounced me thus:
> "Fear not, Macbeth, no man that's born of woman
> Shall e'er have power upon thee."

"What's he / That was not born of woman?" he demands, and mocks all weapons "Brandished by man that's of a woman born"; he insists, "I bear a charmed life which must not yield / To one of woman born." The phrase is present in all versions of the story and the sources of the play, but this repetition is introduced by Shakespeare, and in repetition it takes on weight.[36] We wait for it and anticipate how it may unravel.

As the Bible promises, in the book of Job, "Man that is born of woman, is of short continuance, and full of trouble," and this is only the start of the play's wide plunder. When Macbeth hears of the death of his queen, he mourns: "all our yesterdays have lighted fools / The way to dusty death. Out, out, brief candle, / Life's but a walking shadow." The keywords of Job chime through these lines. The candle echoes Job's "The light shalbe darke in his dwelling, and his candle shalbe put out with him"; the dust of death follows Elihu's promise, "All flesh shall perish together, and man shall return unto dust." Job notes that "we are but of yesterday, and are ignorant for our days upon earth are but a shadow," giving Shakespeare yesterday's slide into shadow, and the image of a disappearing shadow as death runs through Job, from "he vanisheth also as a shadow, and continueth not" to "the shadow of death," a phrase repeated five times in the book.[37] The play is a patchwork and echo chamber of the language of Job.

Macbeth speaks the above allusions, but other characters in the play share this habit. He is not safe, of course, from men who were born of woman. Macduff explains that he was "from his mother's womb / Untimely ripped," and both the word "untimely" and its application to a sudden premature birth are borrowed from Job's anguished demand: "Why was I not hid, as an untimely birth, either as infants, which have not seen the light?" (5.10.15–16; Job 3:16). The witches hail Banquo as "Lesser than Macbeth, and greater," and they promise "Thou shalt get kings, though thou be none." They too have been reading Job, where Eliphaz prophesies "that thy seed shall be great, and thy posterity as the grass of the earth. Thou shalt go to thy grave in a full age, as a rick of corn commeth in due season into the barn" (1.3.63, 65; Job 5:25–26). Where scripture equates the greatness of the present with the greatness of future generations, the witches uncouple the two, promising the former solely to Macbeth and the latter solely to Banquo. Macbeth's later realization—"my way of life / Is fall'n ino the sere, the yellow leaf"—returns to the image of ripe corn but inverts it, as the ripeness of future generations here has withered (5.3.23–24).

This is dictionary work but there is a deeper logic here, a skeleton beneath the skin. Critics of the play have tended to assume that Macbeth's sin—his Aristotelian fatal flaw—is ambition. As A. C. Bradley blustered in his classic study *Shakespearean Tragedy* (1904), "Who ever doubted Macbeth's ambition?" and few have dared to do so; that Macbeth is ambitious is a high school English class default in analysis of the play, and all those who assume so are only following early modern exegeses of Job, which routinely explicate the book as a warning against worldly ambition.[38] Bishop Bonner's homilies illustrate their teaching against "man's vain glory, and pride, which of all vices, is most universal" by reference to Job's "homo natus de muliere."[39] Calvin moralizes Job as a parable of ambitious worldliness:

> We see how ambition reigneth in the world. If a man have many children: he is glad that he hath so many reasonable creatures to be under him at his commandment. If he have wherewith to find a great household: he liketh well of himself for it. But what? All is but mere Ambition or vainglory.[40]

A side note in the influential Protestant translation known as the Geneva Bible glosses Job in the same terms: "He noteth the ambition of them, which for their pleasure, as it were, change the order of nature, & build in most barren places, because they would hereby make their names immortal."[41] As Macbeth complains, "Upon my head they placed a fruitless crown, / And put a barren sceptre in my grip" (3.1.62–63). The play is doubly structured on Job in the skin of its language and the bones of its plot.

One step deeper now, down into the DNA. The book of Job had one specific application in the Reformation church. The key phrase that echoes through *Macbeth*—"man that is born of woman . . ."—was the centerpiece of traditional and reformed liturgies of burial. Regnault's 1531 Sarum primer includes this line as the fifth reading for the office of the dead: "Homo nat de muliere: brevi vivens tempore / repletur multis miseries." In the woodcut that illustrates the text are three characters with speech bubbles: "Homo natus de muliere" comes from the mouth of a woman holding a baby; "Brevi vivens tempore" declares a man in his sick-bed, surrounded by devils; and "Repletur Multis Miseriis" adds a man with one leg and a crutch, looking on. A short text underneath glosses the scene in English:

> Every man / that born is of woman
> Fulfilled is of all misery
> Sure of death / but how / where / nor when
> It is so short as it is seen daily.

The effect is that the key phrase has been repeated three times. Other traditional primers vary the format—Vostre's 1488 *Heures a l'Usiage Romme* includes the reading without the woodcut while his 1517 *Les presentes heures a lusiage de Chartres* adds in a border a dance of death—but always retain the same line.[42] All English primers include the phrase, and it is implicit in the opening lines of the order for the burial of the dead in the Book of Common Prayer from its first edition on: "Man that is born of woman hath but a short time to live, and is full of misery."

Other readings from Job come and go in burial rites. The *Office of the Blessed Virgin Marie*, the 1599 traditional primer that was printed in Antwerp but widely distributed in England, has six separate readings from Job, where the 1539 *Manual* has four and the first Book of Common Prayer three. But Job is always part of Christian burial, and most often—as in the Book of Common Prayer, which only cites Job as part of the burial rite—exclusively so. This is the specific resonance of this phrase. It is not chance but a commonplace. We must hear not its strangeness but its familiarity and then turn back to the oddity that Macbeth apparently does not know this line, given that he spends the play inside the logic and language of the burial rite.

What Macbeth understands as a promise of immortality is an echo of the words said by the priest as he welcomes the corpse. They are the perfect sound of his mortality. What for Hamlet and Ophelia offers a kind of consolation—the old narrative of bonding, of touching the dead—is replayed for Macbeth as a nightmare: a feast at which the dead are present, a funeral at which the corpse will not stay still. The fragments of the old rite return to him as a brutal music. There is no single *Hamlet* and perhaps no single *Macbeth*: the play is broken by rival interpretations, alternate understandings of the same scenes, and these grow upon the language and concerns of the liturgy. The Book of Common Prayer did not inaugurate the tensions I have sketched here—between the community of the living and the community of the dead; between fear that some may not sit to the feast, and fear that too many will. But it did perfectly embody those tensions, in its whispered linkage of the rites for Communion and burial, and in the curious, fraught moment of administration in the 1559 prayer book: when the body is both present and absent, both remembered and here with us. From the prayer book Shakespeare took many things. He learned that mourning like marriage has a narrative, a set vocabulary of phrase and gesture, and that concern over the community of the living bears within it worry over the dead. This is a curious dramatic paradox. At the ceremonies for the dead we worry most of all about the living; and at ceremonies for the living we worry about the dead. Perhaps simplest of all he learned that theology can never be single.

In May 1605, during Whitsun week, in a small town called Allens Moore just outside Hereford in the west of England, a woman called Alice Wellington was buried. According to the pamphlet rushed to the press within a month of her death, she was "a simple woman, and void of true grounds of Learning or Divinity," and had in her simplicity fallen prey to local recusants. "Seduced by the witcheries of Baal's Priests," she refused to receive Communion at the parish church. "It pleased GOD to visit this Alice Wellington with sickness, and to lay his hand so heavy upon her," the pamphlet recounts, "that she died excommunicate." Because she had not communicated, the vicar of the parish church refused to bury her in the churchyard, "alleging, that he should incur the penalty and danger of the Law, if he should yield thereunto."

So far we have the same web of tensions as at the burial of Ophelia: a reluctant, rule-bound priest who resists the demands of those who care for a woman who has died outside the strict community of church order. But unlike *Hamlet*, this is a story not about longing but about fear, and like all nightmares it is, at heart, a story about power. As the pamphlet continues, at an hour before dawn the next morning, the vicar is woken by "the sound of a little bell, and being unacquainted with such a sound, and wondering what it might be, he started by, and looked out the window." He watches the scene in the churchyard below:

> Some forty or fifty persons accompanying a Coarse [corpse] round about the Church, one of which company had a Saints-bell, another bare a Crosse, fastened (as it seemed unto him) upon the end of a Staff; before the coarse some carried Tapers burning, and other such trumperies.

The vicar has here relinquished his traditional dramatic position. He has become a spectator rather than an actor, and as he watches, Alice Wellington is buried with the full panoply of traditional rites— the saint's bell, the crucifix, the burning tapers—in his own churchyard. After the body is buried, the vicar "spake unto them, blaming them for their boldness," but the recusant congregation reply: "they little regarding his words, gave him many reviling terms, and bade him get him gone, if he tendered his own life." The vicar, "seeing so many weaponed in offensive manner," fled.[43] His name, although the pamphlet never gives it, was Richard Heyns.

At certain times—at the hot moment of grief or love, in pain or joy—the performance of liturgy is seized from the hands of the priests and reworked, by extraclerical figures who care deeply about liturgical propriety, into an unorthodox dramatic event. Those recusant mourners in Herefordshire share their care with Rosalind in *As You Like It*, and with Hamlet and Laertes they share a longing for the full form of the traditional burial rite. If we are willing to shift our perspective, then we may see here, too, some strange dumbshow of

Macbeth. The devotional community has fractured precisely at the failure of Communion to reconcile all participants in a single liturgical structure, and the vicar is an onlooker, a powerless witness to a rite underpinned by violence. He is the extra man at the feast. The burial rite is a twofold story, torn between piety and grief, and it is divided upon itself between the living and the dead. Shakespeare did not give drama to liturgy, for it was already dramatic; nor did he simply borrow that which was in the liturgy. What he learned perhaps is best seen as a process of condensation, a drawing down upon key motifs, upon holy phrases, upon promises. The Book of Common Prayer is hardly the only place where a man may learn about grief, nor is it the only way in which a community worries over its borders, but it was a perfect expression of these hurts and fears in Reformation England. There are two plays inside *Macbeth*, and they are rivals. There is not and can never be any single song.

PART III *The Ministration of Baptism to Be Used in the Church*

MINISTER: Will thou be baptised in this faith?
ANSWER: That is my desire.

The Book of Common Prayer (1559), Cummings, 144.

Graunt that whosoeuer is here dedicated to thee by our office and ministery, may also be indued with heauenly vertues, and euerlastingly rewarded, through thy mercie, O blessed Lord God, who doest liue ⁊ gouerne all things, world without end. Amen.

Lmightie euerliuing God, whose most dearely beloued Sonne Iesus Christ, for the forgiuenesse of our sins, did shed out of his most precious side both water and blood, and gaue commaundement to his disciples that they should go teach all nations, and baptize them in the name of the Father, the Sonne, and of the holy Ghost: Regard, we beseech thee, the supplications of thy Congregation, and grant that all thy seruants which shall be baptized in this water, may receiue the fulnesse of thy grace, and euer remaine in the number of thy faithfull and elect children, through Iesus Christ our Lord. Amen.

*Sanctifie this water to the mysticall washing away of sin, grant that this child now to be baptized therein

Then the Priest shall take the childe in his hands, and aske the name: and naming the child, shall dip it in the water, to it bee discreetly and warily done, saying.

N. I baptize thee in the Name of the Father, and of the Sonne, and of the holy Ghost, Amen.

But if they certifie that

And if the childe be weake, it shall suffice to powre water vpon it, saying the foresaid words.

N. I baptize thee, in the Name of the Father, and of the Sonne, and of the holy Ghost. Amen.

Then the Priest shall make a Crosse vpon the childes forehead, saying. *Then shall the Priest say:*

Ee receiue this child into the congregation of Christs flocke, and doe signe him with the signe of the Crosse, in token that hereafter he shall not be ashamed to confesse the faith of Christ crucified, and manfully to fight vnder his banner, against sin, the world and the deuill, and to continue Christs faithfull souldier and seruant vnto his liues end. Amen.

*Here the Priest shall make a crosse vpon y child's forehead.

Then

CHAPTER 6 ❦ *Graceless Sacraments*

I
n the Bodleian Library at Oxford is a 1604 octavo Book of Common Prayer. This was the third edition printed after the Hampton Court Conference, and the first octavo; it is bound with a 1603 psalter. It is a clean copy but for three marginal annotations in a pale and spidery hand. I have read prayer books where jottings sprawl across the page in lovely excess; where profuse notes show the passion and the intimacy of early modern devotion. This book, however, and these annotations are remarkable for their restraint. Where others tailored the text of liturgy to their confessional taste, or to express regard—or disregard—for the tangle of revision inside the Book of Common Prayer, this anonymous worshipper made three small marks.

We may learn much from these ghostly traces. They date from between 1604, when this volume was printed, and 1662, when a new edition arrived; that these and these alone were considered worth noting suggests that what is marked here is important. Their poverty makes this point. Each of the three concern the theology of baptism— the rite at which we may hope for the remission of sin—and the baptism rite changes little over successive editions. What is in 1549 is almost exactly what is in 1604. This does not mean that baptism was not contested, but it does suggest that its controversy was of a particular style. The words themselves were widely agreed upon, but their implications under debate.

Each of the annotations is identical: the phrase "Conf. H. C." In Morning Prayer's instruction "The absolution or remission of sins, to be pronounced," the words "remission of sins" are underlined, and the phrase appears in the margin. In the rite for Private Baptism, the opening warning "that without great cause and necessity, they procure not their children to be baptized at home in their houses" is given the same marking; the words "they procure not their children" are underlined. Later in the rite for Private Baptism, the words "lawful minister" from a direction beginning "First, let the lawful minister call upon God for his grace and say the Lord's Prayer" are underlined, and the same marginal comment appears. "Conf. H. C." is of course the Hampton Court Conference, where each of these lines was emended. In the 1559 Book of Common Prayer, the first stands as "The Absolution"; the second runs, "without great cause and necessity they baptize not children at home"; and the third instructs, "First let them that be present."[1] The annotations note, without commentary, the places of change.

These were not the only alterations to the prayer book discussed or decided upon at Hampton Court, nor are they even all the changes made to the baptism rite. They signal to us now, however, the delicacy of this controversy. Baptism is the beginning of a Christian life: in the traditional homily, "the gate of entry by which we must and do enter into the church and unto the other sacraments."[2] It transfers us from the state in which we are born into a purer one but each of the elements of this process is troublesome. First is the question of the degree of spiritual washing. "Absolution" implies a perfect cleansing; the etymological link between "absolute" and "absolution" indicates this completion, and a sin absolved is surely a sin vanished. "Remission," however, is of a lesser degree, and a remitted sin may remain implicitly present. By including both terms, the 1604 prayer book retreats—just a step—from any perfect washing. Second is the question of who may perform the rite. Private baptism takes place at home and was most often used in cases of emergency, after the birth of a child who was not expected to survive until the following Sunday, when they could be baptized in church. As all editions prior to 1604 instruct at this moment, "let them that be present call upon God for his grace and say the Lord's Prayer, if the time will suffer. And then one of them shall name the child, and dip him in the water." Any person present could say the words, "I baptize thee in the name of the Father, and of the Son, and of the Holy Ghost." But the 1604 edition amends "them that be present" to "the lawful minister." Now, for the first time in the English Church, only a priest may perform the rite.

These were the old controversies over the baptism rite: the 1604 prayer book sits at the end of a catalogue of tightenings, of little changes to the form and its interpretation. The two alterations depend upon one another. According to the traditional homily, even a sinner may perform a baptism. "We must understand and know, that although he which doth minister the sacrament, be of a sinful and evil conversation, yet the virtue and effect of the sacrament, is thereby nothing diminished or hurted," it insists (N.iii.v). If anyone may perform the rite, then its function arises not from the operator but from something internal to it. That is, if a sinner may say the words then their blessing must arise from within the words themselves. If you believe in the words you need not believe in the speaker. If, however, we diminish the force of the words, then we must increase the necessary sanctity of the speaker.

All versions of public baptism begin by invoking two great floods. There was the one that destroyed all the world but Noah and his ark and then, in the words of the 1549 version, "when thou didst drown in the read sea wicked king Pharaoh with all his army, yet (at the same time) thou didst lead thy people the children of Israel safely through the midst thereof." The image remains constant but its explanation evolves. In 1549, the priest continues:

> whereby thou didst figure the washing of thy holy Baptism: by the Baptism of thy well beloved son Jesus Christ, thou didst sanctify the flood Jordan, and all other waters to this mystical washing

away of sin: We beseech thee (for thy infinite mercies) that thou wilt mercifully look upon these children, and sanctify them with thy holy ghost, that by this wholesome laver of regeneration, whatsoever sin is in them, may be washed clean away, that they, being delivered from thy wrath, may be received into th'arke of Christ's church.

Here the washing is complete. The metaphor implies perfection and sin is "washed clean away." The 1552 prayer book strips down the explication, and now the priest says:

figuring thereby thy holy Baptism; and by the Baptism of thy well-beloved son Jesus Christ, didst sanctify the flood Jordan, and all other waters, to the mystical washing away of sin: We beseech thee for thy infinite mercies, that thou wilt mercifully look upon these children, sanctify them and wash them with thy holy ghost, that they, being delivered from thy wrath, may be received into the Ark of Christ's Church.[3]

This lessens both the intensity and quantity of descriptions of the cleansing. No longer is sin washed clean away, nor is there any wholesome regeneration; the later version presents this process only as a metaphor, and "this mystical washing away of sin"—a process taking place before us—becomes "the mystical washing away of sin," a historical episode. This is no real washing, where things become clean; rather it is a blessing from the Holy Ghost, a sign, and the 1559 and subsequent prayer books follow this.

"Washing" describes the process of cleaning and also its achievement; it suggests both an action and its result. One way to consider the revision of the baptism rite is to see it as a shift in emphasis between these two different meanings. The 1549 prayer book—like the traditional theology of the Roman Catholic Church—stresses the result of washing; reformed theology as reflected in subsequent editions of the prayer book instead emphasizes the process. All versions of the baptism rite share a vocabulary. Their disagreement is not with words but with their implications and specifically with how we understand "wash."

In allowing baptism to be performed by women or in private houses, the Elizabethan rite for private baptism suggests that the cleansing power of the sacrament arises from the form of words and elements. In 1578, however, curious copies of the prayer book appeared. They were published by the official printer, Christopher Barker, and in the official format with a dedication to the queen. In them, the term "minister" is substituted for "priest," and the orders for private baptism, confirmation, and churching of women are omitted. As the great historian of English Protestantism Patrick Collinson explains, these versions perfectly follow Puritan conceptions of the sacrament. The Puritans insisted that baptism must only be public and never administered by midwives. Collinson concludes that these prayer book travesties must have had some official sympathy in order to appear under the royal imprint; more recently, Ian Green has suggested that they were marketing ploy by Christopher Barker, who wished to sell as many copies as possible and hoped that the excised version might please godly buyers.[4] We might take this expurgated edition, however, as a sign of both the flexibility of the Book of Common Prayer and the ongoing paradox of private baptism. It was neither absolutely necessary nor entirely irrelevant to the orthodox Anglican liturgy.

The Puritan objection to private baptism was that this was traditional superstition, one of the "men's devices, popish ceremonies, and Antichristian rites" still in the English Church. The 1572 *Admonition to the Parliament* specifically names "private baptism, baptism ministered by women" as an English rite in need of reformation, and the same demand—"baptism not to be ministered by women"— appears also in the Millenary Petition presented to James.[5] The Puritans objected to the implicit claim that it was necessary, since that in turn suggests it has a magic power; the Jacobean church objected to this rite that did not need a priest because it was a sign of the limit of their authority. They differ over motives but they share a cause.

At the Hampton Court Conference, as William Barlow recounts, when the issue of private baptism was raised:

> if private for place, his Majesty though it agreed with the use of the primitive church: if for persons, that any but a *lawful minister* might baptize any where, he utterly disliked: and in this point his Highness grew somewhat earnest against the baptizing by women and Laics [laymen].[6]

Like the Puritans, James is passionately against women performing baptism, but he separates the issue into two parts—of place and of agent. Baptism may take place in a private house; it may not be performed by anyone other than a priest.

This is the curious paradox of the reformation of baptism. In insisting that only a minister could perform the rite, the early Stuart church simultaneously curtailed the agent's role in the process. The revisions made, following the conference, are slight, and they concern the second paragraph of the opening rubric. The 1549, 1552, and 1559 versions of this rubric instruct: "also they shall warn them, that without great cause and necessity they baptize not children at home in their houses. And when great need shall compel them to do so, then they minister it on this fashion." The same rubric in the 1604 prayer book stands:

> And also they shall warn them, that without great cause and necessity they cause not children to be baptized at home in their houses. And when great need shall compel them to do so, that the Curate, or lawful Minister present it on this occasion.[7]

The second revision insists that only a minister of the church may perform a baptism: it may not be a midwife, or any other person. The first revision however lessens any claim to status; it insists that the effect of baptism is performed not by the minister but rather the word of God. The minister is not he who baptizes but who causes baptism to take place.

The tension is over the extent to which the church is willing to imagine a rite outside its control. The 1604 prayer book does not abolish private baptism; it restricts its agent. This characteristic is epitomized, as we have seen, during the marriage rite. Where traditional marriages took place outside, in the churchyard, all editions of the Book of Common Prayer insist that "the persons to be married shall come into the body of the church." Liturgy may be read as a catalogue of common gestures, all joined by this same impulse to bring the many strains of human devotion into the form of the church. Private baptism suggests the opposite movement, a movement outside and away. This was a rite, in the early versions, which required neither priest nor church, and the 1604 revision brings it back into some pattern of control. Here, the Book of Common Prayer's desire is in tension with its theology. It seeks to define the circumstances under which a church rite might leave the church even while suggesting that none of its power is ever accessible to any of us.

PUBLIC BAPTISM BEGINS with the Red Sea. The figure is included in all versions of the prayer book, and as he explains the theology of baptism in his *Treatise of the Sacraments* John Jewel emphasizes the transformation of the water.

> Through the power of God's working the water is turned into blood. They that be washed in it receive the remission of their sins: their robes are made clean in the blood of the Lamb. The water itself is nothing; but, by the working of God's Spirit, the death and merits of our Lord and Saviour Christ are thereby assured unto us.

He explains this transformation by the liturgy's same image. "A figure hereof was given at the Red Sea: the children of Israel passed through in safety; but Pharaoh and his whole army were drowned," he notes. The Red Sea is made red even as it makes pure. This prayer is Cranmer's fairly free translation of an earlier prayer by Martin Luther, but the image did not originate with him. According to the Jesuit historian of liturgy Jean Danielou, crossing the Red Sea is an old typological figure for baptism, present in the writing of the church fathers Origen, Ambrose, and St Cyprian. The early Anabaptist leader Hans Hut used it in his 1526 *On the Mystery of Baptism*:

> Just as in the time of Noah, God slew the whole world through the flood, drowning all evil and washing it away; just as happened with Pharaoh and the Egyptians, in the baptismal bath of the Red Sea, where they sank to the bottom like lead.

This is a wholly conventional trope for the working of the baptism rite.[8]

All this sits just beneath the surface of the play. Returning from the murder of Duncan Macbeth looks down and asks: "Will all great Neptune's ocean wash this blood / Clean from my hand?" Here is the rite's promise, half-familiar; its vocabulary of blood and a sea are present but jumbled and he goes on:

> No: this my hand will rather
> The multitudinous seas incarnadine
> Making the green one red. (2.2.63–66)

Editors commonly footnote the word "incarnadine." Shakespeare is using the adjective as a verb for the first time in English. As a verb, "incarnadine" is the process by which the green sea turns red; but taken as an adjective, Macbeth is also describing the baptism rite's Red Sea, and the line break invites us to read it this way: "seas incarnadine." It is unusual but not impossible in English to place the adjective after the noun, and he names it again in the following line: "the green one red." "Making . . . red" is the process the lines describe—a bloodstained hand causing the green seas to turn scarlet—but even inside the syntax of the line an opposite is remembered—a sea that was already red. The Folio tries to clarify this by punctuating the line "Making the Greene one, Red." But without that awkward comma the ambiguity remains, and since the 1673 Quarto and F4 of 1685, all editions omit punctuation from the line. Try reading it aloud and I suggest you will twice hear the Red Sea.

The most famous treatment of these dense lines is by the southern poet and dazzling close reader John Crowe Ransom in his 1947 essay "On Shakespeare's Language." Ransom observes that here is combined what he calls "native English" in "Making the green one red"—those blocky Anglo-Saxon sounds—with the "Latinical explosion" of "multitudinous seas incarnadine." This last word, notes Ransom,

> is the French name for a pigment, here used by Shakespeare— probably for the first time—as a verb meaning to color to the shade of that pigment. But its proximity to *multitudinous* induces Latinity into our consciousness so that we stop and reflect upon its Latin meaning: to paint to the color of blood.

The curiosity of the phrase is deliberate. Shakespeare, he argues, "stopped the reduction of latinical words into common words, and held them in a state of perpetual suspension and arrest. They are in the language but not quite of it."[9]

What makes this phrase powerful as poetry makes it controversial as liturgy: its attachment to an imagined past. After the publication of the 1549 prayer book, Cranmer invited the European theologian Martin Bucer to comment. Bucer's reply, the *Censura Martini Bucer super libro Sacrorum*, was completed in 1551, and in it Bucer attacks the Red Sea's spiritual washing. "In these words it is recited that through the baptism of his blessed son Jesus Christ God sanctified the waters of Jordan and all other waters, to the mystical washing away of sin," he begins, quoting the prayer, and continues:

> But scripture does not say this, and words like this tend to support the superstitious notion that by the baptism of Christ some kind of sanctifying power was imparted to the waters: for men are always disposed to believe in magical changes in things, as the fiction of transubstantiation witnesses, and the esteem in which almost all things are held which the Papists publicly consecrate, such as water, salt, herbs, candles, bells, and other things which

the priests with some show of devotion are accustomed to bless and consecrate.[10]

For Bucer, the Red Sea prayer was part of the bric-a-brac of traditional theology, and it promotes one of the old church's sustaining fictions: that there might be magic in what he repeatedly calls "things," that the elements might be holy. That fiction is the product of language, and Bucer objects most of all to the possible misreading "words like this" might invite. He dislikes, that is, the pliability of the image.

Although many of Bucer's revisions were incorporated into the 1552 Book of Common Prayer, this prayer remained. The 1572 *Admonition to the Parliament*, a Puritan attack on the "Popish Abuses" inside the Elizabethan church, specified this particular prayer as representative of all that was wrong. "The public baptism, that also is full of childish & superstitious toys," the petition declares:

> First in their prayer they say that God by the baptism of his son Jesus Christ, did sanctify the flood Jordan, and all other waters, to the mystical washing away of sin, attributing that to the sign which is proper to the work of God in the blood of Christ, as though virtue were in water, to wash away sins.[11]

Again, the prayer is quoted, and the specific image drawn out; again the point of objection is one possible implication of this phrase— that water is efficacious rather than a sign of divine power. As before, the trouble is a way of reading rather than any explicit declaration. To escape this trap of suggestion the radical Protestant Zwinglian community in Middelberg in the Netherlands published their own expurgated prayer book in 1584:

> Baptism was ordained to be ministered in the element of Water, to teach us, that like as water outwardly doth wash away the filth of the body, so inwardly doth the virtue of Christs blood purge our souls from that corruption and deadly poison, wherewith by nature we were infected

instructs this version of the rite, and in case its explicit metaphoricity—
"like as water"—is insufficient to deter wayward readers, a short
editorial note follows. "Not that we think any such virtue or power to
be included in the visible water or outward action," it explains.[12]

What these Puritans are objecting to is the suggestion of the traditional rite for baptism. This rite as set out in the Sarum primer opens
with a lengthy blessing of the elements. "Exorcizo te, creatura aquae,"
it begins, "ut fias aqua exorcizata as effugandam omnem potestate
inimici" ["I exorcise thee that you may be able to fight all the power
of the enemy"]. The elements are blessed since they contain power—
"potestate"—for evil or for good; the washing arises from their application. Traditional baptism is a narrative of influence and effect.
A Summe of Christian Doctrine, the 1592 primer by the Jesuit Peter
Canasius, asks "what profit and effect doth Baptism yield?" and
answers:

> by Baptism both sins are remitted, & the Spirit is given, whereby
> both the old man is extinguished, & a new creature is made in
> Christ. For Baptism rightly received doth not only yield this, that
> all sins be fully pardoned & taken away from the wicked man;
> but also that he once being baptized, is perfectly renewed, &
> made truly innocent, just, holy, & worthy in Christ of the heav-
> enly glory.[13]

The perfect cleaning of traditional baptism is built upon faith in the
efficacy of the elements.

The traditional church considered a sacrament a sign of grace
that contains both an image and the cause of that grace; reformed
theology separates the image from the cause. In his *Treatise of the
Sacraments* John Jewel explained, "A sacrament is an outward and
visible sign, whereby God sealeth up his grace in our hearts, to the
confirmation of our faith," and he goes on to isolate the elements
from their effects. "The water wherein we are baptized doth not
cleanse the soul," he writes and repeats: "Not the water, but the blood
of Christ, reconcileth us unto God, strengtheneth our conscience,

and worketh our redemption. We must seek salvation in Christ alone, and not in any outward thing." Reformers often fall to negatives when they define baptismal theology. They seek to define by that which does not take place. "Can water be a spiritual washing for our soul?" demands Calvin in his exegesis of Job, and answers immediately "NO."[14]

Here is the divide between the ideal forms of theologies; but as we have repeatedly seen, devotional practice was always more ragged than this. While the Elizabethan church abandoned the mechanical efficacy of traditional theology, the Book of Common Prayer retained the signifiers of that efficacy such as the Red Sea prayer. Beneath the complaints and criticisms of the liturgy runs a genuine uncertainty. In their attacks on this specific prayer the Puritan and reformed voices imply that the baptism rite promises some efficacy. They see evidence of a magic they wish were not there. Conversely, Counter-Reformation polemicists mocked the English Church for its failure to provide the reassurances of efficacy. They attacked the liturgy for its lack of power. As the polemicist John Brerely wrote in 1664 in his doggerel *Mirror of New Reformation*:

> Your sacraments, you say, do only sign,
> Witness, and seal the promises divine;
> And, even to him who faithfully repents,
> Conferred no grace; o graceless Sacraments![15]

We do not have to take Brerely's description of Anglican theology as sincere or accurate; but it only works as satire if it has identified a point of worry, over the uncertain effect of the promise of washing in the Book of Common Prayer.

"Will all great Neptune's ocean wash this blood / Clean from my hand?" asks Macbeth and answers, "No." This is also Calvin's call-and-response: "Can water be a spiritual washing for our souls? NO." The careful patterning of the scene—the keyword "wash," the allusion to the conventional image of the Red Sea prayer—invokes the prayer book's rite for baptism as a literary construct, a skeleton of language and suggestion. But the rite stands too upon a wider debate about the relation between language and effect. Macbeth believes that no washing can take place, and his imagination spools out a grander scene: his bloodstained hand turning all the seas to red. Like the Puritan critics of the prayer book, he is thinking within the images of the Red Sea prayer and yet resisting their implication. Following Calvin, we might simply concur that no washing will take place. But little in liturgy is this certain, and in the play, too, there are two sets of hands. As Macbeth speaks, his wife enters. She has been back to the scene of the murder, to "gild the faces of the grooms" by smearing them with the king's blood, and now she tells him, "My hands are of your colour." She shares her husband's blood-stained hands but not his assumption of futility. "A little water clears us of this deed," she insists brightly: "How easy it is then!" (2.2.54, 63, 65–66). Here are two washings packaged into one, split by the understanding of what is taking place.

Shakespeare writes invisible stage directions. There are cues for movement within the dialogue, and what the actors say makes inevitable what they do. "Hold, take my sword," Banquo tells Fleance. These work also as cues for the audience. "Light thickens, / And the crow makes wing to th'rooky wood," says Macbeth later in the play, and we are being told that it is dusk (3.2.51–52). This scene after the murder does not give us such clarification. Their hands are surely bloody, but their washing is uncertain. "Retire we to our chamber," says Lady Macbeth: "A little water clears us of this deed." She might here be proposing a future action, that once they have returned to their private chamber they will there wash their hands. "How easy it is then!" she declares hopefully. But these lines might also be read as an account not of the effect but the process. She could in this be describing the moment of washing, and now her exclamation greets her success. We cannot tell between what might happen and what has already taken place.

One audience member at an early modern performance assumed that they both failed to wash the blood away. The eccentric herbalist and astrologer Simon Forman saw *Macbeth* in 1610. In his notebook he describes the scene:

> And when Mack Beth had murdered the king the blood on his hands could not be washed of by Any means, nor from his wives hands which handled the bloody daggers in hiding them By which means they became both much amazed & Affronted.[16]

It might be easy to dismiss this as inaccurate, to assume that Forman is imagining action that does not take place. Lady Macbeth is not amazed, at least in the version of the play that we have now. Later in the play she sleepwalks, and then is found repeatedly and thwartedly washing her hands; perhaps Forman is jumbling two separate washings, and seeing the failure of the second in the achievement of the first. But perhaps his reading is more willful than that. He sees what should be done on stage. For Lady Macbeth, she and her husband are faced with a literal problem: how to clean the blood from their hands. Taken as a literal problem, the answer is water. There is a hard common sense to her, but it is technically correct. "Go get some water," she commands her husband: "And wash this filthy witness from your hand." The problem however they are faced with here has a moral depth, and those bloodstained hands are the proof of murder; they are guilty. Forman refuses to read like Lady Macbeth: he reads literally that which the play offers as metaphor.

What we see here is the conflict of two mentalities. Lady Macbeth refuses to see beyond the tangible world, and her belief that guilt can be transferred rests upon an absolute literalism. "Wash this filthy witness" she commands, as if the trouble were the sign. "I'll gild the faces of the grooms," she declares, "For it must seem their guilt," but gilding—here a kind of grotesque painting with blood—is not quite the same as guilt. The true action of the scene takes place at the limits of the visible. "In baptism the water is the sign; and the thing signified is the grace of God," argues Jewel in his *Treatise of the Sacraments*: "We see the water, but the grace of God is invisible; we cannot see it." Macbeth, by contrast, is lost upon a flood of metaphor, hardly able to see the world for all the symbols that cluster in his way.

Lady Macbeth briefly exits to return the daggers and now a sound interrupts this dense scene. "Whence is that knocking?" demands Macbeth, alone on stage, and it continues after she returns. "I hear a knocking," she announces, and again, "More knocking," and here are Shakespeare's invisible stage directions. This is something to be noted. As they exit, Macbeth mocks, "Wake Duncan with thy knocking," and, just like Macbeth, all who have read this scene have taken the knocks as somehow extraneous. Thomas de Quincey in a famous essay wondered why the knocking filled him with such dread. Here, he wrote, "the human has made its reflux upon the fiendish," and with growing excitement, "the pulses of life are beginning to beat again; and the re-establishment of the goings-on of the world in which we live, first makes us profoundly sensible of the awful parenthesis that had suspended them."[17] The knocking continues into the start of the following scene, and the porter comes slowly to the gate. "Knock, knock, knock," he mimics. It is Macduff and Lennox, coming late to the castle. This is the porter's only scene in the play. He is full of bawdy, of crass jokes—"drink, sir, is a great provoker, of three things," he announces, for he is drunk or perhaps only hung over— and the odd little episode has been read for a range of symbols. A knocking at the gate, they say, is an image of the arrival of death, or a leftover stage prop from the morality tradition of the hell-gate, but it has a far simpler liturgical echo.[18] It literalizes a powerful image from the baptism rite.

The knocking begins as Macbeth is speaking a travesty of the Red Sea prayer and the baptism rite follows this with an address by the priest over the child. He says:

Receive them (O Lord) as thou hast promised by thy well-beloved Son, saying, Ask and you shall have; seek and you shall find; knock and it shall be opened unto you. So give now unto us that ask. Let us that seek find. Open the gate unto us that knock; that these infants may enjoy the everlasting benediction of thy heavenly washing (Cummings, 142).

The liturgy is here following Matthew 7:7—"knock and it shall be opened unto you"—and when early modern biblical commentators glossed these lines, they emphasized the promise that prayer is a sure means to God. Erasmus in his paraphrase upon the gospels insists upon the divine and miraculous plenty offered to the believer: "He denieth not these things to them that seek them diligently: he restraineth not from this treasure, them that knock importunately." The side note to this phrase in Matthew in the Geneva Bible runs "Prayers are a sure refuge in all miseries," and Calvin's *Harmonie* agrees:

> This is an exhortation to prayer . . . nothing shall better encourage us to pray, then a certain assurance of obtaining. For it cannot be that they should pray diligently, that doubt: yea prayer, without faith, is but a vain and sporting ceremony. Christ therefore that he might effectually stir us up to this part of our duty, he doth not only command us what we ought to do: but promiseth that our prayers should not be in vain.[19]

Inside the exhortation "knock and it shall be opened unto you" is a promise of success, and once more the Book of Common Prayer holds out the surety of grace, upon the condition of faith.

The knocking scene is built upon one movement in the rite. If we do not hear the knocking as a liturgical promise, or if we only consider the blood to be a practical problem, then we are seeing only half the scene. We are reading as Lady Macbeth: hard, disenchanted. If we see this scene only as spiritual, however, as if there were no humans here, then we are reading as Macbeth, and where before he was direct and violent, now he is credulous, flourishing in symbols. What play and prayer book share here is a condition of uncertainty. None knows what completes an action, what gesture becomes real. The scene of the play feeds upon both the promises and the failings of liturgy. Its particular weird density is a product of the rite.

THE APPARATI BY which we know the plays are often new additions. Modern editors improvise stage directions, prompted by the words the actors speak (*Banquo hands Fleance his sword; Lady Macbeth washes her hands*). This is of course most grandly true of productions, which are made up of choices by actors and directors; they offer a splendor of literalizations lit up on the stage. All these seek to clarify the action patterned here. In dividing the play into discrete movements, however, they may obscure another skeleton just beneath the script. The act and scene divisions were added in 1623, in the Folio. Often in the earlier quartos, there are not such breaks; or they stand in different places, giving the play a slightly different rhythm. *Macbeth* was first published in the Folio, so we do not have an earlier version; we do not have a version without divisions into acts and scenes. This does not mean, though, that we must entirely respect them. The handwashing scene runs into the next; the knocking is continuous, and as Macbeth and Lady Macbeth leave the stage, the porter enters. "Here's a knocking indeed," he declares and demands: "Who's there i'th'name of Beelzebub?" "This place is too cold for hell," he complains for at least in hell is "th'everlasting bonfire," and "I'll devil-porter it no further." He opens the castle gate to Macduff and Lennox and asks for a tip: "Remember the porter" (2.3.1–18).

In the 1549 rite for public baptism, the prayer of knocking is followed immediately by an address to the devil. "I command thee, unclean spirit," the priest demands: "that thou come out, and depart from these infants, whom our Lord Jesus Christ hath vouchsaved." He goes on: "Therefore thou cursed spirit, remember thy sentence, remember thy judgment, remember the day to be at hand, wherin thou shalt burn in fire everlasting" (Cummings, 48). The devil is a powerful figure in traditional baptismal theology. He embodied the sin that here was washed away, and folded inside the traditional baptism rite was an exorcism. There was no standard Roman rite for baptism until the 1614 *Rituale Romanorum*, but in the pre-Reformation English Church the widespread Sarum rite suggests the paradigm of traditional baptisms. There must be at least one godparent present; the name given to the child must be a saint's name; the salt is blessed; the priest touches the child with his own spittle; and he pours water over the child's head and signs the cross three times. The elements must be blessed—the salt, the font, the water—for in them the devil may reside; the salt, once blessed, is used to exorcise the devil.[20]

As Peter Martyr Vermigli wrote in *Common Places*: "seeing the scripture hath no where commanded, that exorcisms should be joined with baptism, it is not to be attempted unto us."[21] Reformers objected to the joining of these rites: the efficacy of exorcism might suggest that baptism was effective too. In the 1549 Book of Common Prayer the priest declares, "I command thee, unclean spirit," and dips the child in the font three times; in the 1552 version, followed in 1559 and 1604, there is no address to the devil, and the child is dipped only once (Cummings, 48). This is not to say that the devil disappears. For later in all versions of the rite, the godparents are summoned to the font. "Be their sureties," the priest instructs, "that they will forsake the devil and all his works, and constantly believe God's holy Word," and then he asks them to speak on behalf of the child. In the first question—"Dost thou forsake the devil and all his works, the vain pomp, and glory of the world, with all covetous desires of the same, the carnal desires of the flesh, so that thou wilt not follow, nor be led by them?"—the devil is remembered and renounced (144).

We have seen this story before. The Book of Common Prayer keeps some elements of traditional theology but in retention transforms their understanding. In the traditional rite and in 1549, the priest speaks directly to the devil: "I command thee." In the revision of the rite, the priest and congregation speak only for him. As the Reformation historian Susan Karant-Nunn argues, the shift between traditional and reformed baptism describes a shift in the status of the devil. "Satan was becoming steadily more figurative and thus, in one sense, more abstractly metaphorical," she notes, for where he once was an interlocutor he becomes a metaphor for sin.[22] He is, in 1552 and after, something like a quality—of vanity, of covetousness, or carnal desire; a figure of the pomp and glory of the world. "Dost thou forsake the devil and all his works?" asks the priest, and the proper answer comes: "I forsake them all." The devil is not here separately mentioned; he melts into his works.

This transition between a present character and a metaphor was inevitably only imperfectly achieved; the separation of exorcism and baptism in the prayer book was troubled and incomplete. We can see the mixed status of the devil in Cranmer's 1548 *Catechism*, a precursor of the first Book of Common Prayer. At the beginning of the seventh petition—"But deliver us from evil"—there is a woodcut by Hans Holbein of Christ performing an exorcism. He leans forward and gently raises his left hand; beneath him, a man twisted into an awkward half crouch, and from his mouth leaps a winged figure, half insect and half man. Here is quite literally an evil spirit. But Cranmer's gloss on this petition is wholly metaphorical. There is no mention of exorcism, and Cranmer instead instructs that we must abandon worldliness: "many men settle all their mind upon riches, and wealth of this world, which maketh them proud and high minded, full of revenging, idle and slothful, pitiless to the poor." Sin here is an abstraction, a pattern of behavior and interest, and Cranmer goes on to insist that evil is not of any single form. "The evils of this miserable life, be so many, that we can neither number them [nor] know them, not rightly judge of them," he notes, and it is precisely to assist our human limited comprehension that Christ has prepared for us a simple parable: "our Master Christ (which forbiddeth us to use many words in our prayers) hath as it were knit up together in one fardel all the plagues and adversities that can happen unto us in this world, and hath taught us to say this short prayer."[23] Evil is a metaphor for suffering, a single figure arranged by Christ. Within the term is glossed a whole world of sin and sadness.

Exorcism remains implicit to all acts of baptism, a reminder of the troubling possibility that the devil, like all those stained glass windows, will not so easily go away. In the spring of 1585 and the summer of the following year, six demoniacs were exorcised by Catholic priests in the houses of recusant gentry in Buckinghamshire. Stephen Greenblatt's seminal essay "Shakespeare and the Exorcists" traces the language shared between *King Lear* and a skeptical account of those exorcisms, Samuel Harsnett's *Declaration of Egregious Popish Impostures*. Harsnett, argues Greenblatt, wished to expose the fraudulence of exorcism "to drive the practice out of society's central zone, to deprive it of its prestige, and to discredit its apparent efficacy," and he does so by presenting it as a kind of carefully directed theater. The pamphlet insists upon "the theatricality of exorcism" to show its rite as fake, as ineffective.[24]

Harsnett's attacks, like the Jesuit exorcists, are liturgically precise. In turning from the pamphlet to the play, Greenblatt notes that "*King Lear* is haunted by a sense of rituals and beliefs that are no longer efficacious," but he does not note which (Greenblatt, 119). According to Harsnett, the Jesuits explain to Friswood and Sara, the two maids who are exorcised, "that their baptism they had received in the Church of England, must be amended, in regard it wanted many rites, ceremonies & ornaments, belonging to the baptism of the Church of Rome." Exorcism, the Jesuits promise, will compensate for the insufficiency of reformed baptism. Harsnett's attack on the exorcists is therefore also an attack on the traditional rituals, and he interrupts his account of the exorcism of the two servant girls to declare: "In my opinion, there was never *Christmas-game* performed, with more apish, indecent, slovenly gauds, then your baptising, and super-baptising ceremonies are." He lists in disgust, "the impure stinking breath of a soul impure belching swain, your enchanted salt, your charmed grease, your sorcerised chrism, your loathsome drivel, that you put upon their eyes, ears, noses, and lips." The "sorcerised chrism" and "enchanted salt" are the ingredients of traditional baptism. Harsnett goes on to describe the specifics of the exorcism as a traditional baptism, carried out very formally, with the priest in an alb placing salt in her mouth and spittle upon her eyes and nose.[25] The drama and power of the ritual share a source: the popular missing of the reassurance of old rites; the faith that a form of words might drive the devil away.

"I command thee, unclean spirit," declares the priest in the first Book of Common Prayer. "Seyton!" commands Macbeth later in the play: "Seyton, I say!"[26] The play tells a story about a broken rite. The vocabulary is present but the process is not, as if baptism were only theater, its power only phantom. And, in the mirror fallacy, as if theater were only hollow, a puppet show. With this play we are beyond a single story of cause and effect in which Shakespeare follows liturgy or the prayer book is simply a source. The rite is haunted by the specter of its incompletion and the play is haunted, too. *Macbeth* knows the rite like children know their nightmares: as immediately as we all know our fears.

"IT MUST BE BLOODY" declares Thomas Bilson, the bishop of Winchester, in his meandering 1599 polemic *The effect of Certaine Sermons Touching the Full Redemption of Mankinde*: "Almost all things are by the law purged with blood, and without shedding of blood is no remission." The mythic origin of baptism lies in pagan blood-washing ceremonies, at which an initiate was doused in animal blood; the Christian rite replaces that with water, and this is its first metaphor. Bilson is here describing the expiatory quality of Christ's blood shed on the cross—its power to clean away sin, its resilience—and he proceeds by expansion into analogy. He continues:

> For if the blood of bulls and goats sanctifieth as touching the purifying of the flesh; how much more shall THE BLOOD OF CHRIST, who through the eternal spirit offered himself without

spot to GOD, PURGE YOUR CONSCIENCES FROM DEAD WORKS to serve the living God?[27]

The orthodox English theology of baptism is built upon a sequence of displacements. Water stands in for blood, and borrows from its force; water, like blood, is washing, but not literally; that which is washed is invisible but described as a "spot," something we commonly might see. The power of baptism arises from this action of supplanting. In his exposition of the Thirty-Nine Articles—the defining tenets of the Church of England, first set out in 1563—the orthodox chaplain Thomas Rogers explains that "Baptism is unto us as circumcision was unto the Jews," and it replaces that older rite. "By Baptism we are buried into the death of Christ" argues Andrew Willet, but this is not an end, for "Christ by his death triumphed over the Devil," and baptism makes us heirs to his success. George Joye, the translator of the psalms, too insists that baptism's holiest metaphor is the crucifixion. "Ye baptism beareth in its self Christs death his burial & his resurrection to be practised in our bodies and souls perpetually while we live" he writes in his *Fruitful treatise of baptism*, and all agree that baptism is powerful because it is not itself.[28]

"It will have blood they say" declares Macbeth in his fit at the disrupted feast: "blood will have blood." The play has a staggered, repetitive tone, echoic and redundant, and many have been struck by this. Emrys Jones describes "a movement suggestive of a pre-ordained ceremony"; for Frank Kermode, in *Macbeth* "perhaps more than in any other of Shakespeare's plays, an idiosyncratic rhythm and a lexical habit establish themselves with a sort of hypnotic firmness."[29] "Fair is foul, and foul is fair" chant the witches in the opening scene, and when Macbeth enters he begins, "So foul and fair a day I have not seen." Later, Lady Macbeth promises "All our service, / In every point twice done and then done double," and the witches borrow this. "Double, double toil and trouble," they repeat.[30] The play flirts with ritual; it flaunts its own echoes. This is something like a parody, which points to another form, and something like an echo, which remembers origin. It is trying to remind us of something just outside itself.

Macbeth is first introduced in report of battle, where he and Banquo fought with great violence. "They doubly redoubled strokes upon the foe," says the wounded captain:

> Except they meant to bathe in reeking wounds
> Or memorise another Golgotha,
> I cannot tell. (1.2.38–41)

His description tips the careful balance of metaphors inside the Anglican theology of baptism. Where bathing in blood was for Bilson the symbolic event beneath the washing, here the two soldiers apparently intend that literal action; where for Willet and Joye baptism's spiritual power arises from its memory of Christ's death at Golgotha, here the soldiers perhaps wish to kill him again. "I cannot tell," he says. All is equivalent: soldiers fighting in great violence; the holy stories of the church. The wounded captain speaks as if devotion were made of metaphors, hollow and fluid, available for application to any object; they are without grace. This is precise demolition. The captain takes these images as only poetry, as convenient and colorful ways of describing war.

Here is the image of a disenchanted style of theater, in which plays prey upon the tropes of liturgy, borrowing and spending them without regard. The church's graceful words are transposed onto the graceless stage, and this moment might in turn stand as evidence for a reading of the larger relation between theater and liturgy: here we have a Shakespeare who takes from the Book of Common Prayer and hollows its phrases out. This might be a comforting model, as it would in the end celebrate Shakespeare's transcendent genius. It would imply that literature is the summation and liturgy its prompt. This seems to me unsatisfactory as it diminishes both. The prayer book was, as we have seen a great many times, an arena for controversy, both the product of disagreement and the occasion for more;

it was never still or fixed. Debate comprises it. This is its origin and its texture, and central to all liturgical debate is a complex working through of the relation between symbolic actions and literal effects, between what we do and what is done.

In traditional baptism the priest makes the sign of the cross over the infant's head; all versions of the Book of Common Prayer retain the practice. "We receive this child into the congregation of Christ's flock," explains the priest, "and do sign him with the sign of the cross, in token that hereafter he shall not be ashamed to confess the faith of Christ crucified, and manfully to fight under his banner against sin, the world, and the devil." John Jewel, among other first-generation reformers, insisted that the sign has no spiritual effect. "Whether the infant be signed with the sign of the cross," he explains in the *Treatise of the Sacraments*, "it maketh nothing to the virtue of the sacrament: they are no part thereof: without these the baptism is whole and perfect." This unenthusiastic defense failed to satisfy the Puritan opponents of the liturgy, for the instruction that the sign must be present surely confers sacred value upon it. "They do superstitiously and wickedly institute a new sacrament, which is proper to Christ only, marking the child in the forehead with a cross," the 1572 *Admonition to the Parliament* claimed, and the Millenary Petition presented to James before the Hampton Court Conference concurred. "The cross in baptism" it curtly notes, "as superfluous, may be taken away."[31]

At Hampton Court the Puritans objected to the sign of the cross first for its novelty. The bishop of Winchester in reply traced its use back to Constantine and, as Barlow recounts, James was convinced by this: "if it were then used, saith his Majesty, I see no reason, but that still we may continue it." But its history is too part of its problem. It was contaminated by use. "The *Cross* should be abandoned," argued Reynolds, the Puritan spokesman, "because, in the time of Popery, it had been superstitiously abused." The king replied in one of the ponderous jokes at the Puritans' expense that mark the royal style. "They used to wear hose & shoes in Popery," he observed "merrily": "therefore, you shall, now, go barefoot."[32]

This is only half of a defense. The sign's presence within the rite implies that it is needed there, and next the Puritans questioned its necessity. Here the conversation at the Conference—at least in Barlow's deeply partial report—was hurried along, with no pause to deliberate the paradox. James insisted that baptism is "fully and perfectly finished, before any mention of the *Cross* is made," which can only indicate that it is unnecessary but does not justify why it remains. The bishop of Winchester declared "a Church may institute and retain a sign significant," but the Puritan John Knewstub questioned this. If the church may add signs to the rite, he asked, then did this not limit the individual's "*Christian Liberty*?" This is perhaps the moment when the Puritans go too far, and James rushes to close. "I will have one Doctrine and one discipline, one Religion in substance and in ceremony," he declared: "therefore I charge you, never speak more to that point" (Barlow, 70–71).

The defense of the cross in baptism hinges upon what it is not. Its role remains mysterious; it looks outside itself, pregnant and evocative. Following the Hampton Court Conference the English Church issued a new set of canons in 1604. "The use of the sign of the cross in baptism, being thus purged from all popish superstition and error, and reduced in the Church of England to the primary institution of it," the canon sets out:

> we hold it the part of every private man, both minister and other, reverently to retain the true use of it prescribed by public authority: considering that things of themselves indifferent do in some sort alter their natures, when they are either commanded or forbidden by a lawful magistrate.[33]

The sign of the cross is in itself indifferent; since it has been commanded by the magistrate, it assumes some power. Such signs "in some sort alter their natures," explains the canon, but this is deliberately obscure. It is simply something more than immaterial to the rite. Martin Fotherby was chaplain to James, and his 1608 collection of *Four sermons, lately preached* includes a short pamphlet called "An answer unto certain objections of one unresolved, as concerning the use of the Crosse in Baptism." This had been composed, the title page explains, in 1604 and was now printed by royal command. In it Fotherby returns to the role of the cross in baptism, beginning with the redefinition of indifference. "Whosever disobeyeth the law of man," Fotherby writes, "commanding in things of indifferent nature, he therein transgresseth the law of God." The actions described in liturgy are not arbitrary. They contain some sanctity, some elements of grace because, as Fotherby warns, "not only sacraments, but also ceremonies too, ought to have their spiritual signification, of which if they be destitute, they utterly degenerate into vain and idle gesticulations."[34] The ceremony itself has value. If it did not, church rites would only be a dumbshow of vain and idle gestures, pointlessly repeated to no effect.

These are small episodes within a longer story. In the early years of the Reformation, the Edwardian church moved toward a stark and Calvinist model of devotion, and this was largely inherited by Elizabeth. The Jacobean church, however, was marked by an increasing regard for ceremony, and Fotherby's defense of "spiritual signification" expresses the more conservative sacramentalism of the early seventeenth-century church. The historian of religious practice and devotion Lori Anne Ferrell has traced the move of what she calls "an anti-Calvinist, sacramentalist minority" to "mainstream orthodoxy" in the Jacobean court. "James's England emerges," she writes, "not as a haven for religious consensus, but as the rhetorical laboratory for the development of an increasingly powerful and strident anti-Reformation politics."[35] The English Church first abandoned and then returned toward sacramental efficacy, and the Book of Common Prayer embodies each of these shifts. The sign of the cross is a scripted moment, a piece of liturgical theater, controversial not for the form of its gesture but for the ambiguity of its meaning. Inside the baptism rite is ambiguity over spiritual ambition; over the extent to which sacraments may produce the effects they describe.

"Here's a spot," announces Lady Macbeth, and she commands: "Out, damned spot!" The mark she finds and tries to wash is a reminder of the murder. "Here's the smell of the blood still," she says, and its trace will not quickly leave. "What, will these hands ne'er be clean?" she demands, and raves, "To bed, to bed. There's knocking at the gate." The closing homily in the rite for the solemnization of matrimony instructs:

> Ye husbands love your wives, even as Christ loved the Church, and hath given himself for it, to sanctify it, purging it in the fountain of water, through thy Word, that he might make it unto himself a glorious congregation, not having spot or wrinkle, or any such thing, but that it should be holy and blameless,

and here a "spot" is the sign of sin; the Communion for the Sick, which is the Anglican substitute for traditional last rites, wishes that "whensoever his soul shall depart from the body, it may be without spot presented unto thee," and a spot is that which may be washed away at baptism.[36]

This is the last time that we see Lady Macbeth on stage; we might by now recognize the pattern of her actions, for the play has taught us them. A washing, and an imagined knocking; the repeated keyword "spot." Here are the old actions and vocabulary of the baptism rite. Her speech recapitulates her earlier promises of washing, but where before the process was literal—"A little water clears us of this deed"—and the actions sure—"How easy it is then!"—now the same movements are empty. "Out, I say!" she commands: "One, two." The pieces are scrambled and she must fumble for their proper pattern. She repeats to herself, "Wash your hands." Ritual has for her become a script.

"What is it she does now?" asks the doctor: "Look how she rubs her hands." He is puzzled by these hollow gestures, and the gentlewoman explains, "I have seen her rise from her bed, throw her nightgown upon her, unlock her closet," for Lady Macbeth has done these things before. This audience of two, upon the stage, who watch and comment, remind us quite how strange this is, how odd and arbitrary, this panoply of gestures mimed to no effect. They remind us that this is all theater. The gentlewoman continues, "It is an accustomed action with her, to seem thus washing her hands" (5.1.23–25). Lady Macbeth repeats this because it is comforting, or because it is old, and the gentlewoman draws a careful distinction, as much for us as for the doctor. Lady Macbeth is not washing her hands, for even that phrase would imply the chance of success; rather, she is ghosting the action, she is only seeming thus. Her movements have no grace. Once she has left the stage, the doctor gives his diagnosis. "More she needs the divine than the physician," he observes (5.1.64). The power of cleaning that she seeks does not inhere in these physical forms.

We may choose to see the spiritual here, or we may pity the actions of a mad unhappy woman. A modern pathology might give us a differently clarifying vocabulary, might call this neurotic, an obsessive compulsive disorder; or we might see in her stuttered gestures a liturgical counterpart. The scene is necessarily double. One character hopes that actions carry grace, others look on in doubt. The theology was double: blurred, uncertain, strategically obscure, and running beneath much of the liturgical debate are the fears and the fantasies of what does not happen. The tension inside the rite is the drama of the play.

A child as he takes to speech is a king in language. The first talking is naming, and he lists each item of his world, careful, counting in nouns. His knowledge is its empire, his vocabulary its borders. When God first hands some power to Adam, as told in Genesis, he brings the animals to him, "to see how he would call them: for howsoever the man named the living creature, so was the name thereof" (2:19). The first human power is the power of naming.

"What is your name?" is the first question of the catechism in the rite for confirmation, and the child answers. "Who gave you this name?" is the second question. The child is supposed to reply: "My godfathers and godmothers in my Baptism, wherein I was made a member of Christ, the child of God, and an inheritor of the kingdom of heaven" (Cummings, 151). Names are how we identify ourselves but they do not make us unique; they are the gift of others, and they are shared. "We are men, my liege," the murderers tell Macbeth, and he replies:

> Ay, in the catalogue ye go for men,
> As hounds, and greyhounds, mongrels, spaniels, curs,
> Shoughs, water-rugs, and demi-wolves are clept
> All by the name of dogs. (3.1.92–96)

All are dogs, but many types fall within a single name. In Shakespeare's England a quarter of all men were called William.

The naming of a Christian begins at baptism but it ends at confirmation; there is a stutter in the rite, which begins with godparents. "Wilt thou be baptized in this faith?" asks the priest, and here addresses not the child but the godparents who have carried the child to the font, and they must reply, "That is my desire." The priest continues, "Grant that the old Adam in these children may be so buried, that the new man may be raised up in them." A new identity is given but it is borrowed. The prayer book instructs, "Then shall the priest take the child in his hands, and ask the name, and naming the child, shall dip it in the water," and again there is a blur here, a haze around the object. The priest asks the godparents for the name, which they must say aloud, so it is perhaps too simple to claim that the priest names the child, given that the godparents say it first. Names are not a sign of separateness; names are how we are bound. As Will Coster notes in his astonishingly thorough study of spiritual kinship, "some 90 percent of the children of late medieval English noblemen shared the names of one of their godparents," and this trend did not decline until the early seventeenth century. In the late sixteenth century, in the parish of St. Margaret's in York, "145 of 197 (78.7 percent) male children, and some 155 out of 161 (94.4 percent) female children were given the same name as a godparent."[1]

The baptism rite excludes the natural parents. The mother could not attend as she was confined at home for the ritual month of lying-in after childbirth, and the only father mentioned in the prayer book is the heavenly Father. According to Canon 29 of 1603, "no parent shall be urged to be present, nor be admitted to answer as godparent for his own child," and it is in answering, in their patterned responses, that godparents claim the center of this rite. They supplant the parents and speak for the children. "What can be more vain, foolish, and ridiculous?" demanded the puritan Henry Barrow, and called it "wicked and impious" that "popish gossips" [spiritual sponsors] should assume such a role. The Millenary Petition, shortly before the Hampton Court Conference, asked for the abolition of "interrogatories ministered to infants," and the 1572 Puritan *Admonition to the Parliament* described godparents as "childish and superstitious" for making promises "which is not in their power to perform."[2]

So far this is the familiar story, and one more Puritan objection to the traditional elements retained in the Book of Common Prayer. At the Hampton Court Conference, however, the chief opposition to the curiously doubled structure of baptism came not from the Puritan petitioners but from the king himself. On the first day, before the Puritans were permitted to enter, James opened with a speech; the fawning, Osric-like Barlow describes it as "a most grave and princely declaration of his general drift in calling this assembly." James called for clarification of the prayer book, beginning with a list of queries:

> First about *Confirmation*; first, for the name, for if arguing a confirm-
> ing of Baptism, as if this Sacrament without it, were of no validity,
> then it were blasphemous: Secondly, for the use, first brought upon
> this occasion; Infants being baptized, and answering by their *Patrini*,
> it was necessary they should be examined, when they came to years
> of discretion.

The bishops reply with a strategy repeated throughout the confer-ence: by misdirection, and by reference to the patristic church. They insist upon the "antiquity" and "lawful use" of confirmation. The bishop of Durham brings evidence from the gospels and suggests they might change the name to "an *Examination* with a *Confirma-tion*." They do everything, that is, but refer to James's central objec-tion to a baptism repeated at Confirmation, and a double answering by which godparents speak for speechless children and then later the child speaks for himself.

The conversation moves on to private baptism, held at home in the case of emergency, and now James recalls an argument he had, "14 months ago in *Scotland*." There "a pert Minister asked me, if I thought Baptism so necessary, that if it were omitted, the child should be damned?" This minster was challenging James for the assump-tion of baptismal efficacy, and James continues with his anecdote: "I answered him no: but if you, being called to baptize the child, though privately, should refuse to come, I think you shall be damned." The first day ends, and the second begins. The Puritan petitioners enter, and among their objections include "*Interrogatories in baptism, propounded to Infants,*" and here the bishops cite Augustine on the rite's history. But James remains unsatisfied; baptism troubles him like a scratch, and later he returns to it. In response to one Puritan complaint, James cut them off: "it smelled very rankly of *Anabaptism.*" They reminded him, that is, of the sect notorious for adult baptism and radically communal politics.[3] Baptism is a particular kingly care.

"What is thy name?" asks Young Siward, storming Dunsinane, late in *Macbeth*. He is an echo of the catechizing priest. But Macbeth pauses before responding. "Thou'lt be afraid to hear it," he replies. Macbeth is now in armor, perhaps unrecognizable. He is also a man of uncertain name. He is Macbeth, and Glamis, and Cawdor; he is also the king, and much of the play's plot is a procession through this sequence of names. Each haunts him. Returning from the first murder, of Duncan, he tells his wife a fantasy. "Methought I heard a voice cry," he describes:

> Still it cried, "Sleep no more" to all the house;
> "Glamis hath murdered sleep, and therefore Cawdor
> Shall sleep no more." (5.7.5–8; 2.2.33–41)

Here is a jumble for he is each of these, an incomplete, repeated man. "My name's Macbeth" he says, now just before his death.

"NO MORE THAT Thane of Cawdor shall deceive / Our bosom interest," declares Duncan, after the rebellion has been defeated. He strips the traitor of his title and grants it to another. "Go," he commands Ross, "with his former title greet Macbeth." Taken literally, Ross is ordered to address Macbeth by a new name, and in this action his status shall be transformed. When Ross comes to Macbeth in the following scene, he first greets him, "The king hath happily received, Macbeth, / The news of thy success," for this is as yet his name. He waits and only then reports, "He bade me, from him, call thee Thane of Cawdor" (1.2.63–65; 1.3.87–88, 103). He is cautious and the phrase awkwardly particular for it is doing work. Ross notes with care the origin of this power. "*He* bade me, from *him* . . ." he explains, redundant.

Kings name and kings are named; the power of one depends upon the power of the other. The coronation of an English monarch culminates in unction, the traditional and sacramental anointing of the monarch with oil, and then a blessing and the sign of the cross. This first ceremony of kingship is built upon traditional Roman practice, so coronation presents an awkward challenge to a Protestant monarch. Thomas Cranmer anointed Edward VI at his coronation on 20 February 1547 and then immediately followed the unction with a short, apologetic address in which he insisted, "The solemn rites of coronation have their ends and utility, yet neither direct force nor necessity," and "The oil, if added, is but a ceremony." The day after the coronation a violently anti-papal play was staged at court.[4] Elizabeth hid her face in a handkerchief during her own anointing and as the Venetian ambassador Giovanni Scaramelli noted on 4 June 1603 the accession of James opened again the troublesome issue. "The question of the Coronation is coming up," he reports, with slight glee at the tangle in which England finds itself:

> As anointing is a function appointed by God to mark the pre-eminence of Kings it cannot well be omitted, and they cannot make up their minds what expedient they should adopt. The people loath the priestly benediction be it in oil or in water, nor do they admit the sign of the cross except in baptism.

Unction is a new baptism: a second blessing, liquid placed upon the head, again the sign of the cross, and with its ceremonies it retains all the ambiguity and debate of the baptism rite.

The trouble with unction is that it promises transformation; it hints at the magic of the Roman Catholic forms. Scaramelli explains:

"The King is an ardent upholder of these objections, and he says that neither he nor any other king can have the power to heal scrofula, for the age of miracles is past, and God alone can work them." English and French kings traditionally claimed the power to cure scrofula in a rite of healing known as the king's touch or royal touch, the king's evil being the disease itself. The healing suggests that a human may harness divine power and turn it to a literal effect—cure a disease—and so opposes the reformed notion of a symbolic sacrament. As a petition presented to James before his coronation had insisted, "Healing the king's evil" is "a thing offensive and ridiculous in making some use of the Word of God as a charm." The simple solution might be to forgo this rite on theological grounds, and yet James decided otherwise. "However he will have the full ceremony," Scaramelli continues, "so as not to lose this prerogative, which belongs to the Kings of England as Kings of France."[5]

As the recusant Richard Broughton wrote in his *English Protestants Recantation*, a sacrament is a vehicle for power:

> That eternal visible ceremony, by imposition of hands upon ordinary men, whereby power is given them, above all others from Christ, to translate from darkness into glory, to make invisible grace of visible Elements, daily to give the holy Ghost, to dispose of the flesh, and blood of Christ, and giveth power which no potentate on earth, can give, and the like prerogatives, above all humane power, is to be esteemed a Sacrament.[6]

The description is dizzied and dizzying, and through it tolls one word: power. This wild and otherworldly force, far beyond that of any "potentate on earth," may be reserved for God but it may, too, be mobilized through the set phrases of the liturgical rite. Beyond the divide between traditional and reformed notions of sacramental efficacy lay this common ground—that liturgy was a point of access to great force.

It is a commonplace to say that this was an age of deeply held faith. It was certainly so, and one of the ways this world most resists our modern reading is in its conviction that devotion could explain all. Yet we must never let this diffuse faith cloud one simpler truth. At certain times the expression of belief is strategic; faith may be opportunistic, and nowhere more so than in the use of liturgical forms. We dismiss this age if we see its men only as holy fools. If there is a single constant in the story I am telling, it is that devotion may be used, may be turned to particular taste and occasion. It should not surprise us, then, that kings care for power, and that even an apparently Protestant king such as James should follow a Roman Catholic practice.

The first accounts of an English king touching for scrofula appear in twelfth-century histories of Edward the Confessor (1003–1066). According to William of Malmsbury and three anonymous clerical biographers, Edward dipped his hand in a vase of water and made the sign of the cross over a woman whose neck was swollen, and the swelling disappeared. The rite was always a political gesture. "The royal miracle stands out above all as the expression of a certain concept of supreme political power," writes the hugely influential French social historian Marc Bloch, and traces its development to the eleventh-century Gregorian reforms of the church. The Gregorian reformers "were trying to deprive kings of their pretended ecclesiastical character and reduce their functions in the church to those befitting a layman," and the royal touch, which displayed the unique and spiritual character of the monarch, was a useful reassertion of kingly might.[7]

The royal touch claims a special power and its vocabulary is liturgy. Henry VII introduced the set ceremony for the touch, and while his successors made minor changes it kept its basic shape. The rite was originally performed in Latin. Elizabeth was the first monarch to perform it in English. It begins with two readings from the gospels: from Mark, describing Christ blessing the children— "Suffer little children to come unto me," he says—and the opening lines of John; then the king or queen makes the sign of the cross, and gives a royal token to the sufferer. In each detail this is a loose copy of the baptism rite. The sign of the cross was traditional and contested, as we have seen; however, the same reading from Mark is kept in all versions of baptism in the Book of Common Prayer. The lines from the Gospel of John—"In the beginning was the Word and the Word was with God"—are part of the traditional baptism rite but were removed from the Book of Common Prayer due to their association with exorcism, and the phrase survives as the centerpiece of the Counter-Reformation exorcism rite.[8] The royal touch is a special baptism, unique to the king.

James first performed the touch in October 1603, three months before the Hampton Court Conference. He repeated it on 17 November 1604—the anniversary of Elizabeth's death—and again on 4 May 1606, each time with a single alteration to the conventional form. He did not perform the sign of the cross; instead he said the words from the gospels and gave the sufferer a gold coin.[9] This was his rite, and therefore his to edit; the gesture he retained in the prayer book he avoided here. If at Hampton Court James was particularly concerned with the proper form of baptism, this may simply be because he had been performing it himself.

A king who baptizes is a powerful, sacred king. The only scene in *Macbeth* to take place outside Scotland is at the court of the English king Edward. Malcolm and Macduff are in exile and discussing their homeland. "This tyrant, whose sole name blisters our tongues," says Malcolm: "He hath not touched you yet." Macbeth spreads disease, blisters with his touch. They are interrupted by the entrance of a doctor, who reports that Edward is curing the sick. "What's the disease he means?" asks Macduff and Malcolm explains:

'Tis called the Evil.
A most miraculous work in this good king,
Which often since my here-remain in England
I have seen him do. How he solicits heaven
Himself best knows, but strangely visited people
All swoll'n and ulcerous, pitiful to the eye,

The mere despair of surgery, he cures,
Hanging a golden stamp around their necks
Put on with holy prayers. (4.3.12–14, 147–55)

It is a curious and almost redundant scene. It has no bearing on the plot and often in stage productions is simply cut, but it is precisely when Shakespeare seems superfluous that we must pay closest attention. Here, "this good king" performs the royal touch by saying the lines from the gospel and by giving a golden coin, but with no mention of the sign of the cross. This is Edward, within the logic of the play, but he is performing the gesture as James, and a king is made sacred by the continuity of this miniature rite.

The play is suffused with metaphors of holy kingship; its sensibility is a vision of royal power. When Duncan is killed Macduff calls this "Most sacrilegious murder," and refers to the body as "The Lord's anointed temple." This is one more reminder of his unction and even Macbeth the murderer is caught up in the royalist frenzy. Macbeth describes the king's "silver skin laced with his golden blood / And his gashed stabs looked like a breach in nature," and the scandal of the killing of a king sends the whole country into sickness. It is a wounded, broken state, where day is night—"By th'clock 'tis day / And yet dark night strangles the travelling lamp"—and horses turn wild and flee from their stalls. "Bleed, bleed, poor country," Macduff despairs, of Scotland under Macbeth, and Malcolm concurs: "It weeps, it bleeds, and each day a new gash / Is added to her wounds." As they march on Dunsinane the Scottish lords under Malcolm describe themselves as "the med'cine of the sickly weal" for they come to heal.[10]

This was James's language too. As Patrick Collinson has noted, the image of a king as a spiritual physician was one of James's "favorite metaphors." In *Basilikon Doron*, the manual of statecraft that James wrote for his son, he describes a king as "a good Physician, who must first know what peccant humours his Patient naturally is most subject unto, before he can begin his cure" and goes on to describe the "natural sickness" of each of the estates: the church, the nobility, and the merchants. In calling for further reformation of the English liturgy the Millenary Petition flattered James by quoting this image. "The king, as a good physician, must first know what peccant humours his patient is most subject unto before he can begin his cure," the Puritans noted, and during the Hampton Court Conference James returned to this trope in what was perhaps intended as a humorous flourish. "His purpose therefore was, like a good Physician, to examine & try the complaints, and fully to remove the occasions thereof, if they prove scandalous, or to cure them, if they were dangerous," he declared.[11]

It is no coincidence that James paid particular attention to baptism at Hampton Court for royal power was constituted upon a baptismal model. The rite offers a vocabulary of phrases and metaphors through which to articulate power. Liturgy, however, is never a single story, and baptism hints too at the disruption of any worldly absolutism. The most resonant metaphor for royal power in this absolutist age was also perhaps the simplest—that of the king as father to his family, the state. As James wrote in his pamphlet *The True Law of Free Monarchies*

> The king towards his people is rightly compared to a father of children, and to a head of a body composed of diverse members. For as fathers the good Princes, & magistrates of the people of God acknowledged themselves to their subjects. And for all other well ruled common wealths, the stile of *Pater patriae* [father of his country] was ever, & is commonly used to kings.[12]

The play reminds us of this: Macduff twice describes Duncan as "Your royal father" to Malcolm (2.3.93; 4.3.108). More broadly the play literalizes the metaphor. Duncan, a father and a king, is killed by a wrongful king, Macbeth; this wrongful king, who has no children, is in turn succeeded by a rightful king who happens to be Duncan's son. The right king is also a father. At Hampton Court, James asked about godparents, but he did not use that term. Rather, he called them "Patrini," little fathers. He was watching, tracking the play of this image, its flow through the Book of Common Prayer. It is in a king's interest to assert the primacy of fathers, their place as stand-in gods.

The theology of baptism lightly challenges this metaphor. For Thomas Aquinas, baptism separates worldly and spiritual family. "Just as in carnal gestation a person is born of a father and a mother, in spiritual generation a person is born again a son of God as Father, and of the Church as mother," he wrote, and during the Reformation theologians glossed the rite as a break in the bloodline. For Thomas Becon, in his catechism, to be baptized was "to be admitted to the household of God," while for John Donne "to be baptized therefore into the name of Christ, is to be translated into his family." In closing the rite for public baptism the priest gives thanks "most merciful Father, that it hath pleased thee to regenerate this infant with thy Holy Spirit, to receive him for thy own child by adoption, and to incorporate him into thy holy congregation," and at each the narrative of a direct family process is disrupted. According to Will Coster, "the implicit concept of community presented in late medieval baptism was twofold. First, there were the acknowledged bonds of natural kinship, the legal affinity and sexual consubstantiality between parents and the 'blood' tie of consanguinity to the child," and here is the model of this, our world, "where rights of property and systems of hierarchy functioned and were sustained." There was however a rival to this, "a hidden, holy and in some ways ideal world, which paralleled the first."[13] Baptism promises transport from one world to the other; at baptism, our ties to human kings are tested.

At Hampton Court King James declared, "I will have one Doctrine and one discipline, one Religion in substance, and in ceremony," and at the close of the second day he threatened those who would not subscribe to the new prayer book. "I shall make them conform themselves," he said, "or I will harry them out of this land, or else do worse."[14] He who controls liturgy is powerful, but baptism resists this worldly power; it suggests other forces. All this is remembered beneath the surface of *Macbeth*: a parade of fears and symbols, the whole vocabulary and language of an absolutist vision of power; a whole babble of debate and claim, of metaphors proposed and unraveled, of kings as healers, kings as fathers, the family as a state. The play of guilt and the killing of a king is also a play of baptism, and we cannot quickly unstitch its thick texture of allusion; I think we are not meant to. When Macbeth returns from killing the king, his wife addresses him. "Had he not resembled / My father as he slept, I had done't" says Lady Macbeth (2.2.12–13).

"GO," DUNCAN COMMANDS Ross, "with his former title greet Macbeth." The king has stripped the traitor of his title but he is not quick enough. The witches get there first. "Hail to thee, Thane of Cawdor" they greet Macbeth, and by the time Ross meets him—"He bade me, from him, call thee Thane of Cawdor"—the king's news is old. There is no power in naming if you are not first. In the following scene Duncan nominates his successor—"We will establish our estate upon / Our eldest, Malcolm, whom we name hereafter / The Prince of Cumberland"—but the witches have already named their own heir to the throne of Scotland. "All hail Macbeth, that shalt be king hereafter," they told him. Kings and witches are struggling here over what shall be hereafter; they share the word and habit. Now Macbeth sends a letter to his wife, and it shows the same confusion. She reads aloud his account of meeting the witches: "Whiles I stood rapt in the wonder of it, came missives from the king who all-hailed me Thane of Cawdor, by which title before these weird sisters saluted me and referred me to the coming on of time, with 'Hail, king that shalt be.'"[15] The "missives from the king" are first Ross and Angus but the hasty syntax of Macbeth's report elides royal envoys into weird sisters: as the second clause turns to the third its subject slips because of "these." The missives were sent first, but the weird sisters first greeted him. The line suggests that the king sent the witches. Either they are doing his work, or he is doing theirs.

The witches do not quite belong. "Round about the cauldron go; / In the poisoned entrails throw," they chant, and in a play marked by great swathes of stately pentameter their stuttering mash of iambic and trochaic tetrameter might come from another world. They sing:

> Toad, that under cold stone
> Days and nights has thirty-one
> Sweltered venom sleeping got,
> Boil thou first i'th'charmed pot

and the rhyme is the only decorum (4.1.6–9). This verges upon nonsense, as if the form came first and the words were filled in later. The actual subject of the song—a poisonous toad that slept under a cold stone for a month—is so specific as to be absurd. What matters is the tone of rhyme and menace, the music of dark ritual.

That the witches sound different is a commonplace in criticism of the play. G. Wilson Knight in 1953 described "the weird note that characterizes the prophecies and incantations of the witches," and Terry Eagleton has more recently emphasized "their riddling, ambiguous speech," which makes them the "heroines" of the play: "their teasing word-play infiltrates and undermines Macbeth from within, revealing in him a lack which hollows his being into desire." This sense of strangeness, of difference, is central to more recent accounts of the authorship of the play. In his New Cambridge edition A. R. Braunmuller notes "the almost inarguable presence of one other author's writing in Folio *Macbeth*," and Gary Taylor includes this play in his 2007 edition of the collected works of Thomas Middleton. As Taylor explains, the play was written by both Shakespeare and Middleton. Eleven percent of the *Macbeth* we now have is what he calls "Middletonian or mixed writing," and he argues that Middleton adapted or revised the play in about 1616, and that he added 151 lines. The scenes that most show the signs of joint authorship are those involving the witches. Taylor hears Middleton in the first scene of the first act, in the ways the witches speak; Hecate's song in the third act and then return at the start of act 4 were, he argues, Middleton's. Not all agree. In response to Taylor's claims, and giving extensive stylistic analysis and paying particular attention to line-endings, Brian Vickers, Marina Tarlinskaya, and Marcus Dahl have insisted that "the claimed Middletonian additions to *Macbeth* look no different than the rest of the play."[16] This is at heart a debate about style: not so much whether this is Shakespeare as whether it is Shakespearean, as if the author were an adjective rather than a noun. They disagree over what sounds like what and over what a phrase recalls.

"When shall we three meet again?" begins the play, begins one witch, and from the first their central principle is repetition. They are familiar. "Fair is foul, and foul is fair" they chant and when Macbeth enters he declares, "So foul and fair a day I have not seen." They hail him as Glamis and they hail him as Cawdor and they hail him as "king hereafter," and when he returns to Dunsinane and enters to his wife she greets him: "Great Glamis, worthy Cawdor, / Greater than both by the all-hail hereafter," as if all were listening to one another, as if the world were one script (1.1.10; 1.3.36; 1.5.52–53). They are designed to sound almost like but not quite something else. "Double, double toil and trouble, / Fire burn and cauldron bubble," they chant, and they repeat this twice (4.1.10–11, 20–21, 35–36). They establish a sound from the first scene that never leaves the play; it lingers and is remembered, hovering through fog and filthy air, always half heard.

If all are quoting the witches then this suggests that the witches have some power, and in their chants they promise that there is much they may do. "I'll do, I'll do, and I'll do" sings the first witch. "The fables of witchcraft have taken so fast hold and deep root in the heart of man, that few or none (nowadays) with patience endure the hand of God" writes the Protestant Member of Parliament Reginald Scot in his *Discovery of Witchcraft* (1584): "Certainly, it is neither a witch, not devil, but glorious God that maketh the thunder."[17] It might be easy to believe in powerful witches but to do so is to muddle spiritual causation. We may believe that witches have powers only if we believe that forces other than God cause spiritual effects. As the Puritan preacher George Gifford insists in his *Discourse of the Subtle Practises of Devils by Witches and Sorcerers* (1587), "the devils are not able to create any thing, though never so small, much less those great things." All they may do is trick us, is exploit our credulity, and in his *Dialogue concerning Witches and Witchcrafts* (1593) Gifford explains that the devil is simply a good observer. "There be natural causes of torture and grief, of lameness, and of death in the bodies of man and beasts," he writes,

> which lie so hid and secure, that the learnedest of Physicians can not espy them, but the devil seeth them, and can conjecture very near the time, when they will take effect. Then doth he ply it, to bring the matter about that it may seem he did it.[18]

The devil and his allies claim a power they do not have.

Belief in witches feeds upon belief in the efficacy of the sacraments, and in particular the ceremonies of the baptism rite. Scot lists the charges held against witches. "They give their faith to the devil, and they worship and offer sacrifice unto him," he records, and "They sacrifice their own children to the devil before baptism." Their wickedness is sacramental. "They boil infants (after they have murthered them unbaptized) until their flesh be made potable," he reports, and "They eat the flesh and drink the blood of men and children openly." These are the crimes that many believe witches guilty of. They are also travesties of church rites, and Scot's point is not that the witches are wicked but that they are not real. Sacraments— their source of power—simply do not work like that. His target here is the belief and not the witches. The ceremony at which a witch is made, Scot explains, is commonly understood to reverse the effects of baptism, but this is hardly necessary. "I marvel at how they take on to preserve the water poured on them in baptism," he observes, with careful cynicism: "and yet I think it is commonly wiped and washed off, within four and twenty hours after baptism: but this agreeth with the residue of their folly." The folly is to believe that baptismal water has literal effect.

The scholar of Renaissance Italian literature Walter Stephens has explained witchcraft as "a countersacrament": "Witchcraft theory and Protestantism emerged between 1400 and 1600 as manifestations of the same crisis of confidence in the efficacy of the sacraments, that is, in the reality of their energies and effects." The Roman Catholic Church developed their theory of witchly power in response to popular heresies, which doubted the automatic efficacy of the sacraments. Witches would not only eat unbaptized children if baptism conferred no spiritual power, and so the witch in this inverted logic proves the truths of the traditional church. "On her shoulders," writes Stephens, "fell the task of defending the sacramental efficacy of baptism and, by extension, the goodness and providence of God."[19]

Witches may have their uses; they may do the king's work, and James himself wrote a book about witchcraft. In *Daemonologie* (1597), he describes witches who make things happen. "Witches can by the power of their master, cure or cast on diseases," he wrote and he famously believed that witches had caused the storms that nearly sank the boat in which he and his new queen were returning from Denmark in 1590. We cannot unravel this notion of effective witches from traditional conceptions of sacramental efficacy, and in *Daemonologie* James parades each of the traditional qualities that Scot had mocked. Witches, he writes, "have shaken off them the sacred Water of Baptism, and willfully refused the benefit thereof."[20] This runs against his own theology as expressed elsewhere—as shown in his nervous querying of the necessity and influence of the baptism rite at the Hampton Court Conference—and yet it serves one vision of royal power. Witches are the proof of an enchanted world. If they may cast or cure disease, then surely kings may, too.

The conventional priorities of a historically minded literary criticism run in one direction only. History is the ground, the backdrop, and while it may be complex those complexities serve in turn the purposes of the play. If the context is tense, then the play feeds upon tension; if the context is ambiguous, then the play may reflect doubt. The play becomes the reward for our schooling in a little history. History is what makes the play legible; history is the servant.

Until now I have tried to tell a story in one direction: the story of Shakespeare's apprenticeship by the Book of Common Prayer. We may trace a narrative of learning: how from the comedies of the mid-1590s he began to adopt its structures and its irresolution; how throughout he dwelled upon its hottest and most controversial moments; how as a dramatist in a society fixed by devotion he found a way to write plays that were both strangely familiar and wildly new; how his originality was at times bound, learned through a kind of puppet-work when characters for a moment say words that are not their own. *Macbeth* stands at the end of this. It is the finest product of one strand of his career, but if it is the apex it also is the evening. The plays written after this—*Antony and Cleopatra, The Winter's Tale, The Tempest*—show less imprint of liturgy. The Book of Common Prayer subsides as his most powerful source.

Macbeth borrows freely. The play like the king takes things that are not his—from the rite for marriage and the burial of the dead, from the Psalms and from Job, so that much liturgical language clusters beneath its surface. But the play depends most of all upon the baptism rite: both the pattern of its words and the structure of its associations, the particular linkages through which it imagines the world, so that kings are tied to doctors, witches to rites, washing to family. Until now I have taken liturgy to tell a story about the plays. But to see the prayer book as a simple source for *Macbeth* is too poor a read. They are too tightly bound. "I am in blood / Stepped so far that should I wade no more, / Returning were as tedious as go o'er," says Macbeth and the play, too, at times threatens to topple into liturgy (3.4.135–36). Its concerns are the concerns of liturgy, as are its vocabulary and actions; at times the two are indistinguishable, illegible without the other. The play is not simply immersed in the prayer book. Rather, it is beginning to tell a story about the power we admit to patterns of language and arrangements of ritual.

Macbeth begins in civil war and in its second scene a wounded captain brings news to the king of Scotland. He reports the state of battle, pauses exhausted, and Duncan commands: "Go get him surgeons" (1.2.44). We have a king and a wounded man; the king calls for another to help. Many scenes later in the play, the king of Scotland is again faced with civil war, and in his castle his wife is suffering. Now the king is Macbeth, and he turns to one of his attendants. "How does your patient, doctor?" he asks. "Not so sick," the doctor reports, "As she is troubled with think-coming fancies," and Macbeth commands, "Cure her of that" (5.3.39–42). Where the first is a simple sickness—the wounded soldier has been injured in battle, so his hurts are surface, of the flesh—the second is of a different quality, a trouble of the fancy. An action echoes, across time and character. We have a king who cannot cure, who calls another to heal, and the play makes the point by a division of characters: on stage both a king and doctor, apart.

There is no whole science by which to gauge literary affiliation; we must each decide whether we find these moments incidental or resonant. We each read how we will, and as Macbeth goes to exit, he offers his.

> If thou couldst, doctor, cast
> The water of my land, find her disease,
> And purge it to a sound and pristine health,
> I would applaud thee to the very echo
> That should applaud again.—Pull't off, I say!

he commands, as if he could not quite resist the metaphor between his unwell wife and suffering country (5.3.52–56). He makes injury political; he is not only a bad doctor but also a bad king, and his land is sick. The essence of liturgy is repetition and here as the action repeats it asks us to complete the echo. James believed that kings could cure and those Puritans who petitioned him before the Hampton Court Conference held this as superstition. The idea of a healing king, they wrote, is "a thing offensive and ridiculous in making some use of the Word of God as a charm," and the play becomes an arena for the struggle between beliefs. Liturgy gives us no safe base from which to judge the play; the play rather reveals the flexibility of all liturgical positions. If we believe that kings are healers, then these are wrongful kings; if we do not then we see the absurd superstition. If we believe that witches have power then we see the need for kings, and at each point the play returns us to liturgy.

We are in the chamber only of what is seen and heard. The play presents one healing monarch, "the most pious Edward," "the holy king." "Sanctity hath heaven given his hand," reports one more doctor and Malcolm explains, " 'tis spoken / To the succeeding royalty he leaves / The healing benediction" (3.6.27, 30; 4.3.145, 156–57). The royal cure is described but the ritual kept off stage; we never meet Edward, nor see him heal, and here in miniature is an effect we have seen so often before. The church rite is remembered and absent. The ritual leaves behind its shadow, its skeleton. An imprint remains like a scar, a déjà vu, like the sound of fears, and what seemed corporal melted, as breath into the wind.

Here, then, are the elements of Shakespeare's last reckoning with liturgy. For kings and dramatists, church ritual is opportunity: a weighted, tense symbolic language that promises access to great power. For each, it is remembered beneath the surface of action: when a king kneels or heals, when a character goes to wash her hands or to mourn the dead in set phrases. In each of these Shakespeare binds his plays to liturgy, but in *Macbeth* he succeeds from its forms. In doubling and redoubling, the play explodes any decorum of liturgical order. The Act for the Uniformity of Service and Administration of the Sacraments was printed at the front of prayer books to remind all that it is illegal to "in any interludes, plays, songs, rhymes, or by other open words, declare or speak anything in the derogation, depraving, or despising of the same book," and the witches are not precisely this. They are rhythmic and nasty; they sing and offend. "Pour in sow's blood, that hath eaten / Her nine farrow; grease that's sweaten / From the murderer's gibbet throw / Into the flame," one sings and all reply, "Come high or low" (4.1.80–83). In their chants the play approaches countersacrament. They parody the hope that in rites we might find order, and mock in repetition all that kings have said, all that priests may promise, and they are therefore at the end of Shakespeare's great engagement with the Book of Common Prayer. He can go no farther.

BAPTISM IS A ritual of what anthropologists call fictive kinship. It arranges a new family, apart from the ties of blood. At confirmation the child affirms those spiritual bonds that were first set at baptism, before he could speak or choose. Godparents replace parents, a physical washing recalls a spiritual one, and the rite upon these stages builds up to a grand analogy. In closing, the priest exhorts the godparents to remember "that baptism doth represent unto us our profession, which is to follow the example of our Savior Christ, and to be made like unto him, that as he died and rose again for us, so should we which are baptized die from sin, and rise again unto righteousness" (Cummings, 149). Baptism is a ceremony of resemblance. It draws together disparate things and suggests that devotion is the acceptance of their similarity. It is a dance of metaphors, a style of symbolic thinking, and one might with only slight exaggeration describe all that I have done here as an act of fictive kinship. I have proceeded, throughout this book, by asserting the resemblances between patterns of language and action. I have speculated about cause and effect, and at all times emphasized familiarity.

This play attracts a particular style of associative thinking. Shakespeare wrote *Macbeth*, lectures Stephen Daedelus in the library, "with the coming to the throne of a Scotch philosophaster with a turn for witchroasting."[21] The scene is of course in James Joyce's wild novel *Ulysses* (1922), and nobody since has been able to resist the same association. Shakespeare wrote a play about witches and Scottish kings just as a Scottish king who was scared of witches arrived on the English throne. Criticism of the play has been ruled by an elegantly circular argument: because the play is so ostenta-tiously topical, ostentatious topicality must be its point. As criticism this hinges upon a faith in similarity. One Scottish king is like another, a stage battle is a symbol. Resemblance does the work of argument, and analogy becomes analysis.

In *The Royal Play of Macbeth* (1948) Henry N. Paul quotes Mal-colm's account of the holy king Edward and his healing touch, and notes with sour dismay: "It would be hard to point to any passage in the plays of Shakespeare more irrelevant to the drama." This is a puzzle—Shakespeare cannot be irrelevant; and so Paul continues, presenting his conclusion as a neutral observation in the second half of the sentence, "and more obviously intended to serve some topical interest." Paul sketches some of the same context I have given above—James was reluctant at first to perform the royal touch, but in time did so—and concludes that Shakespeare must, in writing the play, have been prompted by some royal councilors who wished to "bring the king to their way of thinking concerning the royal touch." This is a strict story of cause and effect, and the dramatic imagination. We have a biddable Shakespeare, literal-minded, obe-dient; we have some shadowy councilors, whispering behind an arras. Even as the scenario suggests that Shakespeare had little con-trol over his own plays, it also implies that his plays were powerful political tools, capable of convincing the king. This is biography dressing up as history and the play is made equivalent to its context. There is no gap between the two. "The entire play," concludes Paul, is "a compliment to the king."[22]

These are the fictions of a particular season. As Alvin Kernan nar-rates in *Shakespeare, The King's Playwright* (1995), the King's Men were at Greenwich in late July 1606. Christian of Denmark was vis-iting James, and the players performed twice before the pair of kings. On 5 August, the royal party heard Lancelot Andrewes preach upon the text, "It is He that giveth salvation unto Kings," and two days later the royal party went upriver to Hampton Court where they saw a play that evening. "It is most likely," Kernan writes, "that the play on this latter occasion was *Macbeth*," and the claim is followed by one name in parenthesis: "(Paul)." Once the timing has been established more certain assertions follow. *Macbeth* "was probably written especially for this occasion," Kernan notes, and a play written for a king is surely royalist. The play was designed to flatter James's "cult of divine right," and as a whole it represents "the synthesizing work of the propagandist."[23] There is a mighty single-mindedness to this reading of the play. Surely Duncan, constantly asking questions, is shown as weak? It is, however, dictated by Kernan's understanding of the relation between theater and political power. The playwright bids for kingly approval even at the expense of the play itself. The play is best seen, notes Kernan, as "basic patronage work" and a "consummate piece of patronage art."

It is perhaps too tempting to hear history in this play, to see the play as troublingly, provocatively close to the court. Braunmuller notes that "Nothing stronger than hypothesis and circumstantial evidence joins *Macbeth* with either James's accession or Christian's visit," but the play is dominated by a reading bound to time. Literary critics and historians assume in passing that what explains the play is its royal context. We see this habit when one study notes that the play uses "concepts and rhetoric made topical by James' accession in order to make political points about kingship as such," and equally when an historian observes, "*Macbeth* was first performed shortly after the accession of James I, and many critics have speculated about the local political meanings that may have been placed upon it," and, as if she cannot help herself, she tumbles into speculation: "Perhaps one of these could have been derived from the fact that James had himself believed that he was under attack from witches in league with the devil."[24] Some read the play for its resistance of royal power: for its emphasis upon "the vulnerability of sacred kingship" or the implicit republicanism the play retains from its sources, or as a response to James' lavish bestowal of titles shortly after accession.[25] All concur that what sets this play apart from any other by Shakespeare is its particular involvement in the courtly politics of a moment.

I do not wish here to propose a new date of composition for the play; all the available evidence agrees that it was finished at the latest by the end of 1606. But beneath the confidence that this play is the product of the politics of this moment lies a separate and unexamined assertion: that Shakespeare, always cautious, always wary of engagement, chose now to write a wildly controversial play. He took a great deal—perhaps more than we can reckon up, more than we can recover—from the Book of Common Prayer, and this at heart imagines the story of a life. It is deeply concerned with time and its passing for it marks the thresholds of the journey it imagines we all take. From baptism through confirmation, then marriage and a funeral, each punctuated by Communion, our progress is its pattern. It is a work of and about human time, both a record and a template. At the Hampton Court Conference, liturgy assumed a different style of topicality. Here debate over the prayer book's language was simultaneously argument over politics: the arrangement and institution of the state embodied in a turn of phrase. At the start of his study *Shakespeare's Language* (2000) Frank Kermode pauses to dismiss the "presumptuous" notion that "to make sense of Shakespeare we need first to see the plays as involved in the political discourse of his day." He continues by insisting that attention to contemporary politics can only distract us from the real object of study: "Shakespeare's words, which are, as I say, only rarely invoked."[26] The Conference showed this to be a false opposition. There, the king and bishops paid tight attention to language; there the great force of words themselves was cautiously surveyed. This is the time of *Macbeth*.

We may take one more step. There is a deeper network of liturgical logic beneath the play, a skeleton of lovely links and associations. The play is about the relation between politics and morals, and about their divorce; about reading the spiritual kingdom in the political, and what it means to be an heir to one but not the other. In the baptism rite we fight as "Christ's faithful soldier" and are made "inheritor of thine everlasting kingdom." Its language is the language of worldly politics but it points toward another state, and the baptism rite is about the transport between those worlds. It is the only Anglican sacrament to promise transformation, to touch upon the old medieval magic; this is why it was so feared and followed by kings and this is why in the play the spirit world comes so whisperingly close, threatening, shaking its gory locks, riddling upon the heath. The play is built upon the concerns of baptismal liturgy and its controversies. It invites and then thwarts any political reading. Baptism asks a reckoning with the world, our world and the next. It is the drama of affinity: of the bonds of duty and the bonds of faith and the bonds of the state. It strains how we imagine each affiliation. "Cancel and tear to pieces that great bond / Which keeps me pale," says Macbeth.[27]

It is anachronism to isolate Elizabethan and Jacobean politics from the Book of Common Prayer. Royal power in this period was a story about baptism, and the liturgy and theology of baptism tell a story about power. The two are twinned and together make the foundation for this play, and this is in turn the play which gives literature its greatest metaphor for the perils of attachment. The wounded captain reports to Duncan the state of battle: "Doubtful it stood, / As two spent swimmers that do cling together / And choke their art" (1.2.7–9). There is danger in this image, and beauty too. There is no way to tell between the soldiers, between the warring men; no way to read apart the strands of battle here; there is no way to unravel the strands of this play, when liturgy echoes civil war, when murder is a ritual. Its art—and this is an old term, out of fashion now in literary criticism, but one that still may do some work for us—is the art of association, of analogy, of affiliation. The power of the throne is the power of the rite; the power of the rite is the power of the play.

THE PLAY ENDS in a flurry of echo, a parting resonance, and its closing ceremony begins the succession of one order by another. "Hail, king of Scotland," declares Macduff and all repeat, "Hail, King of Scotland." He is greeting Malcolm, but he has in his hands another king.

He entered only lines before with this same greeting—"Hail, king, for so thou art"—and as the stage direction explains, "with Macbeth's head." Each naming is a doubling and every time a stutter in the rite. "Behold," he says, "Th'usurper's cursed head. The time is free" (5.11.20–25). Surely by now we are wise to these moves, and ready for the reference; Shakespeare has by now trained us as readers. "Hail, King of Scotland," say the lords and attendants, and as they do so behind them whisper the witches: "All hail Macbeth, that shalt be king hereafter." Each phrase is a palimpsest, too stuffed with history. All is familiar.

The king is named and then he names. "My thanes and kinsmen," he commands: "Henceforth be earls, the first that ever Scotland / In such an honour named." Thanes now are earls, and here he gives Macbeth one more name too. He has been Glamis and he has been Cawdor, and he has been king, but Malcolm now points to the corpse and calls him "This dead butcher." In naming he asserts an order but also more than this. He promises the possibility of order in this broken place. In the play's final lines Malcolm vows to redress the troubles of his kingdom:

> this and what needful else
> That calls upon us, by the grace of Grace
> We will perform in measure, time, and place.
> So, thanks to all at once and to each one,
> Whom we invite to see us crowned at Scone (5.11.28–30, 35,
>   37–41).

Kingship is ritual. He will perform the proper actions "in measure, time, and place"; and he will be crowned, will take unction and assume all the liturgical force that underpins a king.

Inside the command is a promise, and perhaps as this comes at the end there is a valediction too. Here are some of the things that the Book of Common Prayer gave Shakespeare: a poetry and web of association, a vocabulary and a bundle of gestures; ways in which to walk, and measure, time, and place; the idea of order and the means for its undoing; a pattern of many things and through them all a fine thread running, fair and dark. Here he says farewell. After this his plays shed the particular liturgical density and resonance of this time. His concern turns to the drama and consequences of fading marriages, not their union, and to growing old. He still will write of young lovers meeting, until the end, but they will not be bound in elaborate formality; he still will write of grief, but it will slip from set expression. His uses of liturgy were momentary, only as solid as an echo. They fade from us and they fade from the plays. But for a time at the closing of Elizabeth's reign and the start of the new king James, the Book of Common Prayer was at the heart of Shakespeare's imagination.

Perhaps *Macbeth* was first performed for an audience of kings at Hampton Court Palace in August 1606. Like so much in Shakespeare, we cannot wholly know. But we can be sure that this playwright knew perfectly the book that was the most controversial and adored of his lifetime. If we place Shakespeare and the Book of Common Prayer back in close relation, some sparks from the rub between these two may throw a light that will permit us to see both anew.

EPILOGUE ❧ *Five or Six Words*

T he beginning of the ending of the Book of Common Prayer was 4 January 1645. "The Lords and Commons assembled in Parliament, taking into serious consideration the manifold inconveniencies that have arisen by the Book of Common-Prayer in this Kingdome," begins the government ordinance issued on that day:

> and resolving, according to their Covenant, to reform Religion according to the Word of God, and the Example of the best Reformed Churches, have consulted with the Reverend, Pious, and Learned Divines called together to that purpose; And do judge it necessary, that the said Book of Common Prayer be abolished.

I have been tracking here those "manifold inconveniencies": all the strange rich flourish of debate and theater that flowed from the Book of Common Prayer, which was provoked by liturgy into being, in Elizabethan and in Jacobean England, a blush upon the stern face of the church. The ordinance continues, "The said Book of Common-Prayer, shall not remain, or be from henceforth used in any Church, Chapel, or place of public Worship, within the Kingdome," it instructs, and in the shift of verbs is a little ontological uncertainty.[1] This prayer book is a practice that may be "abolished"; it is an object that "remains"; it is a tool that may be "used." It is each of these and while the ordinance strains to describe it the Book of Common Prayer slips quietly from grasp.

"By 1641," notes Timothy Rosendale, "reconciliation between the royalist, Anglican, liturgical right and the parliamentary, Puritan left seemed all but impossible." These were precisely the two sides who met at Hampton Court, and we might view the English Civil War as the failure of the Hampton Court Conference. The struggle divided over liturgy. By now, popular attachment to the once-controversial Book of Common Prayer was deep and widespread, but parliament sought to end it through prohibitions and penalties stricter than those previously imposed upon Puritans and non-conformists by the church. Possession of the prayer book became an offense.[2] In the ordinance abolishing the prayer book, the parliamentarians present themselves explicitly as the heirs to earlier Puritans. The ordinance calls for "further Reformation," and lists a sequence of by-now-familiar complaints against the orthodox liturgy. "Long and sad Experience hath made it manifest, That the Liturgy used in the Church of England (notwithstanding all the pains and Religious intentions of the Compilers of it) hath proved an offence," they note with apparent reluctance, but go on to emphasize "the many unprofitable and burdensome Ceremonies, contained in it." Above all it failed to be *common* prayer, for "Sundry good Christians have been by the means thereof, kept from the Lords Table, and divers able and faithful Ministers debarred from the Exercise of their Ministry."[3]

In the place of the prayer book the ordinance here introduces the *Directory of Public Worship*. This is not a new liturgy; it is a new conception of liturgy. The *Directory* suggests but does not define public worship. Under this order, the cycle of services and set forms of prayer are built upon a combination of readings from the Bible and sermons. It instructs the minister in broad rubrics, laying out instructions to follow but not set forms, and in so doing it isolates common prayer from any prayer book. At baptism, for example, the *Directory* explains that "the Minister is to use some words of Instruction, touching the Institution, Nature, Use and ends of this Sacrament," but does not define what those must be. "He is also to admonish all that are present," it continues, "to look back to their Baptism; to repent of their sins against the Covenant with God, to stir up their faith," but again these are suggestions in the place of a script ("An Ordinance for taking away the Book of Common Prayer," 594–95). At the funeral all is barer still. "When any person departeth this life, let the dead body, upon the day of Burial, be decently attended from the house to the place appointed for Public Burial," it commands, "and there immediately interred without any Ceremony" (604). "What ceremony else?" demands the anguished Laertes. The single moment of set language in the *Directory* is at the marriage rite.

"O lamentable!" wailed one pamphlet in response. Called *A Dirge for the Directory, Written by one of King James ancient Protestants*, it continues:

> what times do we live in? when the Church is without true discipline, Gods Laws quite taken from us, no Lords Prayer, no Creed, no Common Prayer allowed, but Master *Presbyter* to do as his fickle brain serves him, the sacrament of the Lords Supper not administered once in half a year, and when it is delivered wonderful out of order it is; the Sacrament of Baptism celebrated as any would have it that is in fee with Master Parson; the dead body buried with five or six words at the most.[4]

It is easy to strike a note of nostalgia, to mourn the lost cadences and to tell a story of cultural diminishment. The politics of such a move are royalist, conservative, and my concern in tracing here that which was lost is not, I hope, sentimental. Rather, it is with the shift in the relation of dramatic word and gesture and between language and faith. The pamphlet laments that a burial may be performed in "five or six words," and the sadness here is not only that they are few; it is that they are variable, that they are casual, five *or* six. "The Minister is to pray to this or the like effect," the *Directory* instructs. "All which he is to endeavour to perform with suitable affections answerable to such an holy Action, and to stir up the like in the people" ("An Ordinance," 595, 598). Without the particular orchestration of word and gesture, there is no possibility of parody, and this is why the *Directory* does not include a ruling at the start against the appropriation or mockery of its contents. Parody requires specificity, familiarity, and tension; once we remove all this, there is no chance of theater. Where the Book of Common Prayer established roles for the congregation— their responses and movements, their involvement—the *Directory* is addressed only to the minister. It is his book, not theirs, and so surviving copies of the *Directory* tend to be perfectly clean. They are not worn by the passage of hands, not debated nor inscribed. They have no annotations for they have not passed through history.

During the Interregnum (1642–60) the Book of Common Prayer was banned, but this did not finish its use. The historian John Morrill estimates that more churches held onto the Book of Common Prayer than took up the *Directory*, and there was growing use during the 1650s. By 1659, dispossessed Anglican ministers were returning to their old churches and leading service according to the Book of Common Prayer. In April 1661, Charles II was crowned at Westminster Abbey, and in December parliament passed the Corporation Act, which dictated that all municipal office holders must receive Anglican Communion.[5] That month, at the Savoy Conference, Presbyterians met with Anglican bishops to discuss the new form the liturgy should take. The puritans objected to the usual areas— the sign of the cross, the use of the ring in the marriage service, and the word "worship"—and they were overruled. "And thus the conference ended without any accommodation," noted the royal proclamation. On 19 May 1662 the Act of Uniformity reinstated the Book of Common Prayer as the official liturgy of the English Church. The 1662 prayer book was very largely the same form as that of 1604—and therefore in turn the liturgy of 1559—although was slightly more traditional in its theology. The Communion service once more included the commemoration of the dead; a service for the baptism of adults was added, and no longer did a newly married couple have to receive Communion on the day of their solemnization. Its strictness is most clear in one simple addition. Now, for the first time, every clergyman in England was ordered to stand in front of his congregation and announce: "I do here declare my unfeigned assent, and consent to all, and every thing contained, and prescribed in and by the book entitled, The Book of Common Prayer."[6]

Any history that takes as its center the Book of Common Prayer must inevitably become as much a catalogue of the fictions told about the prayer book as an account of actual liturgical practice. At each appearance, from 1549 on, the prayer book announces itself in relation to a past of disappointing liturgical use. According to the Act of Uniformity of May 1662, "by the great and scandalous neglect of ministers in using the said liturgy or order so set forth and enjoined as aforesaid, great mischiefs and inconveniences, during the time of the late unhappy troubles, have arisen and grown." There is a surprising narcissism here—as if the lack of Book of Common Prayer caused the Civil War—but it is the necessary counterpoint to the following optimism. "Nothing conduces more to the settling of the peace of this nation (which is desired of all men), nor to the honour of our religion, and the propagation thereof," claims the act, "than an universal agreement in the public worship of Almighty God" ("Act of Uniformity," 601). This is the oldest fantasy of liturgy: That there ever was or might be universal agreement, or that all men might fold their worships inside the narrows of a single form, and while the fiction might have persuaded some in 1549, or 1552, or even 1559, precisely what the *Directory* ended was this faith in form. In its vagueness and variation it broke the link between set text and salvation, and after this it could not be convincingly restored. In April 1687, twenty-five years after the restoration of the king and Book of Common Prayer, and shortly before he abdicated the throne, James II issued his Declaration of Indulgence. It promised to all subjects "the free exercise of their religion," and suspended all penalties for nonconformity. The act explains this measure as the only reasonable lesson of the history of the prayer book. "After all the frequent and pressing endeavours that were used to reduce this kingdom to an exact degree of conformity in religion, it is visible the success has not answered the design, and that the difficulty is inevitable," it notes in resignation.[7] A carefully circumscribed toleration was in turn enshrined as law by the Act of Toleration in 1689, which repealed the penalties for dissent and permitted "some ease to scrupulous Consciences in the Exercise of Religion" in the hope that this "may be an effectual means to unite their Majesties Protestant Subjects in Interest and Affection."[8]

The 1662 Book of Common Prayer remains today the official liturgy of the Church of England. It is not, however, the only form that the church permits. The Act of Toleration promised "some ease" in patterns of worship, and then in 1928 the Church proposed a sequence of alternative liturgies—not to replace the 1662 prayer book but to stand alongside it. This is a radically new conception of liturgy, but it is the direct consequence of toleration, which was in turn made inevitable by the *Directory of Public Worship*. Each law steps yet farther from any force of form. Parliament rejected the Church's plan until 1965, when they passed the Alternative and Other Services Measure, and the following year the Church adopted a set of alternative liturgical forms, known as "Series One." In 1974, under the terms of the Church of England Worship and Doctrine Measure, parliament granted to the Church of England permanent authority to introduce new forms of service, and in return the Church agreed to the permanent protection of the 1662 prayer book. The 1662 Book of Common Prayer can only ever now be one of several. In 1980 the Church introduced the first full new rival liturgy, the Alternative Service Book.

We have seen the phases of this struggle at each and every step. Perhaps this is the single continuity of the prayer book's history: the struggle over who controls its shape, who has the right to dictate its inclusions, and who is allowed to place upon it a limit. We see it in the prefaces and the Acts of Uniformity. We see it just as powerfully in the penalties for parody—one hundred marks for the first offence, in 1559—as when Elizabeth Lettisham finds a love letter in the margin of her liturgy, or when Timothy Levett uses his copy to learn maths. I have argued that we see it when Shakespeare writes *Macbeth*. This is simply the most beautiful of all human responses to the liturgy, but it is of the same kind as marginal scribbles and royal decrees, only an infinitely higher degree of intensity and craft. We see it each time a worshipper has said the words, and in the end it does not matter whether that worshipper stands in an English church and is marrying now or if he is an actor playing Orlando; what matters is the voice that says the lines, and each time this is different. The history of the Book of Common Prayer is no history of perfect form, and nor is it even most meaningfully a history of uniform worship; but it is the history of ideas about and appropriations of each of these, and above all it is a history of response. As the Bishop of Winchester wrote in the early 1990s, in a collection of essays discussing the future of liturgical revision: "there never was as much common prayer in the past as we sometimes now imagine."[9] The prayer book was only ever completed in the variation of individual use.

Now, common prayer takes a thousand forms. On the first Sunday of Advent in 2000 the Church of England introduced a new set of liturgies. This is a project rather than a prayer book: Common Worship is available as a series of books or on a website, and it is composed of a collection of possible pieces from which congregation and ministers may assemble the service they choose. The rites are now a forest of options, and many paths may be taken. At the burial of the dead, "The minister introduces the service in these or other suitable words," and "may say one of these prayers." "A hymn may be sung," "Silence may be kept," and there are two available versions of the Lord's Prayer. All is delicate, careful; nothing is set or fixed. At a wedding the priest may first address the congregation like this: "In the presence of God, Father, Son and Holy Spirit, we have come together to witness the marriage of N. and N., to pray for God's blessing on them, to share their joy and to celebrate their love." He may begin with something simpler: "We have come together in the presence of God, to witness the marriage of N and N, to ask his blessing on them, and to share in their joy." He may also repeat the traditional phrases as preserved in the 1662 version: "Dearly beloved, we are gathered together here in the sight of God, and in the face of this congregation, to join together this Man and this Woman in holy Matrimony."[10] All the versions hold in common a pool of vocabulary, phrases, and movements, but with the possibility of choice each of these has lost its heat.

Some of the change is perhaps best described as translation. In the 1559 Book of Common Prayer, at the burial, the priest declares, "Man that is born of a woman hath but a short time to live, and is full of misery. He cometh up and is cut down like a flower; he flieth as it were a shadow, and never continueth in one stay. In the midst of life we be in death," and this becomes, in one of the possible matching prayers in Common Worship, "We have but a short time to live. Like a flower we blossom and then wither; like a shadow we flee and never stay. In the midst of life we are in death." This keeps the major images but simplifies them; and it keeps the hendiadys of the earlier version, the doubling back and forth by which the sentences balance within themselves. It is too conservative to say that in this translation what is lost is poetry, for it retains the same techniques and form, and yet absent from Common Worship is the strictness of its predecessor. There is no mention now of "misery," the condition in which we live, and now man is not cut down but rather we wither, and here perhaps is the distinctive change. Now it is "we" where previously it was "he," and beyond the obvious point about male and female pronouns here is a quiet transformation. The rite was once about a single representative figure—and at a burial this is inevitably the body in the ground—and now it looks out at all the congregation. We make this liturgy as we will and in turn it describes us.

In the beginning was the Book of Common Prayer, but this was built of older works and from its first issue in 1549 it was given into the hands of worshippers who fought and contested it. Liturgy lives only in the voices and actions of a thousand others, and so Common Worship sits at the end of all this story. It is a history of the tugs of use and the turbulence of worship; of adaptation and revision, the great and strange flowering of liturgical poetics from thumbprints and genealogies in the margins of prayer books to the plays of Shakespeare. Common Worship finishes what the Book of Common Prayer began. It enshrines the process of abdication, when each takes to himself the words of faith and reworks them into something new yet old, pious and profane. "See," wrote Shakespeare, long ago, "a book of prayer in his hand." He is instructing us to look at one great and defining practice of his moment, and then he puts it down. Perhaps the only final proof of all that I have written here would be if we were to discover Shakespeare's own annotated copy of the Book of Common Prayer. But among the paper mountains of the records from his time, there is no trace of this. We do not have his prayer book. Instead, we have the plays.

Acknowledgments

This book began as a PhD dissertation, and has been many years in the preparation. I'd like first to thank two teachers of mine, who taught me a very great deal about Shakespeare, early modern religious debate, and how to write and think about the two: Peter McCullough at Lincoln College, Oxford, and James Shapiro at Columbia University.

Molly Murray and Alan Stewart at Columbia, and Richard McCoy at the CUNY Graduate Center were generous, insightful readers; I owe particular gratitude to David Scott Kastan. At Columbia, I benefited greatly from the advice and friendship of Tom Festa, Karl Saddlemire, Stefanie Sobelle, Andrew Tumminia, and Tiffany Werth.

Much of this was written while on sabbatical from Skidmore College. I would like to thank my colleagues in the English department, and particularly April Bernard. I am grateful to Michelle Aldredge and The MacDowell Colony, where I very happily wrote a section of this book, and to the Whiting Foundation and the Folger Shakespeare Library, who supplied very generous fellowships during the research. David Bevington and Jonathan Bate were expert second readers.

I would also like to thank David Godwin and—at Oxford University Press—my editor, Tim Bent, and his assistant, Keely Latcham. I am deeply grateful to my parents for their support.

Notes

Abbreviations

BL	British Library
BOD	Bodleian Library, Oxford
CSP	Calendar of State Papers
CUL	Cambridge University Library
EETS	The Early English Texts Society
F	Folio
f	folio page
HMSO	Her Majesty's Stationery Office
NA	The National Archives, London
NYPL	New York Public Library
Q	Quarto
r	recto
SPCK	The Society for Promoting Christian Knowledge
v	verso

Documentation of sixteenth- and seventeenth-century sources refer to archival/ library systems: capital letters indicate the page signature when a volume does not have page numbers. Authors' names in abbreviated forms often appear on the source title page (Ste B, for example). Roman numerals refer to the volume number or the page number within a stated volume. Other abbreviations (Rel, Adv, and the like) are call letters given by various archives and libraries. Because early texts predate the Dewey decimal system, each library has its own system of arranging these pre-eighteenth-century sources.

Prologue

1. John Stow, *The Annals of England* (London, 1605), 1425.

2. Edward Cardwell, *A History of Conferences and Other Proceedings Connected with the Revision of the Book of Common Prayer* (Oxford: Oxford University Press, 1849), 161; Patrick Collinson, "The Jacobean Religious Settlement," in *Before the English Civil War: Essays on Early Stuart Government and Politics*, ed. Howard Tomlinson (London: Macmillan, 1984), 40.

3. Ernest Law, *The History of Hampton Court Palace* (London: George Bell and Sons, 1885), 2:12–30; J. T. Murray, *English Dramatic Companies 1558–1642* (London:

Constable, 1910), 1:146–49; F. P. Wilson, *The Plague in Shakespeare's London* (Oxford: Clarendon Press, 1927), 85–113; Alvin Kernan, *Shakespeare, the King's Playwright: Theater in the Stuart Court, 1603–1613* (New Haven, CT: Yale University Press, 1995), 27, 29.

4. Peter Cunningham, ed., *Extracts from the Accounts of the Revels at Court in the Reigns of Queen Elizabeth and King James I* (London: Shakespeare Society, 1842), xxxv.

5. Kernan, *Shakespeare, the King's Playwright*, 203–4, 31.

6. "Diary of the Journey of Philip Julius, Duke of Stettin-Pomerania, through England in the year 1602," in *Transactions of the Royal Historical Society* (London: Longmans, Green, and Co., 1892), new series, vol. 6, 53, 55; *A Journey into England by Paul Hentzner in the Year MDXCVIII*, trans. Horace Walpole (Strawberry Hill, 1762), 82; William Camden, *Britain, or A Chorographicall Description of the Most Flourishing Kingdomes, England, Scotland, and Ireland* (London, 1610), Mm4v; John Stow, *Annals of England*, 885.

7. Ernest Law, *Historical Catalogue of the Pictures at Hampton Court Palace* (London, 1881); *Hampton Court Palace: A Hand-List of the Pictures* (London: Her Majesty's Stationery Office, 1958); Cunningham, *Extracts from the Accounts of the Revels at Court*, xxxiv.

8. John Speed, *The Theatre of the Empire of Great Britain* (London, 1611), f.29; Hentzner, 80, 81; "Diary," 55.

9. Cunningham, *Extracts from the Accounts of the Revels at Court*, 23, 28, 59.

10. NA CSP 14/6, f.21–22; Horatio F. Brown, ed., *Calendar of State Papers and Manuscripts, relating to English Affairs, existing in the Archives and Collections of Venice* (London: Longman, 1894), 10:129; John Nichols, *The Progresses, Processions, and Magnificent Festivities of King James I* (London, 1828), 4:1061.

11. Katherine Duncan Jones, *Ungentle Shakespeare: Scenes from His Life* (London: Arden Shakespeare, 2001), 170.

12. Murray, *English Dramatic Companies 1558–1642*, 1:178; E. K. Chambers, *The Elizabethan Stage* (Oxford: Clarendon Press, 1923), 4:139; W. J. Lawrence, "Was Peter Cunningham a Forger?" *Modern Language Review* 19, no. 1 (January 1924). See also either Samuel A. Tannenbaum, *Shakespeare Forgeries in the Revels Accounts* (New York: Columbia University Press, 1928), who describes the revels accounts as "Forgeries from beginning to end" (5), or A. E. Stamp, *The Disputed Revels Accounts* (Oxford: Oxford University Press, 1930), who with equal vehemence insists: "I have long been convinced that the documents are genuine, and I have lately realized that their genuineness is capable of proof" (8).

13. Samuel Daniel, *The True Description of a Royall Masque Presented at Hampton Court* (London, 1604), A3v.

14. *Calendar of State Papers and Manuscripts . . . Venice*, 10:7, 10.

15. NA CSP 14/1, f.159; Parsons expresses the same optimistic sentiments in the preface to his *Treatise of Three Conversions of England from Paganisme to Christian Religion* (1603), *3v.

16. NA CSP 14/1, ff.121–22, 127–29; 14/1, ff.127–31.

17. NA CSP 14/1, f.110r–v; British Museum MSS Ayscough's Catalogue, 4108, 67.

18. Thomas Betteridge, "Puritanism," in *The Oxford Encyclopedia of British Literature*, ed. David Scott Kastan (Oxford: Oxford University Press, 2006), 4:299. In his classic study *The Elizabethan Puritan Movement* (Berkeley: University of California Press, 1967), Patrick Collinson defines the movement by its dedication to further reform: "In that they were organized to secure reform in the whole body of the Church, and by means of public authority, the puritans intended to complete the English Reformation" (13).

19. BL Additional MS 28571, ff.175–76; BL Egerton MS 2877, f.174.

20. William Barlow, *The Summe and Substance of the conference: Which it pleased his Excellent majestie to have with the lords, bishops, and other of his clergie at Hampton Court* (London, 1604), 1–2.

21. Alan Stewart, *The Cradle King: A Life of James VI and I* (London: Chatto and Windus, 2003), 200.

22. *Calendar of State Papers . . . Venice*, 131; Sir John Harington quoted in Stewart, *Cradle King*, 200.

23. "A Briefe relacon of ye conference 1603 held at Hampton Court," BL Egerton MS 2877, f.173; letter from Matthew to Hutton, BL Add. MS 4272, f.233r. Italics added.

24. Duncan-Jones, *Ungentle Shakespeare*, 9; Peter Ackroyd, *Shakespeare: The Biography* (London: Chatto and Windus, 2005), 67; Park Honan, *Shakespeare: A Life* (Oxford: Oxford University Press, 1998), 34; Stephen Greenblatt, *Will in the World: How Shakespeare Became Shakespeare* (New York: W. W. Norton, 2005), 42, 45–46.

25. Kernan, *Shakespeare, the King's Playwright*, 51.

26. Nicholas Tyacke, *Aspects of English Protestantism, c. 1530–1700* (Manchester: Manchester University Press, 2002), 111. The phrase "the end of a movement" comes from Collinson, *Elizabethan Puritan Movement*.

27. Kenneth Fincham and Peter Lake, "The Ecclesiastical Policy of James I," *Journal of British Studies* 24, no. 2 (April 1985): 171–73; Patrick Collinson, "The Jacobean Religious Settlement," 32. See also Mark Curtis, Hampton Court Conference and Its Aftermath," *History* 46, no. 156 (February 1961); F. Shriver, "Hampton Court Revisited: James I and the Puritans," *Journal of Ecclesiastical History* 32 (1982); Kenneth Fincham, *Prelate as Pastor: The Episcopate of James I* (Oxford: Clarendon Press, 1990); and Lori Anne Ferrell, *Government by Polemic: James I, the King's Preachers, and the Rhetoric of Conformity* (Stanford, CA: Stanford University Press, 1998).

28. *By the King: A Proclamation for the authorizing and uniformitie of the Booke of Common Prayer to be used throughout the realm* (London, 1604).

29. Barlow, *Summe and Substance*, 38; "An Anonymous Account in Favour of the Bishops: Hampton Court Conference," in *The Reconstruction of the English Church*, ed. Roland G. Usher (London, 1910), 2:338.

30. John Stow, *Annals of England*, 1427–28.

31. Jesse M. Lander, *Inventing Polemic: Religion, Print, and Literary Culture in Early Modern England* (Cambridge: Cambridge University Press, 2006), 126.

32. "A declaration of the conference had before the kings most excellent Majesty and divers of his most honorable privie counsel," in Usher, *Reconstruction of the English Church*, 2:341–54.

33. Judith Maltby, *Prayer Book and People in Elizabethan and Early Stuart England* (Cambridge: Cambridge University Press, 1998), 4.

34. "To the right Reverand fathers in God the Lord Bishopps of the Church of England The humble Petition of sundry Ministers of the same" (April 1604?), BL Add MS 38492, f.94v.

35. *A Survey of the Booke of Common prayer, By way of 197 Quares grounded upon 58 places* (London, 1610), Br.

36. W. P. M. Kennedy, *Studies in Tudor History* (London: Constable, 1916), 70.

37. William P. Haugaard, *Elizabeth and the English Reformation: The Struggle for a Stable Settlement of Religion* (Cambridge: Cambridge University Press, 1968), 70–78. See also Elizabeth Gilliam and W. J. Tighe, "To 'Run with the Time': Archbishop Whitgift, the Lambeth Articles, and the Politics of Theological Ambiguity in Late Elizabethan England," *Sixteenth Century Journal* 23, no. 2 (Summer 1992): 325–40.

38. "The exceptions of the London puritans to the booke of common prayer the booke of ordination and the booke of homilies. 1606." BL Add. MS 29975, ff.14r–v.

39. *A Survey of the Booke of Common Prayer, By Way of 197. Quares grounded upon 58. places*, F2r.

40. Thomas Hutton, *The Second and Last Part of Reasons for Refusall of Subscription* (London, 1606), Br.

Chapter 1

1. 4.5.197. F: "common"; F2, Q2: "commune."

2. *As You Like It* 1.3.109; *Measure for Measure* 4.2.7; *Henry V* 4.8.72–73; *2 Henry VI* 2.62–63; *All's Well That Ends Well* 5.3.190.

3. See, for example: *A Fourme of Common Prayer to be used . . . necessarie for the present tyme and state* (London, 1572); *A Prayer for the good successe of her Majesties forces in Ireland* (London, 1599); *A Fourme of Prayer with Thanksgiving, to be used . . . every year, the 24 of March* (London, 1604); *Prayers and Thanksgiving to be used by all the Kings Majesties loving subjects for the Happy Deliverance of his Majestie . . . from the most traiterous and bloody intended Massacre by Gunpowder* (London, 1605).

4. Ian Green, *Print and Protestantism in Early Modern England* (Oxford: Oxford University Press, 2000), 277.

5. Henry Barrow, *A Brief Discoverie of the False Church* (Dort, 1590), Kr, I4r.

6. Diarmaid MacCulloch, *Thomas Cranmer: A Life* (New Haven, CT: Yale University Press, 1996), 221–22, 328–33.

7. Stanley Morison, *English Prayer Books: An Introduction to the Literature of Christian Public Worship* (Cambridge: Cambridge University Press, 1945), 5, 8–10.

8. Henry Gee and Williams John Hardy, eds., *Documents Illustrative of English Church History* (London: Macmillan and Co., 1914), 360.

9. Eamon Duffy, *The Stripping of the Altars: Traditional Religion in England 1400–1580* (New Haven, CT: Yale University Press, 1992), 464.

10. Gee and Hardy, *Documents Illustrative*, 369.

11. Roy A. Rappaport, *Ritual and Religion in the Making of Humanity* (Cambridge: Cambridge University Press, 1999), 32.

12. Richard Bancroft, *A Sermon Preached at Paules Crosse the 9. of Februarie being the first Sunday on the Parlement, Anno. 1588*, 54; Andrew Willet, *Synopsis Papismi* (1594), Zz6v–Zz7r.

13. *Titus Andronicus* 1.1.121–24; *Romeo and Juliet* 4.1.109–11; *Much Ado About Nothing* 4.1.206–7, 5.3.23; *Hamlet* 5.1.205.

14. Lisa Jardine and Anthony Grafton, "'Studied for Action': How Gabriel Harvey Read His Livy," *Past and Present* 129 (1990): 32, 33; William H. Sherman, *Used Books: Marking Readers in Renaissance England* (Philadelphia: University of Pennsylvania Press, 2008), xiv.

15. The educational theories of early modern reading have been thoroughly surveyed by Eugene R. Kintgen in *Reading in Tudor England* (Pittsburgh: University of Pittsburgh Press, 1996) while the politics of literacy—who was allowed to read what, and when?—are discussed in Heidi Brayman Hackel, "'The Great Variety of Readers' and Early Modern Reading Practices," in *Companion to Shakespeare*, ed. David Scott Kastan, and in *Literacies in Early Modern England*, a special issue of *Critical Survey* 14, no. 1 (2002), ed. Eve Rachele Sanders and Margaret W. Ferguson. These works focus on the skills involved in reading rather than the activity itself. See also William H. Sherman, *John Dee: The Politics of Reading and Writing in the English Renaissance* (Amherst: University of Massachusetts Press, 1995) and Kevin Sharpe, *Reading Revolutions: The Politics of Reading in Early Modern England* (New Haven, CT: Yale University Press, 2000) for portraits of individual readers.

16. Sherman, *Used Books*, 5.

17. Philip Sidney, *The Countess of Pembrokes Arcadia* (London, 1598), ff.154–56.

18. In *Used Books*, Sherman identifies eight different categories of readers' marks in printed Bibles: "Ownership notes," "Penmanship exercises," cross-references to other books, instructions for reading in lectern Bibles, "Numberings of pages, chapters, verses, columns," "Corrections," "Polemical notes," and "Dating of various kinds." I have chosen not to follow his categories here because prayer book annotation seems to fall into different patterns: specifically, one major category of prayer book annotation—my second category, updating the liturgy—is not relevant to the Bible. More broadly, I do not see a clear distinction between "Ownership notes" and "Penmanship exercises": Which of these two categories would include, for example, the repeated marginal practice of a name or signature? I argue that personalization, defined very broadly and displayed in various forms, is the most powerful motive behind early modern prayer book annotation. Sherman devotes chap. 5 of his excellent book to an MS copy of the prayer book and psalter, from the early 1560s, now in the Huntington Library. It is simply a copy, by hand, of a 1559 Book of Common Prayer. This is a volume, Sherman argues, "full of vexing bibliocultural mysteries"

and goes on to demand: "Why would someone bother to make—or have made for them—a manuscript copy of the recently printed and readily available Book of Common Prayer and Psalter (and its 598 pages of closely written text could not have been either easy or cheap to produce)?" (Sherman, 94, 87). He argues that "as a manuscript— which is to some extent inherently customized and privatized—this volume cuts against the very nature and purpose of the printed Book of Common Prayer" (Sherman, 100). In reference to early modern habits of annotation, there is no mystery here at all but rather the sign of a widespread cultural practice. This is an extreme example of a tendency we see throughout the annotated and marked-up prayer books of the period: the desire to make liturgy one's own.

19. BL C108.f.10.

20. NYPL *KC 1606 (BCP).

21. BOD C.P. 1552 d.6. Mary Lane's prayer book is now in the Huntington Library: Huntington 438000.815.

22. CUL Sel.3.218; BL C.18.a.9.

23. Folger 16410.

24. BCP (1552), 42.

25. BOD C.P. 1552 d.6, B.v.r; BL 1609/4817, A2r.

26. BL C.175.dd.1, A.vi.r, B.ii.v; BOD Douce C.P.e.1606, D3r, D5v. The same emendation appears in NYPL *KC 1615.

27. BOD Douce C.P. f.1604, C5v, U5v.

28. BL C.183.a.18. (1). There are two similarly updated Restoration prayer books in CUL: Adv.a.50.2, Adv.bb.28.1.

29. BL C108.f.10.

30. Huntington Library 438000:7.

31. NYPL *KC + 1600.

32. BOD C.P. 1552 d.6, C.ii.r, p.i.v.

33. BL C.175.dd.1, A.r, A.v.

34. CUL Rel.a.60.3; Adv.a.50.2.

35. CUL Sel.3.220, P.i.v, B.v.r.

36. A. W. Pollard and G. R. Redgrave, *A Short-Title Catalogue of Books Printed in England, Scotland, & Ireland and of English Books Printed Abroad, 1475–1640* (London: Bibliographical Society, 1976–91), 2:68.

37. Bruce Holsinger, "Liturgy," in *Oxford Twenty-First Century Approaches to Literature: Middle English*, ed. Paul Strohm (New York: Oxford University Press, 2007), 296, 309, 305, 312.

38. Elizabeth L. Eisenstein, *The Printing Revolution in Early Modern Europe* (Cambridge: Cambridge University Press, 1993), chap. 3, "Some Features of Print Culture," 42–91.

39. Adrian Johns, *The Nature of the Book: Print and Knowledge in the Making* (Chicago: University of Chicago Press, 1998), 31.

40. Columbia Special Collections, B264.03 C4754, C6r, Dr; the 1632 edition is Columbia Special Collections, B264.03 C4711. Italics mine. In a 1604 prayer book

now in the Huntington Library, a smaller printing error has similarly been corrected by hand. Verse 17 of Psalm 31, set for Morning Prayer for the sixth day, is printed as "My tine is in thy hand, deliver me from the hand of mine enemies"; a marginal annotation emends the line to "My tyme . . ." (438000:815, Y5r).

41. Eisenstein, *Printing Revolution*, 78, 64; Johns, *Nature of the Book*, 19.

42. Glynne Wickham, ed., *English Professional Theatre 1530–1660* (Cambridge: Cambridge University Press, 2000), 34, 50, 69–70.

43. John Donne, *Biathanatos: A Declaration of that Paradoxe, or Thesis, that Selfe-homicide is not so Naturally Sinne, that it may never be otherwise* (London, 1644), 47.

44. Richard B. Donovan, *The Liturgical Drama in Medieval Spain* (Toronto: Pontifical Institute of Medieval Studies, 1958), 6; V. A. Kolve, *The Play Called Corpus Christi* (Stanford: Stanford University Press, 1966), 48; Gail McMurray Gibson, *The Theater of Devotion: East Anglian Drama and Society in the Late Middle Ages* (Chicago: University of Chicago Press, 1995).

45. David M. Bevington, *From Mankind to Marlowe: Growth of Structure in the Popular Drama of Tudor England* (Cambridge, MA: Harvard University Press, 1962), 57; Louis Montrose, *The Purpose of Playing: Shakespeare and the Cultural Politics of the Elizabethan Theatre* (Chicago: University of Chicago Press, 1996), 28, 25.

46. E. K. Chambers, *Elizabethan Stage*, 1:255.

47. *Sermons of Master John Calvin, upon the Booke of Job*, trans. Arthur Golding (London, 1574), A.vi.v.

48. Thomas Cranmer, "Answers to the Fifteen Articles of the Rebels, Devon, Anno 1549," in *The Works of Thomas Cranmer*, ed. John Edmund Cox (Cambridge: Cambridge University Press, 1846), 2:180; Thomas Becon, "A Comparison between the Lord's Supper and the Pope's Mass," in *Prayers and Other Peeces*, ed. John Ayre (Cambridge: Cambridge University Press, 1844), 356; Andrew Willet, *Synopsis Papismi* (London, 1600), Yy6v.

49. John Ayre, ed., *The Works of John Jewel* (Cambridge: Parker Society, 1848), 3:249.

50. William Prynne, *Histrio-Mastix: the Players Scourge or Actors Tragedie* (London, 1633), 119–20.

51. Philip Massinger, *The Renegado* 5.3.114–15, in *Three Turk Plays from Early Modern England*, ed. Daniel J. Vitkus (New York: Columbia University Press, 2000).

52. *Macbeth* 2.1.56–57; Horace Howard Furness, ed., *A New Variorum Edition of Shakespeare*, vol. 2: *Macbeth* (Philadelphia: J. B. Lippincott and Co., 1873), 93.

53. Kenneth Muir, ed., *Macbeth* (London: Methuen and Co., 1962), 51; Naseeb Shaheen, *Biblical References in Shakespeare's Plays* (Newark: University of Delaware Press, 1999), 72.

54. Abraham Fleming, *The Footepath to Felicitie, Which everie Christian must walke in, before we can come to the land of Canaan* (London, 1581), 77; Robert Crowley, *Pleasure and Payne, Heaven and Hell: Remembre these foure, and all shall be well* (London, 1551), D.v.r.; Alexander Craig, *The Poeticall Recreations of Mr. Alexander Craig of Rosecraig* (Edinburgh, 1609), D3.

55. William Massie, *A Sermon Preached at Trafford in Lancashire at the marriage of the daughter of the right worshipfull Sir Edmonde Trafforde* (Oxford, 1586), A7r; Samuel Hieron, *The Bridegroome* (London, 1613), A8r; Heinrich Bullinger, *The Christen State of Matrimony, moost necessarye & profitable for all them, that entend to to live quietly and godlye in the Christen state of holy wedlock* (London, 1546), C.ii.v; *The seconde tome of homeleyes, of such matters as were promised and Intituled in the former part of the Homeleyes, set out by the auctoritie of the Quenes Majestie* (London, 1563), Vvvv.ii.r.

56. Charles Wordsworth, *Shakespeare's Knowledge and Use of the Bible* (London, 1880), 2.

57. G. Wilson Knight, *The Wheel of Fire: Interpretations of Shakespearian Tragedy* (New York: Routledge, 1989), 89, 108; Hamilton Coleman, *Shakespeare and the Bible* (New York: Vantage Press, 1955), v, vi.

58. Huston Diehl, *Staging Reform, Reforming the Stage: Protestantism and Popular Theatre in Early Modern England* (Ithaca, NY: Cornell University Press, 1997), 98; Jeffrey Knapp, *Shakespeare's Tribe: Church, Nation, and Theater in Renaissance England* (Chicago: University of Chicago Press, 2002), 132; Susan Sontag, *Against Interpretation and Other Essays* (New York: Picador, 1990), 8.

59. Kenneth Muir, *The Sources of Shakespeare's Plays* (New Haven, CT: Yale University Press, 1978), 7; Stuart Gillespie, *Shakespeare's Books: A Dictionary of Shakespeare's Sources* (London: Athlone Press, 2001), 64.

60. Jeffrey Masten, *Textual Intercourse: Collaboration, Authorship, and Sexualities in Renaissance Drama* (Cambridge: Cambridge University Press, 1997), 4; Brian Vickers, *Shakespeare Co-Author: A Historical Study of Five Collaborative Plays* (Oxford: Oxford University Press, 2002), 18; G. E. Bentley, *The Profession of Dramatist in Shakespeare's Time 1590–1642* (Princeton, NJ: Princeton University Press 1972), 199.

61. Samuel Schoenbaum, *William Shakespeare: A Documentary Life* (New York: Oxford University Press, 1975), 62; David Cressy, *Birth, Marriage, and Death: Ritual, Religion, and the Life-Cycle in Tudor and Stuart England* (Oxford: Oxford University Press, 1997), 15–16, 97.

Chapter 2

1. BCP: 157, 159, 160, 162.

2. *A Survey of the Booke of Common Prayer, By way of 197 Quare grounded upon 58 places, ministering just matter of question, with a view of London Ministers exceptions* (London, 1610), I2v.

3. Andrew Willet, *Synopsis Papismi* (1592), 523, 525.

4. Catherine Bates, "Love and Courtship," in *The Cambridge Companion to Shakespearean Comedy*, ed. Alexander Leggatt (Cambridge: Cambridge University Press, 2002), 104; Ann Jennalie Cook, *Making a Match: Courtship in Shakespeare and His Society* (Princeton, NJ: Princeton University Press, 1991), 183. In "Liturgical Quibbles in *As You Like It* and *Much Ado About Nothing*," Richard Levin observes

that these two Shakespeare plays "both come very close to reproducing the actual wording of small portions of the official marriage service appointed to be followed in churches" and adds that "the two marriage ceremonies discussed here are the only ones I have found in the drama of this period that are presented on stage and even include some of the words of the church service" (*Notes and Queries* 254, no. 1 [March 2009]: 53). I argue that Shakespeare often and at length borrowed from the prayer book's marriage rite, but the tentative identification shown by Levin—"come very close . . . small portions"—is representative of a wider critical separation between plays and the prayer book. This is built upon a refusal to see the prayer book as dramatic: there is no sense, that is, of a relation between the theater and the church that is other than predatory, in which the stage dramatizes the inert churchly originals.

5. Edward Berry, *Shakespeare's Comic Rites* (Cambridge: Cambridge University Press, 1984), 1; C. L. Barber, *Shakespeare's Festive Comedy: A Study of Dramatic Form and Its Relation to Social Custom* (Princeton, NJ: Princeton University Press, 1959); René Girard, "Myth and Ritual in Shakespeare," in *Textual Strategies: Perspectives in Post-Structuralist Criticism*, ed. Josue V. Hariri (Ithaca, NY: Cornell University Press, 1979).

6. David Bevington, *Action Is Eloquence: Shakespeare's Language of Gesture* (Cambridge, MA: Harvard University Press, 1984), 142.

7. Anne Barton, "'Wrying but a little': Marriage, Law, and Sexuality in Shakespeare's Plays," in *Essays, Mainly Shakespearean* (Cambridge: Cambridge University Press, 1994).

8. Henry Swinburne, *A Treatise of Spousals, or Matrimoniall Contracts* (London, 1686), 14, 209–12, 35. For biographical information on Swinburne (1560–1623), see the *Dictionary of National Biography* (Oxford: Oxford University Press).

9. Jean H. Hagstrum, *Esteem Enlivened by Desire: The Couple from Homer to Shakespeare* (Chicago: University of Chicago Press, 1992), 348.

10. Edmund Bonner, *A Profitable and necessarye doctrine, with certayne homelies* (London, 1555), B1.i.r; Francis Meres, *Gods Arithmeticke* (London, 1597), A2r.

11. Jewel, *Works*, 2.1128, 2.1129, 3.385–429, 3.405, 3.388.

12. *Certayne Sermons, or homelies, appointed by the Kynges Maiestie, to bee declared and redde, by al persons, Vicares, or curates, every Sundaye in their Churches, where they have cure* (London, 1547), U.iii.r, T.iv.r, U.i.v.

13. Bonner, *A profitable and necessarye doctrine*, Qq.iv.v, Cc.iii.r.

14. William Perkins, *Christian Oeconomie: Or, A Short Survey of the Right Manner of erecting and ordering a Familie, according to the Scriptures* (London, 1609), C4r.

15. William Whately, *A Bride-Bush, or A wedding Sermon* (London, 1617), B2r, F4r.

16. There is, of course, ring-play in other of Shakespeare's works, most notably *The Merchant of Venice*. But in *Romeo and Juliet* it coincides with a specific liturgical language. I am not aiming here for a total coverage; only to trace one arc of Shakespeare's use of prayer book motifs.

17. "An Anonymous Account in Favour of the Bishops," in Usher, *Reconstruction of the English Church*, 2.336; Sir John Harington, "Breefe Notes," in *Nugae Antiquae*, 2.181.

18. *The Abolishing of the Booke of Common Prayer* (1605), Bv; Willett, *Synopsis Papismi* (1592), Nn5r-v; Barlow, *Summe and Substance of the Conference*, L2v.

19. BCP (1559), 294. The psalm is entirely conventional: shared both by the traditional primers and the Puritan prayer book (*The forme of prayers and ministration of the sacraments*, O7r).

20. Louis L. Martz and Richard S. Sylvester, eds., *Thomas More's Prayer Book: A facsimile reproduction of the annotated pages* (New Haven, CT: Yale University Press, 1969), 206; *Decrees of the Ecumenical Councils*, ed. Norman P. Tanner (Washington, DC: Georgetown University Press, 1990), 660.

21. *The Sermons of Master John Calvin, upon the Booke of Job*, trans. Arthur Golding (London, 1574), B.iii.v; *The Folger Library Edition of the Works of Richard Hooker*, ed. W. Speed Hill (Cambridge, MA: The Belknap Press, 1977–82), V.60.3.

22. Jewel, "An Exposition upon the Two Epistles of St Paul to the Thessalonians," in *Works*, 2.818, 819, 822, 827, 833, 835, 836, 837, 847, 849, 863, 886.

23. *The Abolishing of the Booke of Common Prayer* (London, 1641), B2v; Barlow, *Summe and Substance of the Conference*, 75–76.

24. *As You Like It* 3.3.68–69; BCP (1559), 290; Matthew Parker, *An Admonition to all such as shall intend hereafter to enter the state of Matrimonie godly, and agreeable to Lawes* (London, 1605).

25. Geoffrey Bullough, ed., *Narrative and Dramatic Sources of Shakespeare* (New York: Columbia University Press, 1957–75), 2:214.

26. *As You Like It* 3.2.99–100; 3.2.183–86; 3.2.286–87; 5.2.33–35; 5.4.52–55; 5.4.186–87.

Chapter 3

1. Heinrich Bullinger, *The Christen State of Matrimony*, A.iii.r; Peter Martyr, *The Common Places of the most famous and renowned Divine Doctor Peter Martyr*, pt. 2, 470; Ste. B., *Counsel to the Husband: To the Wife Instruction* (London, 1608), C8r; William Perkins, *Christian Oeconomie*, ¶3r.

2. Edward Berry, *Shakespeare's Comic Rites*, 163; Leo Salingar, *Shakespeare and the Traditions of Comedy* (Cambridge: Cambridge University Press, 1974), 17; Lisa Hopkins, "Marriage as Comic Closure," in *Shakespeare's Comedies*, ed. Emma Smith (Oxford: Blackwell, 2004), 36.

3. Aristotle, *Poetics*, 1449a.

4. George E. Duckworth, *The Nature of Roman Comedy: A Study in Popular Entertainment* (Princeton, NJ: Princeton University Press, 1952), 412–18; see also Robert S. Miola, *Shakespeare and Classical Comedy: The Influence of Plautus and Terence* (Oxford: Clarendon Press, 1994) for a thorough consideration of the influence.

5. Frank Kermode, *The Sense of an Ending* (Oxford: Oxford University Press, 1967), 18.

6. Frederick S. Boas, *Shakspere and His Predecessors* (London, 1896), 344, 345.

7. William Witherle Lawrence, *Shakespeare's Problem Comedies* (New York: Macmillan, 1931), 4; Ernest Schanzer, *The Problem Plays of Shakespeare* (London: Routledge and Kegan Paul, 1963), 6.

8. *Certaine Sermons appointed by the Quenes Majesty, to be declared and read* (London, 1563), T.iv.r; X.i.v.

9. William Perkins, *Christian Oeconomie*: "if the parties betrothed, do lie together before the condition (though honest & appertaining to marriage) be performed; then the contract for time to come is, without further controversie, sure and certaine." Claudio's sister Isabella slightly disagrees: she believes they are not yet married but they should be. As she pleads with Angelo: "O, let him marry her!" (1.4.49).

10. Boas, *Shakspere and His Predecessors*, 345; Lawrence, *Shakespeare's Problem Comedies*, 5; Darryl J. Glesy, *Measure for Measure, the Law, and the Covenant* (Princeton, NJ: Princeton University Press, 1979), 212.

11. Lawrence, *Shakespeare's Problem Comedies*, 68–69.

12. See, for example: Marliss C. Desens, *The Bed-Trick in English Renaissance Drama: Explorations in Gender, Sexuality, and Power* (Newark: University of Delaware Press, 1994); Janet Adelman, "Bed Tricks: On Marriage as the End of Comedy in *All's Well That Ends Well* and *Measure for Measure*," in *Shakespeare's Personality*, ed. Norman N. Holland, Sidney Homan, and Bernard J. Paris (Berkeley: University of California Press, 1989); David McCandless, "Helena's Bed-trick: Gender and Performance in *All's Well That Ends Well*," *Shakespeare Quarterly* 45, no. 4 (1994).

13. Christopher Rush, *Will* (London: Beautiful Books, 2007), 435.

14. Greenblatt, *Will in the World*, 134, 143, 136, 123; Germaine Greer, *Shakespeare's Wife* (London: Bloomsbury, 2007), 322, 324.

15. William Henty, *Shakespeare with Some Notes on His Early Biography* (London, 1882), 23; Grace Carlton, *The Wooing of Anne Hathaway* (London: The Mitre Press, 1938), 123; Katherine Duncan-Jones, *Ungentle Shakespeare*, 22, 91; Avril Rowlands, *Mrs. Shakespeare . . . The Poet's Wife* (Malvern: J. Garnet Miller, 2005), 122.

16. Greenblatt, *Will in the World*, 145; Greer, *Shakespeare's Wife*, 325.

17. Carol Anne Duffy, *The World's Wife* (London: Faber, 2001).

18. Emrys Jones, *Scenic Form in Shakespeare* (Oxford: Clarendon Press, 1971), 46, 56.

19. Bullough, *Narrative and Dramatic Sources of Shakespeare*, 7:242.

20. Stanley Cavell, *Disowning Knowledge in Seven Plays of Shakespeare* (Cambridge: Cambridge University Press, 2003), 128, 135.

Chapter 4

1. Thomas Frederick Simmons, ed., *The Lay Folks Mass Book or The Manner of Hearing Mass* (London: EETS, 1879), 2; Nicholas Saunders, *The Supper of our Lord . . . with a confutation of such false doctrine as the Apologie of the Churche of England* (Louvain, 1566), Fii.v.

2. Jewel, "An Exposition upon the Two Epistles of St Paul to the Thessalonians," in *Works*, 2:874; Whitgift, *An answere to a certen Libel intituled, An admonition to the Parliament* (London, 1572), in *The Works of John Whitgift*, ed. John Ayre (Cambridge: Parker Society, 1851), 2:442; Willet, *Synopsis Papismi* (1592), Kk2.v.

3. Paul Strohm, *England's Empty Throne: Usurpation and the Language of Legitimation, 1399–1422* (New Haven, CT: Yale University Press, 1998), 45, 47.

4. Jewel, *Works*, 3:20–21.

5. W. J. Torrance Kirby, "Signs and Things Signified: Sacramental Hermeneutics in John Jewel's 'Challenge Sermon' and the 'Culture of Persuasion' at Paul's Cross," *Reformation and Renaissance Review* 11, 1 (2009): 70. The debate is also surveyed by John E. Booty in *John Jewel as Apologist of the Church of England* (London: SPCK, 1963), 58–82; and Gary W. Jenkins, *John Jewel and the English National Church: The Dilemmas of an Erastian Reformer* (Aldershot: Ashgate, 2006), 70–82.

6. Jewel, *Works*, 1:3, 8, 26, 20–21.

7. Lawrence Humfrey, *Joannis Juelli Angli, Episcopi Sarisburiensis vita & mors* (London, 1573), Liii.r–v; *The Works of the Very Learned and Reverand Father in God John Jewel* (London, 1609), ∃∃3r.

8. Thomas Harding, *A Rejoindre to M. Jewels Replie* (Antwerp, 1566), CCCCi.v.

9. R. N. Swanson, *Church and Society in Late Medieval England* (Oxford: Blackwell, 1989), 51; Nigel Saul, *Death, Art, and Memory in Medieval England: The Cobham Family and Their Monuments, 1300–1500*; Duffy, *Stripping of the Altars*, 301–74. In his study of the reformation of burial rites, Peter Marshall argues that "the ways in which late medieval Catholicism articulated its relationship with the dead may serve as a kind of synecdoche for that religious system as a whole" (*Beliefs and the Dead in Reformation England*, 7).

10. R. N. Swanson, ed., *Catholic England: Faith, Religion, and Observance before the Reformation* (Manchester: Manchester University Press, 1993), 150–57.

11. *Mirk's Festial*, 199.

12. Simmons, *Lay Folks Mass Book*, 45.

13. John Fisher, *Here after ensueth two frutyfull Sermons* (London, 1532), C3r.

14. The standard creed of the Catholic Church was promulgated at the third session of the Council of Trent, on 4 February 1546: Tanner, *Decrees of the Ecumenical Councils*, 1:662; Cummings, 59.

15. Jonathan Bate, ed., *Titus Andronicus* (London: Routledge, 1995), 263.

16. Alan Hughes, ed., *Titus Andronicus* (Cambridge: Cambridge University Press, 1994), xi.

17. E. K. Chambers, *William Shakespeare: A Study of Facts and Problems* (Oxford: Clarendon Press, 1930), 2.261; Charles Gildon quoted in Horace Howard Furness, ed., *A New Variorum of Shakespeare: Hamlet* (Philadelphia: J. B. Lippincott and Co., 1877), vol. 3, pt. 1, 3.

18. *Hamlet* 1.1.31–34, 40, 44, 47, 50, 43, 128, 68; 1.2.214.

19. Duffy, *Stripping of the Altars*, 474–75.

20. Peter Marshall, *Beliefs and the Dead in Reformation England* (Oxford: Oxford University Press, 2004), 18–33; Clive Burgess, "A Service for the dead: the form and function of the anniversary in late medieval Bristol," in *Bristol and Gloucestershire Archeological Society Transactions*, vol. 105 (1987).

21. Francis Proctor and Walter Frere, *New History of the Book of Common Prayer* (London: Macmillan, 1910), 443.

22. Tanner, *Decrees of the Ecumenical Councils*, 2:694.

23. *The Manual of prayers, or the prymer in Englyshye . . . set forth by Jhon late byshoppe of Rochester* (London, 1539), A.a.i.v.

24. *Heures a l'Usiage Romme, avec Calendrier* (Paris [Simon Vostre], 1488); *Les presentes heures a lusiage de Chartres* (Paris [Simon Vostre], 1517) offer few major variations on the burial rite and Dirige according to Sarum use.

25. *This prayer of Salisbury use is set out a long w-out any serchyng / With many prayers / and godly pyctures in the kalendar* (Paris, 1531), f.xc.r–xc.v.

26. Philippe Ariès, *Western Attitudes Toward Death from the Middle Ages to the Present* (Baltimore: Johns Hopkins University Press, 1974), chap. 1, "Tamed Death." On the cult of the saints, Peter Brown writes: "The rise of the cult of saints was sensed by contemporaries, in no uncertain manner, to have broken most of the imaginative boundaries which ancient men had placed between heaven and earth, the divine and the human, the living and the dead." Peter Brown, *The Cult of the Saints: Its Rise and Function in Latin Christianity* (Chicago: University of Chicago Press, 1981), 21.

27. Marshall, *Beliefs and the Dead in Reformation England*, 271.

28. Jewel, "An Exposition upon the Two Epistles of St Paul to the Thessalonians," in *Works*, 2.865–66.

29. John Griffiths, ed., *The Two Books of Homilies appointed to be read in churches* (Oxford: Oxford University Press, 1859), 93; BCP (1559), 309.

30. *Sermons of Master John Calvin, upon the Booke of Job*, trans. Arthur Golding (London, 1574), B.vii.v.

31. Willet, *Synopsis Papismi* (1592), Y5r.

32. Whitgift, *Works*, 3.370.

33. Hooker, *Laws*, V.75.4.

34. *Sermons of Master John Calvin, upon the Booke of Job*, B.vii.v.

35. Hooker, *Laws*, V.75.2.

36. Walter Howard Frere and Charles Edward Douglas, eds., *Puritan Manifestoes: A study of the origin of the Puritan revolt with a reprint of the Admonition to the Parliament and kindred documents, 1572* (London: SPCK, 1954), vii, 21, 28.

37. *A Survey of the Booke of Common Prayer, by way of 197. Quares grounded upon 58 places* (London, 1610), I8v.

38. William Keatinge Clay, ed., *Private Prayers, put forth by Authority during the Reign of Queen Elizabeth* (Cambridge: Parker Society, 1851), 59, 67.

39. William Keatinge Clay, ed., *Liturgies and Occasional Forms of Prayer Set Forth in the Reign of Queen Elizabeth* (Cambridge: Parker Society, 1847), 433.

40. Elaine V. Beilin, ed., *The Examinations of Anne Askew* (Oxford: Oxford University Press, 1996), 190, 180, 184; John Foxe, *Acts and Monuments* (1570), 1608–9.

41. Edmund Bonner, *Homiles sette forth by the righte reverende father in God, Edmunde Byshop of London* (London, 1555), f.64r. Bonner's homily on the Mass similarly insists upon the keyword "remembrance": *A Profitable and necessarye doctrine, with certayne homelies* (London, 1555), S.iv.v; Sanders, *The Supper of our Lord*, Xv.

42. Catherine Gallagher and Stephen Greenblatt, *Practicing New Historicism* (Chicago: University of Chicago Press, 2000), 152.

43. Greenblatt, *Hamlet in Purgatory* (Princeton, NJ: Princeton University Press, 2001), 19.

44. Greenblatt, "The Death of Hamnet and the Making of Hamlet," *New York Review of Books*, 21 October 2004.

45. J. G. Nichols, ed., *The Diary of Henry Machyn, Citizen and Merchant-Taylor of London, from AD 1550 to AD 1563* (London: The Camden Society, 1848), 14, 24.

46. *The Primer, or Office of the Blessed Virgin Marie, in Latin and English* (Antwerp, 1599), P8r.

47. *The Primer in Latin and Englishe (after the use of sarum)* (London, 1555), D.ii.r.

48. The exclusion of suicides from full burial was only specifically articulated in the 1662 edition of the Book of Common Prayer: at the beginning of the rite for the burial of the dead, a note explains, "Here it is to be noted, that of the Office ensuing is not to be used for any that die unbaptized, or excommunicate, or have laid violent hands upon them selves" (Cummings, 451).

49. Roland Mushat Frye, *The Renaissance Hamlet* (Princeton, NJ: Princeton University Press, 1984); Michael MacDonald, "Ophelia's Maimed Rites," *Shakespeare Quarterly* 37 (Autumn, 1986).

50. Bevington, *Action Is Eloquence*, 174; Greenblatt, *Hamlet in Purgatory*, 247.

51. *A Booke of the Forme of common prayers, administration of the Sacraments &c. agreeable to Gods Worde, and the use of the reformed Churches* (Middleburgh, 1584), E4v.

52. Thomas Hutton, *Reasons For Refusall of Subscription to the booke of Common praier* (Oxford, 1605), Dr.

53. *Manual of Prayers* (1539), Cc.iii.v; Willet, *Synopsis Papismi* (1592), Y7r.

54. Ann Thompson and Neil Taylor, eds., *Hamlet: The Texts of 1603 and 1623* (London: The Arden Shakespeare, 2006), 86, 91.

55. Q2 1.1.44; Q1 1.35; F1.1.44.

56. Q2 4.7.175; Q1 15.47; F4.3.149.

57. Q1 16.133.

58. F3.6.24–25; Q2 4.3.22–23; Q1 11.132.

59. Q1 2.47; BCP (1559), 309.

60. Peter Marshall, "Angels around the deathbed: variations on a theme in the English art of dying," in *Angels in the Early Modern World*, ed. Peter Marshall and Alexandra Walsham (Cambridge: Cambridge University Press, 2006), 84–85; Pamela Sheingorn, "'And flights of angels sing thee to thy rest': The Soul's Conveyance to the Afterlife in the Middle Ages," in *Art Into Life: Collected Papers from the Kresge Art Museum Medieval Symposium*, ed. Carol Garrett Fisher and Kathleen L. Scott (East Lansing: Michigan State University Press, 1995).

61. BCP (1559), 262.

62. Griffiths, *Two Books of Homilies*, 337.

Chapter 5

1. *Macbeth* 3.1.11–15, 19–20, 24, 29, 48–49.

2. Jewel, *Works*, 2:1100.

3. Thomas Becon, "A Comparison between the Lord's Supper and the Pope's Mass" in *Prayers and Other Pieces*, ed. John Ayre (Cambridge: Parker Society, 1849), 374.

4. Thomas Cranmer, *An Answer unto a craftie and Sophisticall cavillation, devised by Stephen Gardiner* (London, 1551), in John Edmund Cox, ed., *The Works of Thomas Cranmer*, 2:163; Jewel, *Replie unto M. Hardings answer* in *Works*, 1:118–19; John Rastel, *Beware of M. Jewel* (Antwerp, 1566), G.iv.r.

5. Peter Lake, *Anglicans and Puritans? Presbyterianism and English Conformist Thought from Whitgift to Hooker* (London: Unwin Hyman, 1988), 2.

6. Hooker, *Of the Lawes of Ecclesiasticall Politie*, 5.67.12.

7. Debora Shuger, "'Society Supernatural': The Imagined Community of Hooker's *Laws*," in *Religion and Culture in Renaissance England*, ed. Claire McEachern and Debora Shuger (Cambridge: Cambridge University Press, 1997), 130.

8. BCP, 130; *Macbeth* 2.1.23, 48; 2.3.81; 3.1.124; 3.5.22.

9. *This prayer of Salisbury use*, f.xv.r; Martz and Sylvester, eds., *Thomas More's Prayer Book*, 205.

10. Alan Beesley, "An unpublished source of the Book of Common Prayer: Peter Martyr Vermigli's *Annotatio ad Coenam Domini Mysticam*," *Journal of Ecclesiastical History* 19 (April 1968): 83–88.

11. Griffiths, ed., *The Two Books of Homilies appointed to be read in churches*, 340, 344.

12. Andrew Willet, *Ecclesia Triumphans: that is, The Joy of the English Church, for the happie Coronation of the most vertuous and pious Prince, James* (Cambridge, 1603), B2v.

13. Thomas Blague, *A Sermon Preached at the Charterhouse, before the Kings Majestie* (London, 1603), A8r, A7r–v, B5r.

14. *Macbeth* 3.4.107, 109–10, 118–20; Cummings, 131.

15. Hugh A. Hanley, "Shakespeare's Family in Stratford Records," *Times Literary Supplement*, 21 May 1964, 441.

16. Alexandra Walsham, *Church Papists: Catholicism, Conformity and Confessional Polemic in Early Modern England* (London: The Royal Historical Society, 1993), 11, 85, 12.

17. Alan Dures, *English Catholicism 1558–1642: Continuity and Change* (London: Longman, 1983), 43–46; Edward Cardwell, ed., *Documentary Annals of the Reformed Church of England*, 2.101–16; Walsham, *Church Papists*, 80.

18. James C. Scott, *Seeing Like a State: How Certain Schemes to Improve the Human Condition Have Failed* (New Haven, CT: Yale University Press, 1999), 2, 72.

19. *Macbeth* 3.3.1–2; 1.2.38; 1.6.14–15; 1.7.12; 4.1.10, 20, 35; 2.2.17; 2.1.4–5.

20. BCP (1552), 172, 169.

21. Jewel, *Works*, 1:9.

22. Willet, *Synopsis Papismi* (1600), 590; BL 4473.aa.58: Jewel, *Certaine Sermons preached before the Queene Majestie* (London, 1603). The marginal note, with other annotations in the volume, is dated 14 May 1633.

23. Rosendale, *Liturgy and Literature*, 60.

24. William Strode, "On Fayrford Windows," quoted in Adam Smyth, "'Art Reflexive': The Poetry, Sermons, and Drama of William Strode," *Studies in Philology* 103, no. 4 (Fall 2006): 447–48.

25. "A description of the painted glass in Fairford Church in Gloucestershire," in *Vita D. Thomae Morie Equitis Aurati, lingua Anglicana contexta* (London, 1716), 278.

26. Richard Marks, *Stained Glass in England during the Middle Ages* (Toronto: University of Toronto Press, 1993), 230–37.

27. Eamon Duffy, "Bare Ruined Choirs: Remembering Catholicism in Shakespeare's England," in *Theatre and Religion: Lancastrian Shakespeare*, ed. Richard Dutton, Alison Findlay, and Richard Wilson (Manchester: Manchester University Press, 2003), 48.

28. Margaret Aston, *England's Iconoclasts: Laws Against Images* (Oxford: Clarendon Press, 1988), 294–331; Duffy, "Bare Ruined Choirs," 47.

29. John Webster, *The White Devil*, ed. John Russell Brown (Manchester: Manchester University Press, 1996), 3.2.151–55; Elizabeth Cary, *The tragedy of Mariam, the fair queen of Jewry*, ed. Barry Weller and Margaret W. Ferguson (Berkeley: University of California Press, 1994), 4.1.174–75.

30. Braunmuller here follows the Oxford edition of the play (1990) in footnoting R. W. Dent, *Shakespeare's Proverbial Language: An Index*, B703, 66–67. Kenneth Muir's 1951 Arden edition footnotes Webster.

31. Michael Neill, *Issues of Death: Mortality and Identity in English Renaissance Tragedy* (Oxford: Clarendon Press, 1997); Jeffrey Knapp, *Shakespeare's Tribe*, 132; Diehl, *Staging Reform, Reforming the Stage*, 97, 120.

32. Talal Asad, *Genealogies of Religion: Discipline and Reasons of Power in Christianity and Islam* (Baltimore: Johns Hopkins University Press, 1993), 58.

33. Alison Shell, *Catholicism, Controversy and the English Literary Imagination, 1558–1660* (Cambridge: Cambridge University Press, 1999), 8; Duffy, preface to *Stripping of the Altars*, 2nd ed. (2005), xvii.

34. Greenblatt, *Hamlet in Purgatory*, 240; Roland Mushat Frye, *The Renaissance Hamlet* (Princeton, NJ: Princeton University Press, 1984), 19–20, 160.

35. J. Dover Wilson, *What Happens in Hamlet* (Cambridge: Cambridge University Press, 1935), 70; Butterfield quoted in David Hackett Fischer, *Historians' Fallacies* (New York: Harper and Row, 1970), 139. Fischer describes Whig historiography as a species of "presentism," which he defines as: "the mistaken idea that the proper way to do history is to prune away the dead branches of the past, and to preserve the green buds and twigs which have grown into the dark forest of our contemporary world" (135).

36. *Macbeth* 4.1.95–97; 5.3.3–7; 5.7.2–3, 14; 5.10.12–13; Naseeb Shaheen, *Biblical References in Shakespeare's Tragedies*, 157.

37. Job 14:1, 18:6, 34:15, 14:2, 16:16, 38:17, 12:22, 34:22, 3:5.

38. A. C. Bradley, *Shakespearean Tragedy* (London: Macmillan and Co., Ltd., 1904), 224.

39. Edmund Bonner, *Homilies sette forth by the right reverende father in God, Edmunde Byshop of London* (London, 1555), f.8r.

40. John Calvin, *Sermons of Master John Calvin, upon the Booke of Job*, trans. Arthur Golding (London, 1574), A.vi.v.

41. Geneva Bible (1587), side note to Job 3:14.

42. *This prayer of Salisbury use is set out a long wont any serchyng* (Paris, 1531), f.Xciv; *Heures a l'Usiage Romme* (Paris, 1488), H.viii r; *Les presentes heures a lusiage de Chartres* (Paris, 1517), K.iv.v.

43. Thomas Hamond, *The Late Commotion of certaine Papistes in Herefordshire* (London, 1605), C4r–D2r.

Chapter 6

1. BOD Douce C.P.F 1604, C5v, U5v; Cummings, 104, 147.

2. *A profitable and necessarye doctrine, with certayne homelies*, M.iii.r

3. Cummings, 47; BCP (1552), 174.

4. Patrick Collinson, *The Elizabethan Puritan Movement*, 165, 369; Ian Green, "Puritan Prayer Books . . . an Episode in Elizabethan Publishing," *Transactions of the Cambridge Bibliographic Society* 11 (1998); Green, *Print and Protestantism in Early Modern England*, 247–48.

5. *An Admonition to the Parliament* in Frere and Douglas, *Puritan Manifestoes*, 12, 21; "The Millenary Petition" in J. P. Kenyon, ed., *The Stuart Constitutions 1603–1688: Documents and Commentary*, 132–33.

6. Barlow, *Summe and Substance*, B4v.

7. Cummings, 147; Barlow, *Summe and Substance*, M3v.

8. Jewel, *Works*, 2:1106. Jewel cites Augustine on the same image at 2:732. Luther's prayer is printed in English in J. D. C. Fisher, ed., *Christian Initiation, The Reformation Period: Some Early Reformed Rites of Baptism and Confirmation* (London: SPCK, 1970), 90; and in the original German in F. E. Brightman, *The English Rite*, 2:726–28; Jean Danielou, *The Bible and the Liturgy* (Notre Dame, IN: University of Notre Dame Press, 1956), chap. 4; Daniel Liechty, ed., *Early Anabaptist Spirituality* (New York: Paulist Press, 1994), 77.

9. John Crowe Ransom, "On Shakespeare's Language," *Sewanee Review* 55, no. 2 (April–June 1947): 182–83, 188.

10. E. C. Whitaker, ed., *Martin Bucer and the Book of Common Prayer* (Alcuin Club Collections, no. 55), 88–90.

11. Frere and Douglas, *Puritan Manifestoes*, 26.

12. *A Booke of the Forme of common prayers, administration of the Sacraments, &c. agreeable to Gods Worde, and the use of the reformed Churches* (Middleburgh, 1584), Dr.

13. *Manuale ad usum ecclesie Sarisburiensis* (Paris, 1529), a ii v–a iii r. Peter Canasius, *A Summe of Christian Doctrine* (1592–96), K3v–K4r.

14. Jewel, *Works*, 2:1099, 1106; Calvin, *Sermons of Maister John Calvin, upon the Booke of Job*, trans. Arthur Golding (London, 1574), L.vi.r.

15. John Brerely, *Mirrour of New Reformation* (London, 1634), 4.

16. Samuel Schoenbaum, *William Shakespeare: Records and Images* (London: Scolar Press, 1981), 7–8.

17. Thomas de Quincy, "On the Knocking at the Gate in *Macbeth*," in *The Collected Writings of Thomas de Quincy*, ed. David Masson, 10: 389–94.

18. John Webster Spargo, "The Knocking at the Gate in *Macbeth*: An Essay in Interpretation," in *John Quincy Adams Memorial Studies*, ed. James G. McManaway, Giles E. Dawson, and Edwin E. Willoughby (Washington, DC: The Folger Shakespeare Library, 1948); Glynne Wickham, *Shakespeare's Dramatic Heritage* (New York: Barnes and Noble, Inc., 1969), 214–24.

19. *The Paraphrase of Erasmus upon the newe testament* (London, 1548–49), fiii.v; Calvin, *A Harmonie upon the Three Evangelists, Matthew, Mark and Luke*, trans. Eusebius Paget (London, 1584), O3r.

20. Adrian Fortescue, *The Ceremonies of the Roman Rite Described* (London: Burns Oates and Washburne, 1934), 415–19; William Maskell, ed., *Monumenta Ritualia Anglicanae: The Occasional Offices of the Church of England according to the old use of Salisbury* (Oxford: Clarendon Press, 1882), 1:ccxl–ccxlix; Archdale A. King, *Liturgies of the Past* (London: Longmans, 1959), 276–84. The Rituale Romanorum is printed—"Ordo Baptizandi, Aliaque Sacramenta Ministrandi"—in *Missale pro Sacerdotibus in Anglia, Scotia, & Ibernia itinerantibus* (1626), a Jesuit manual for itinerant recusant priests in Britain.

21. Peter Martyr, *Common Places*, 4:128–33.

22. Susan Karant-Nunn, *The Reformation of Ritual: An Interpretation of Early Modern Germany* (New York: Routledge, 1997), 45–46.

23. Thomas Cranmer, *Catechismus, that is to say, a shorte instruction into Christian religion for the synguler commoditie and profyte of childre[n] and yong people* (London, 1548), f.cci.r.

24. Greenblatt, *Shakespearean Negotiations*, 99, 111.

25. Samuel Harsnett, *A Declaration of Egregious Popish Impostures* (London, 1603), 32–33.

26. Whether "Seyton" is also "Satan" is a matter of critical debate. Kenneth Muir, in his Arden edition's note to this line, claims that the suggestion is coincidental; more recently, A. R. Braunmuller's Cambridge edition accepts the possibility. In *Shakespeare After All* (New York: Pantheon, 2004), Marjorie Garber concludes, in a terrible pun, "I find myself very tempted by the 'Satan' reading" (Garber, 721). I remain convinced that here is at the least an echo. The play is, as I have argued, rich with liturgical echo, and Shakespeare was after all nothing if not keen on puns.

27. Thomas Bilson, *The effect of Certaine Sermons Touching the Full Redemption of Mankinde by the death and bloud of Jesus Christ* (London, 1599), J1v–J2r.

28. Thomas Rogers, *The Catholic Doctrine of the Church of England: An Exposition of the Thirty-Nine Articles*, 279; Willet, *Synopsis Papismi* (1592), 544; George Joye, *A frutefull treatis of baptyme and the Lordis Souper and the use and effect of them* (1541), no page numbers.

29. Jones, *Scenic Form in Shakespeare*, 224; Kermode, *Shakespeare's Language*, 203.

30. *Macbeth* 3.4.122; 1.1.12; 1.3.36; 1.6.15–16; 4.1.10.

31. Jewel, *Works*, 2:1106; *Admonition to the Parliament*, 26–27; "Millenary Petition," 132.

32. Barlow, *Summe and Substance*, 69, 72, 73.

33. Gerald Bray, ed., *The Anglican Canons 1529–1947* (Bury St. Edmunds: The Boydell Press, 1998), 307–9.

34. Fotherby, *Four Sermons, lately preached*, A2r, Br.

35. Lori Anne Ferrell, *Government by Polemic: James I, the King's Preachers, and the Rhetoric of Conformity* (Stanford, CA: Stanford University Press, 1998), 7, 6.

36. *Macbeth* 5.1.27, 30, 42, 37, 56; Cummings, 162, 170.

Chapter 7

1. Will Coster, *Baptism and Spiritual Kinship in Early Modern England* (Aldershot: Ashgate, 2002), 173, 174. The statistic about the number of men called William in early modern England is also from Coster, who notes: "in the late sixteenth and early seventeenth centuries, around a quarter of all males were called William, and over half of all males possessed this name or that of John or Thomas" (168). He continues, "Among girls, a similar process appears to have been taking place, with Elizabeth tending to be the most common name by the seventeenth century, which, together with Mary and Anne, was used for over half of all recorded females."

2. David Cressy, *Birth, Marriage, and Death*, 150, 152–53.

3. Barlow, *Summe and Substance*, 7, 11–12, 17, 63, 71.

4. Cox, ed., *The Works of Thomas Cranmer*, 2.126; Sydney Anglo, *Spectacle, Pageantry, and Early Tudor Policy* (Oxford: Clarendon Press, 1997), 283–96.

5. *Calendar of State Papers*, 10:43–44; NA SP 14/1, f.131.

6. Richard Broughton, *The English Protestants Recantation* (1617), Bb4r.

7. Marc Bloch, *The Royal Touch: Sacred Monarchy and Scrofula in England and France* (London: Routledge and Kegan Paul, 1973), 28; Frank Barlow, "The King's Evil," in *English Historical Review* 95 (January 1980): 15.

8. *The Ceremonies us'd in the Time of King Henry VII For the Healing of them that be Diseas'd with the King's Evil* (1686), A3r–B2r; Raymond Crawfurd, *The King's Evil* (Oxford: Clarendon Press, 1911), 71–74.

9. Bloch, *Royal Touch*, 191; CSP 10.193, 344.

10. *Macbeth* 2.3.63–64, 109–10; 2.4.6–7; 4.3.32, 41–42; 5.2.27.

11. Collinson, "The Jacobean Religious Settlement," 30; Johann P. Sommerville, ed., *King James VI and I: Political Writings* (Cambridge: Cambridge University Press, 1995), 25–26; Cardwell, *History of Conferences*, 131; Barlow, *Summe and Substance*, 5.

12. *The True Law of free Monarchies: Or, the Reciprock and Mutuall Dutie Betwixt a free King, and his naturally Subjectes* (Edinburgh, 1598), D3r.

13. Coster, *Baptism and Spiritual Kinship*, 78, 50–51; BCP (1559), 275.

14. Barlow, *Summe and Substance*, 71, 83.

15. *Macbeth* 1.2.64–65; 1.3.47–48, 103; 1.4.37–39; 1.5.5–8.

16. G. Wilson Knight, *The Shakespearian Tempest* (London: Methuen, 1953), 326; Terry Eagleton, *William Shakespeare* (Oxford: Blackwell, 1986), 2–3; Braunmuller, ed. *Macbeth*, 259; Gary Taylor, *Thomas Middleton and Early Modern Textual Culture* (Oxford: Oxford University Press, 2007), 397; Brian Vickers, Marina Tarlinskaya, and Marcus Dahl, "An Enquiry into Middleton's supposed 'adaptation' of *Macbeth*" (Published on the website of the School of Advanced Study, University of London: www.ies.sas.ac.uk), 35.

17. Reginald Scot, *The Discoverie of Witchcraft*, 25–26.

18. George Gifford, *A Discourse of the Subtill Practices of Devills by Witches and Sorcerers*, D3r; *A Dialogue concerning Witches and Witchacraftes*, E2r.

19. Walter Stephens, *Demon Lovers: Witchcraft, Sex, and the Crisis of Belief* (Chicago: University of Chicago Press, 2002), 184–85, 241.

20. James, *Daemonologie* (Edinburgh, 1597), A3v, L4v; Christina Larner, "James VI and I and Witchcraft," in *The Reign of James VI and I*, ed. Alan G. R. Smith (London: Macmillan, 1973).

21. James Joyce, *Ulysses* (Oxford: Oxford World's Classics, 1998), 196.

22. Paul, *The Royal Play of Macbeth* (New York: Macmillan, 1950), 367, 385, 1.

23. Kernan, *Shakespeare, the King's Playwright*, 72, 76, 78–79, 88.

24. Braunmuller, ed., *Macbeth*, 9; Curtis Perry, *The Making of Jacobean Culture: James I and the Renegotiation of Elizabethan Literary Practice* (Cambridge: Cambridge University Press, 1997), 148; Susan James, "Shakespeare and the Politics of Superstition," in *Shakespeare and Early Modern Political Thought*, ed. David Armitage, Conal Condren, and Andrew Fitzmaurice (Cambridge: Cambridge University Press, 2009), 95.

25. David Scott Kastan, *Shakespeare After Theory* (New York: Routledge, 1999), 178; David Norbrook, "*Macbeth* and the Politics of Historiography," in Kevin Sharpe and Steven Zwicker, eds., *Politics of Discourse: The Literature and History of Seventeenth-Century England* (Berkeley: University of California Press, 1987); John Kerrigan, *Archipelagic English: Literature, History, and Politics 1603–1707* (Oxford: Oxford University Press, 2008).

26. Kermode, *Shakespeare's Language*, viii.

27. Cummings, 145, 146; *Macbeth* 3.2.50–51.

Epilogue

1. "An Ordinance for taking away the Book of Common Prayer, and for establishing and putting in execution of the Directory for the publique worship of God," in *Acts and Ordinances of the Interregnum, 1642–1660*, ed. C. H. Firth and R. S. Tait (London: HMSO, 1911), 582.

2. Rosendale, *Liturgy and Literature*, 130; John Morrill, *The Nature of the English Revolution* (London: Longman, 1993), 163.

3. "An Ordinance for taking away the Book of Common Prayer," 583–84.

4. *A Dirge for the Directory, Written by one of King James ancient Protestants* (London, 1645), 2.

5. Morrill, *Nature of the English Revolution*, 164–65; Tim Harris, *Restoration: Charles II and His Kingdoms* (London: Allen Lane, 2005), 52–53.

6. "Order for the Savoy Conference" and "Act of Uniformity" in *Documents Illustrative of English Church History*, ed. Henry Gee and William John Hardy (London, 1896), 594, 604.

7. Andrew Browning, ed., *English Historical Documents, 1660–1714* (London: Eyre and Spottiswoode, 1953), 399–400.

8. "William and Mary, 1688: An Act for Exempting their Majestyes Protestant Subjects dissenting from the Church of England from the Penalties of certain Lawes," in *Statutes of the Realm: 1685–94* (1819), 74.

9. *The Renewal of Common Prayer* (London: SPCK, 1993), vii.

10. The complete texts of Common Worship are available on the website of the Church of England: www.churchofengland.org/prayer-worship/worship/texts.aspx. I have quoted here the Pastoral Services of Marriage and Funeral.

Bibliographical Essay

The specific sources for particular facts, details, and opinions are given in the endnotes, but my understanding of Shakespeare, the Book of Common Prayer, and the religious and ecclesiastical history of sixteenth- and seventeenth-century England has been shaped by a range of books beyond those that appear there. What follows is my attempt to acknowledge some of those works that have been most formative for me and to direct the interested reader toward further material.

Shakespeare's Life

The key records of Shakespeare's life—including, most interestingly for me, his liturgical traces—are collected in Samuel Schoenbaum, ed., *William Shakespeare: A Documentary Life* (Oxford: Oxford University Press, 1975) and E. K. Chambers, *William Shakespeare: A Study of Facts and Problems* (Oxford: Clarendon Press, 1930). These are the starting-points for any study of Shakespeare's life, although there are also of course many fine full-length biographies. I have relied on Peter Ackroyd, *Shakespeare: The Biography* (London: Chatto and Windus, 2005); Katherine Duncan-Jones, *Ungentle Shakespeare* (London: Arden, 2001); and Park Honan, *Shakespeare: A Life* (Oxford: Oxford University Press, 1998).

The best book about Shakespeare biography—its perils and practices—is Schoenbaum's *Shakespeare's Lives* (Oxford: Clarendon Press, 1970). There are also those who suggest that the person who lived Shakespeare's life was not the playwright; the best book about the authorship controversy is James Shapiro's *Contested Will* (London: Faber, 2010).

The Book of Common Prayer

The most recent and most useful scholarly edition of the Book of Common Prayer is that edited by Brian Cummings (Oxford: Oxford University Press, 2011). This volume includes the texts of the 1549, 1549, and 1662 prayer books and a thorough, hugely insightful introduction; I warmly recommend this volume to anyone interested in the prayer book, the religious history of early modern England, or the Reformation more broadly.

The 1552 prayer book—excluded from Cumming's edition—is reprinted in *The First and Second Prayer Books of King Edward VI* (London: J. M. Dent, 1910). The website of the Anglican Communion (http://justus.anglican.org/resources/bcp/england.htm) includes easily accessible versions of every edition of the prayer book. Edward Cardwell's *A History of Conferences and Other Proceedings Connected with the Revision of the Book of Common Prayer* (Oxford: Oxford University Press, 1849) is the most convenient source for the debates surrounding liturgical revision in England. *Liturgy and Worship: A Companion to the Prayer Books of the Anglican Communion*, edited by W. K. Lowther Clarke (London: SPCK, 1954) is a useful guide to the often-obscure origins of Anglican theology and rites. John Booty's edition of the 1559 Book of Common Prayer (Washington, DC: Folger Library, 1976) includes a handsome version and extensive history of the Elizabethan prayer book.

Timothy Rosendale has noted that the prayer book has "a history of near-spectacular neglect among literary scholars"; his own excellent *Liturgy and Literature in the Making of Protestant England* (Cambridge: Cambridge University Press, 2007) goes a long way toward making up for this omission. Ramie Targoff's *Common Prayer: The Language of Public Devotion in Early Modern England* (Chicago: University of Chicago Press, 2001) is one of the very few critical works to attend to the specifics of liturgy.

The two most revealing books about the English prayer book come from disciplines outside literary studies: Judith Maltby's *Prayer Book and People in Elizabethan and Early Stuart England* (Cambridge: Cambridge University Press, 1998) and Diarmaid MacCulloch's exemplary biography, *Thomas Cranmer: A Life* (New Haven, CT: Yale University Press, 1996), which details the making of the successive versions of the early prayer books.

On specific rites, among many others, I recommend the following: on baptism, Will Coster's *Baptism and Spiritual Kinship in Early Modern England* (Aldershot: Ashgate, 2002); on marriage, Anne Barton's "'Wrying but a little': Marriage, Law and Sexuality in the Plays of Shakespeare," which is in her *Essays, Mainly Shakespearean* (Cambridge: Cambridge University Press, 1994); on Communion, Arnold Hunt's "The Lord's Supper in Early Modern England," in *Past and Present* 161 (1998); and on burial, Peter Marshall's *Beliefs and the Dead in Reformation England* (Oxford: Oxford University Press, 2002).

The English Church and Religious History

The work of Eamon Duffy has inspired much of what I have written here: his groundbreaking *The Stripping of the Altars* (New Haven, CT: Yale University Press, 1992) is perhaps the most important single book about sixteenth-century English history published in the last fifty years. David Cressy's *Birth, Marriage and Death: Ritual, Religion, and the Life-Cycle in Tudor and Stuart England* (Oxford: Oxford University Press, 1997) is an invaluable social history for anyone interested in the period.

On the specifics of Elizabethan and Jacobean doctrine and devotional practice, I have gratefully followed Patrick Collinson, *The Birthpangs of Protestant England: Religious and Cultural Change in the Sixteenth and Seventeenth Centuries* (New York: St Martin's Press, 1988); Lori Anne Ferrell, *Government by Polemic: James I, the King's Preachers, and the Rhetoric of Conformity* (Stanford, CA: Stanford University Press, 1998); Kenneth Fincham, *Prelate as Pastor: The Episcopate of James I* (Oxford: Clarendon Press, 1990); Peter Lake, *Anglicans and Puritans? Presbyterianism and English Conformist Thought from Whitgift to Hooker* (London: Unwin Hyman, 1988); Peter

McCullough, *Sermons at Court: Politics and Religion in Elizabethan and Jacobean Preaching* (Cambridge: Cambridge University Press, 1998); and Nicholas Tyacke, *Anti-Calvinists: The Rise of Arminianism, c. 1590–1640* (Oxford: Clarendon Press, 1987) among many others.

The most important study of the Hampton Court Conference remains Patrick Collinson's essay "The Jacobean Religious Settlement: the Hampton Court Conference," in *Before the English Civil War: Essays on Early Stuart Government and Politics,* ed. Howard Tomlinson (London: Macmillan, 1984). Mark Curtis's "Hampton Court Conference and Its Aftermath," *History* 46 (February 1961) is also informative.

The best way to track the intricacies of theological debate in this period—to discover now what mattered most then, the flashpoints of controversy—is by comparing the successive and growing editions of Andrew Willet's extraordinary compendium *Synopsis Papismi* (1594, 1600, 1614). I recommend also the works of Bishop John Jewel, available in a severe four-volume edition (Cambridge: The Parker Society, 1845–1850). The austerity of their appearance belies the liveliness of their contents: Jewel is a fluid, provocative, and engaging writer and spent his career at the center of Reformation English religious controversy.

The Theater and the Sacraments

Much of this book is an argument for the continuation of something that historians have long assumed ended in the early Reformation: liturgically precise, sacramental theater. My thinking here has been shaped by anthropologists as much as by literary critics, and by studies of medieval literature and culture as much as those of the early modern period.

The Purpose of Playing: Shakespeare and the Cultural Politics of the Elizabethan Theatre (Chicago: University of Chicago Press, 1996) by Louis Montrose is a classic study of the commercial theater's succession from liturgical drama. I highly recommend Bruce Holsinger,

"Liturgy," in *Oxford Twenty-First Century Approaches to Literature: Middle English*, ed. Paul Strohm (New York: Oxford University Press, 2007) and Sarah Beckwith, *Signifying God: Social Relation and Symbolic Act in the York Corpus Christi Plays* (Chicago: University of Chicago Press, 2001) on the relationship between liturgy and literary culture before the Book of Common Prayer.

Talal Asad, *Genealogies of Religion: Discipline and Reasons of Power in Christianity and Islam* (Baltimore, MD: Johns Hopkins University Press, 1993) has many valuable insights on religious ritual; James Scott's *Seeing Like a State: How Certain Schemes to Improve the Human Condition Have Failed* (New Haven, CT: Yale University Press, 1999) is a book that deserves to be read by literary scholars and historians as well as political theorists.

On the interconnected questions of the structures of faith and their cultural role, I particularly recommend Philippe Ariès, *Western Attitudes Toward Death from the Middle Ages to the Present* (Baltimore: Johns Hopkins University Press, 1974) and Peter Brown, *The Cult of the Saints: Its Rise and Function in Latin Christianity* (Chicago: University of Chicago Press, 1981).

Two volumes are invaluable for the stage history of this period: *English Professional Theatre 1530–1660* (Cambridge: Cambridge University Press, 2000), edited by Glynne Wickham, and—slightly more surprisingly—*Documents Illustrative of English Church History* (London: Macmillan, 1914), edited by Henry Gee and William John Hardy. These reprint the Acts of Uniformity, injunctions, and rulings against the theatrical appropriation of liturgy and in doing so tell a revealing history of the English stage. As I argue, it is precisely in considering what is ruled against that we may deduce what was taking place.

The Plays

I have relied primarily upon the *Norton Shakespeare* (New York: W. W. Norton, 1997) but have also been very happily informed by specific editions of single plays: in particular, *As You Like It,* edited by Michael Hattaway (The New Cambridge Shakespeare, 2009); *Hamlet,* edited by Harold Jenkins (Arden Shakespeare, 1982); *Hamlet: The Texts of 1603 and 1623,* edited by Ann Thompson and Neil Taylor (Arden Shakespeare, 2007); *Macbeth,* edited by Kenneth Muir (Arden Shakespeare, 1951); and *Macbeth,* edited by A. R. Braunmuller (The New Cambridge Shakespeare, 1997).

Perhaps the most exciting new field within Shakespeare studies is that of co-authorship: the recognition that Shakespeare worked within a collaborative culture has transformed and will continue to deepen our understanding of both the plays and their world. *Shakespeare, Co-Author* (Oxford: Oxford University Press, 2002) by Brian Vickers and *Shakespeare and Co.* (New York: Allen Lane, 2006) by Stanley Wells describe the collaborative conditions of sixteenth- and early seventeenth-century playwriting. Gordon McMullan's extraordinary *Shakespeare and the Idea of Late Writing: Authorship in the Proximity of Death* (Cambridge: Cambridge University Press, 2007) is not directly about the question of co-authorship but demonstrates the ways in which the idea of Shakespeare as a collaborative author must necessarily transform many of our preconceptions about his work.

It is worth also noting here my debt to Stephen Greenblatt. While I frequently disagree with his findings and conclusions, my thinking about Shakespeare has been powerfully marked by his own extraordinarily imaginative studies, in particular *Renaissance Self-Fashioning: From More to Shakespeare* (Chicago: University of Chicago Press, 1980) and *Shakespearean Negotiations: The Circulation of Social Energy in Renaissance England* (Oxford: Clarendon Press, 1990). Nobody who studies Shakespeare today has not been influenced by his work.

Index

Get **more** out of libraries

Please return or renew this item by the last date shown.
You can renew online at www.hants.gov.uk/library
Or by phoning 0300 555 1387

 Hampshire
County Council

C015901036